Summer

English Earthenware Figures
1740-1840

Falconer

Frontispiece. Falconer, pearlware with overglaze enamel painted decoration, impressed numeral on the base *135*, made in Staffordshire, c.1785-1800, ht. 227mm. *Private Collection; photograph by Gavin Ashworth, New York*

English Earthenware
Figures
1740-1840

Pat Halfpenny

Antique Collectors' Club

Dedication

This book is dedicated to the memory of
Reginald G. Haggar 1905-1988,
my mentor and my friend

British Library Cataloguing-in-Publication Data
A catalogue record for this book is available from the British Library

Designed by John and Griselda Lewis

Printed in England on
Consort Royal Satin paper from Donside Mills, Aberdeen, Scotland, by the
Antique Collectors' Club, Woodbridge, Suffolk IP12 1DS

The Antique Collectors' Club

The Antique Collectors' Club was formed in 1966 and quickly grew to a five figure membership spread throughout the world. It publishes the only independently run monthly antiques magazine, *Antique Collecting*, which caters for those collectors who are interested in widening their knowledge of antiques, both by greater awareness of quality and by discussion of the factors which influence the price that is likely to be asked. The Antique Collectors' Club pioneered the provision of information on prices for collectors and the magazine still leads in the provision of detailed articles on a variety of subjects.

It was in response to the enormous demand for information on 'what to pay' that the price guide series was introduced in 1968 with the first edition of *The Price Guide to Antique Furniture* (completely revised 1978 and 1989), a book which broke new ground by illustrating the more common types of antique furniture, the sort that collectors could buy in shops and at auctions rather than the rare museum pieces which had previously been used (and still to a large extent are used) to make up the limited amount of illustrations in books published by commercial publishers. Many other price guides have followed, all copiously illustrated, and greatly appreciated by collectors for the valuable information they contain, quite apart from prices. The Price Guide Series heralded the publication of many standard works of reference on art and antiques. *The Dictionary of British Art* (now in six volumes), *The Pictorial Dictionary of British 19th Century Furniture Design*, *Oak Furniture* and *Early English Clocks* were followed by many deeply researched reference works such as *The Directory of Gold and Silversmiths*, providing new information. Many of these books are now accepted as the standard work of reference on their subject.

The Antique Collectors' Club has widened its list to include books on gardens and architecture. All the Club's publications are available through bookshops world wide and a full catalogue of all these titles is available free of charge from the addresses below.

Club membership, open to all collectors, costs little. Members receive free of charge *Antique Collecting*, the Club's magazine (published ten times a year), which contains well-illustrated articles dealing with the practical aspects of collecting not normally dealt with by magazines. Prices, features of value, investment potential, fakes and forgeries are all given prominence in the magazine.

Among other facilities available to members are private buying and selling facilities, the longest list of 'For Sales' of any antiques magazine, an annual ceramics conference and the opportunity to meet other collectors at their local antique collectors' clubs. There are over eighty in Britain and more than a dozen overseas. Members may also buy the Club's publications at special pre-publication prices.

As its motto implies, the Club is an organisation designed to help collectors get the most out of their hobby: it is informal and friendly and gives enormous enjoyment to all concerned.

For Collectors — By Collectors — About Collecting

ANTIQUE COLLECTORS' CLUB
5 Church Street, Woodbridge Suffolk IP12 1DS, UK
Tel: 01394 385501 Fax: 01394 384434
or
Market Street Industrial Park, Wappingers' Falls, NY 12590, USA
Tel: 914 297 0003 Fax: 914 297 0068

Acknowledgements

I would like to record my sincere thanks to many people who have helped me write this book. In the early days I was given free access by Reginald Haggar to all his research notes and received great encouragement whenever I began to doubt if I could complete the work; he taught me to seek for the truth, to be objective, and to enjoy pots. I wish I had finished sooner so that he could have judged whether I had learnt my lessons well. I would never have been in a position to have written this book if it had not been for Arnold R. Mountford, former Director, City Museum & Art Gallery, Stoke-on-Trent, who nurtured my love for early Staffordshire pottery and gave me confidence to pursue my own researches.

Many collectors have offered help and assistance and I would particularly like to thank Jean and Wynn Hamilton-Foyn for entering into a spirited exchange of information which provoked much thought and re-examination of my more radical ideas. There are many people and institutions without whose help this book would not have been written and I would like to thank the following:

G.L.W. Beardsley	M. & L. Hillis	M. & C. Sachs
S. Beddoe	J. Homery-Folkes	A.C. Scott
J.N. Black	R. Lane	M. Schkolne
J. Boff	N. Lester	E.N. Stretton
M. Brook-Hart	J. & G. Lewis	P. Turner
G. Coke	M. Longfoot	H.A.B. Turner
J. Critchley	T. Lonton	H. & J. Weldon
T. Cross	D. Napier	S. Whomsley
L. & M.G. Dornfeld	A. Parr	R.B. Wilson
A. Eatwell	R. Pretzfelder	B.G. Wood
M. Evans	V.E. Price	J.W.H. Wright
L. & L. Grigsby	J. Price	D. & C. Zeitlin
G.A. Godden	G. Reed	

Photography studios which have been particularly helpful include A.C.P. Photolabs and Downing Street Studios.

Museums which have been particularly helpful include: Atlanta Historical Society; Colonial Williamsburg Virginia; Laing Art Gallery, Newcastle upon Tyne; Hampshire County Museum Service; Harris Museum & Art Gallery Preston; Royal Pavilion Art Gallery & Museum, Brighton; Southport Museum; Warrington Museum & Art Gallery; Temple Newsam House, Leeds; Wisbech & Fenland Museum; Wolverhampton Art Gallery & Museums; Victoria & Albert Museum, London.

Last but not least I would like to thank Geoff Halfpenny for his patience and support.

Contents

List of Colour Plates

'Frontispiece', Enoch Wood's Manufactory, 1827

Introduction

Images in clay are as old as the history of pottery. The earliest exponents of the plastic art produced animal and human figures for pleasure, devotional and ritualistic reasons. In England the tradition was late in arriving and was stimulated by imports of Oriental and European porcelains which in the eighteenth century set the standard for our embryonic industry.

The earliest response was made by John Dwight in the 1690s, whose saltglazed stoneware pieces were modelled and fired as individual works of art. It has been suggested that Staffordshire's white saltglaze potters were producing figures as early as the 1730s and '40s; we certainly have evidence of their manufacture by the early 1750s, for in William Duesbury's account book of 1751-3 are found records of his painting 'Stone Birds', 'Stafordshir ladis' and 'Staffordshir lar B[ir]ds'.[1]

By far the greatest number of figures produced in the mid-eighteenth century were those in porcelain: Bow, Chelsea and Derby all catered for the wealthy customer. The eighteenth century was a time of great economic change in England. The growth of the merchant and trading classes saw a corresponding increase in the number of people with a small amount of disposable income who required a range of fine wares but cheaper than porcelain; not only were dinner, tea and dessert services demanded but ornamental pieces in the form of vases, candlesticks and figures. The Staffordshire potters sought to fulfil those demands.

The infinite range of the figure makers' output which still remains today is a testament to the huge number of pieces which must have been produced. The private collector tends to favour one class of figure over another and to build up a homogeneous group, but the whole range of complexity, styles and colour can be seen in many museum collections. The figures themselves demonstrate changes in style and fashions and illustrate technical developments in the pottery industry, but there is little other evidence to assist in a serious study of the subject. Primary evidence in the form of marks is most uncommon and it is unlikely that this book will reflect the true ratio of marked and unmarked pieces as I shall rely heavily on marks as a guide to classifying the various groups of figures.

Other primary evidence in the form of excavation occurs very rarely and figures usually are found by chance rather than as the result of a systematic search. Archaeologists have a duty to excavate to help formulate a clearer understanding of life in the past. Excavating a figure manufactory is such a narrow undertaking that it is not likely to receive high priority even if a suitable site is known. Where figures have been excavated and they are known to me I have found them to be a valuable source of information.

Documentary evidence of two sorts may be found; both are fraught with interpretational problems. Primary documentation is that which came into

---

1. Mountford, A.R., *The Illustrated Guide to Staffordshire Salt-glazed Stoneware*, Barrie & Jenkins, 1971, Chap. VIII.

existence during the period in which the figures were produced and includes manuscript and printed sources. Manuscripts may include factory records, personal diaries and parish registers; printed ephemera encompasses a wider range of material of which the most useful are trade directories, newspapers, and broadsheets. Each of these sources has its own problems. Manuscript records are rarely complete so that entries may have to be taken out of context and the problem of deciphering and transcribing can be difficult and subjective. Printed sources are just as problematical, trade directories may for example not always be accurate or comprehensive, we do not know whether they were compiled in the year prior to or the year of publication and they only exist for a few odd years of each century; as far as newspapers are concerned we have no evidence that their reporting was any more accurate or unbiased than it is today.

Secondary sources are those which came into existence at some time after the figures were made and mostly consist of published works of reference. One should always study past literature but never use someone else's conclusions: always test these against the evidence, check all facts at primary source and do not rely on the accuracy of others. I have tried to abide by this rule though no doubt have breached it; I can only urge you to treat my work with the same caution I advocate for others.

Once the sources have been assembled and studied, an overall picture of the earthenware figure making industry emerges. It seems likely that the earliest figures were not made by specialist factories but were produced by makers of dinner, tea and dessert services, therefore one can only conclude that the industry's bread and butter lay with the production of tablewares. From excavated and documentary evidence it can be seen that figures formed a very small part of the output of any factory, presumably they were more prey to the peaks and troughs of the economic climate for in days of restraint one might more easily forgo the purchase of an ornamental figure than the more necessary plate.

By 1796 the first specialist figure maker is recorded. This was Edward Till, toy maker, Smith-Field, Tunstall.[2] In 1800 Allbut's *View of the Staffordshire Potteries* recorded five specialist figure makers, all in the Burslem and Hanley area, setting a pattern for the next fifty years. By 1830[3] the number had risen to fifteen (all but four in the Burslem and Hanley/Shelton area) and by 1841[4] thirty-six manufacturers were recorded but these now included china toy and ornamental manufacturers with a corresponding increase in Lane End and Longton addresses at the china end of the district. Between 1796 and 1841 more than seventy specialist figure makers of all kinds are listed. The specialist

2. *The Staffordshire Pottery Directory*, Chester & Mort, 1796.

3. *National Commercial Directory 1830*, Pigot & Co, 1830.

4. *Royal National & Commercial Directory and Topography of the Counties of . . . Staffordshire 1841*, Pigot & Co, 1845.

figure makers do not include those who made other kinds of ware, for instance potters like Enoch Wood, James Neale or Lakin & Poole, whose names would make the list significantly longer. The growth of figure making did not occur in isolation but reflected the development and expansion of the pottery trade as a whole.

Documentary evidence points to the specialists being very small concerns, often with no more than one making oven and one enamelling kiln. Substantial factories in the 1830s might expect to have as many as eight bottle ovens to fire biscuit, gloss and decoration in a continuous round of production.[5] The situation can still be seen today, where large companies involved in figure production, such as Royal Doulton, still make more tableware than ornamental pieces, and where specialist firms are more likely to be found in older, smaller premises. These businesses rarely register with the British Ceramic Manufacturers Federation and may change hands or close down without anyone realising they have ever existed. In the twenty-first century the same problems will face collectors and students that we experience today.

One of the major problems in studying earthenware figures is finding the sources of their inspiration. There are a number of pieces which can be shown to have an earlier plaster original, a printed source or a corresponding porcelain model, but the vast majority, particularly in the first half of the nineteenth century, seem to be genuinely novel. The subjects may be commonly followed as a matter of fashion but the interpretation is free from plagiarism. Larger factories employed modellers and mould makers to supply their needs, but obviously a small factory might have problems keeping a skilled modeller in full-time employment. It is known that tradesmen were prepared to work a set number of days per week for more than one master and perhaps some modellers solved their employment problems in this way. However, the trade directories show that during the nineteenth century there was a growing number of independent modellers prepared to undertake tasks in return for payment and perhaps they also prepared stock patterns for the figure makers to choose from. If the latter is the case it will be difficult to substantiate the attribution of any figure on style alone.

One modeller who is often associated with early figures is John Voyez, who came to the Staffordshire Potteries in 1768 to work for Josiah Wedgwood. Within a year he had committed an offence for which he was sentenced to three months' imprisonment and on his release he worked for various manufactories as well as working independently. There is no evidence that he ever worked for any of the Wood family. There is also no evidence that Voyez modelled any three-dimensional subjects at all; his reputation for relief modelling is supported by examples of his vases and jugs, as no independent figures are known.

---

5. A notice of sale or letting of Charles Bourne's factory in Fenton appeared in the *Staffordshire Advertiser* at various times during 1829 and 1830 advertising premises with 'three biscuit ovens and three gloss ovens, with hardening and enamelling kilns'.

The Modeller or Sculptor from whose productions are taken casts or moulds for the potter.

'Modelling', Enoch Wood's Manufactory, 1827

Biscuit earthenware sculpture incised in cursive script 'Mr James Copeland China Toy Manufactory New Street Hanley Staffordshire Aged 51 years Herbert Son of the Above Aged three years and 3 Months Modeled by Mr Henry Bentley Sep 1841 Aged 22', ht. 406mm. *City Museum & Art Gallery, Stoke-on-Trent, 18.P.1979.*

14

In 1800 three modellers are recorded in the local trade directory: Ralph Johnson of Mount Pleasant, Burslem, Thomas Heath and Peter Stephan, both of Shelton,[6] each may have provided a varied service to the trade, offering useful and ornamental wares. Of the first two we have no direct evidence that figures were in their repertoire but Peter Stephan was the French modeller Pierre Stephan, who had formerly worked for the Derby porcelain factory and his porcelain figures are discussed in excellent detail elsewhere.[7] It seemed commonplace for craftsmen to move among the pottery making centres of England looking for employment. The 1834 Staffordshire directory records two more former Derby workers, Edward and Samuel Keys, as modellers in Stoke Lane and Upper Cliff Bank respectively.[8] It is not surprising that a number of Staffordshire figures are similar to Derby examples and this is commented on in the text, particularly in connection with Enoch Wood in the 1825-30 period. By 1841 Pigot[9] records fifteen freelance modellers and during this time one or two like Joshua Walton and Henry Mills also appear in lists of toy makers, confirming a direct connection between some modellers and the figure making trade. The use of freelance modellers and the practice of figure makers to hire themselves out as modellers is calculated to afford the greatest confusion when attempting to isolate and identify the unmarked pieces which occur in such profusion. If I were mischievous (which of course I am not), I might suggest that it would be just as accurate and more entertaining to choose a figure maker at random from the appropriate period directory than to trot out the same old well-worn names; this is a game which is not to be taken seriously and should only be practised by consenting adults.

The specialist figure makers became more common in the late 1820s and many were quite poor, as the figure trade was not the most lucrative form of potting. This is most eloquently borne out by the memoirs of Charles Shaw,[10] who, despite the grinding poverty of his childhood, remembered with some pleasure the period he spent working for a toymaker. The toymaker in question was probably George Hood, who took over John Walton's Navigation Road premises after his retirement and is likely to have continued using the moulds left by Walton as well as developing his own range of figures. Charles Shaw wrote:

'The toy manufactory itself was a curiosity in structure and management. It was rusty and grim. As to form, it might have been brought in cartloads

---

6. *A View of the Staffordshire Potteries,* T. Allbut, 1800.

7. Bradshaw, P., *18th Century English Porcelain Animals 1745-1795,* Antique Collectors' Club, Woodbridge, 1981.

8. *History, Gazetteer and Directory of Staffordshire,* W. White, 1834.

9. *Royal National & Commercial Directory and Topography of the Counties of . . . Staffordshire 1841,* Pigot & Co, 1845.

10. Shaw, C., *When I was a Child,* originally published 1903 by Methuen, reprinted by Caliban, 1977.

from the broken-down cottages on the opposite side of the street. The workshops were neither square, nor round, nor oblong. They were a jumble of the oddest imaginable kind, and if there had been the ordinary number of workshops on an average-sized pot-works, placed as these were placed, it would have been impossible to have found the way in and the way out. As it was, though small, it was rather difficult. The one cart-road went round a hovel nearby, and then dived under a twisted archway. Only about a dozen people were employed on this "bank", and if we all turned out[11] together we were thronged in the narrow spaces outside the shops.[12] To be "master" of such a place as this poor G.H. had had to come down from his white horse and from his much larger works in Tunstall...I remember the figure of Napoleon Bonaparte was the leading article of our industry at this toy factory...These Napoleons must have been in large demand somewhere, for shoals of them were made at that time...If all the Napoleons made at this toy manufactory could have had life given them, then England, if not invaded, would have been crowded by military Frenchmen, and of the dreaded Napoleonic type.

At this toy manufactory we did not make many figures so tragic and terrible in suggestion as Napoleon. George H. had designed a little toper publican with his left hand in his breeches pocket, and in his right hand a jug full of foaming beer. The face wore a flabby smile, which carried welcome to all.

We made cats, too, on box lids, representing cushions. We made dogs of all sizes, from "Dignity" to "Impudence". We made the gentlest of swains and the sweetest of maids, nearly always standing under the shade of a tree, whose foliage must have been blighted some spring day by an east wind, as it was so sparse in what seemed to be midsummer time.

It is astonishing what amiable squinting those swains and maids did in pretending not to look at each other. I have never seen squinting so amiable looking in real life. But that was where the art came in. The course of life in this little toy-works was always pleasant. There was nothing strenuous or harsh. "The master" was the president of a small republic of workers. All were equal in a sort of regulated inequality. We did different work, of different grades of importance and value, and yet no one seemed to think himself better than anyone else. We had no drunkenness and immorality such as I had seen elsewhere in the same town at a "bank," which would, if it could, have looked down on our "toy" place as the Pharisee looked down on the publican. There have been worse employers than George H. even in his adversity, and his little place of business was a quiet refuge for a few toilers, and one free from the demoralising influences prevailing in much larger concerns.

---

11. 'turned out', i.e. left the work place.
12. 'shops', i.e. workshops.

I felt a distinct access of better influences while I worked for George H. and though he never spoke of religion, while placing no obstacle in the way of its pursuit, it was easier to follow it there than at some works whose ''masters'' wore broad phylacteries on Sundays.'

Charles Shaw had experienced many truly horrifying events during his childhood and his brief sojourn in the toy-works is obviously remembered with less pain than many other episodes in his book. It is inevitable that the evidence he leaves us has some personal bias but if we are aware of his circumstances, I think we can test his version against some of the known facts and find that by reading his words we are nearer to knowing the environment in which our figures were produced. The decrepit buildings, the small workforce, the owner actively involved in production matters, the Nonconformist religious preferences versus drunkenness and immorality, the harsh master versus the kindly master: all these matters weighed heavily on the mind of a young boy in the Potteries, a boy who was responsible for making at least some of the figures we treasure so much. Perhaps he even had a hand in some of those we own?

Group of musicians, creamware with underglaze oxide decoration, made in Staffordshire, mid-18th century, ht. 160mm. *Henry Weldon Collection.*

Side view of a musician showing fire-cracks along the seam line, made in Staffordshire, mid-18th century, ht. 155mm. *City Museum & Art Gallery, Stoke-on-Trent, 141.P.1949.*

Group of musicians showing use of slip to colour the eyes and to decorate musical instruments, made in Staffordshire, mid-18th century, ht. 160mm. *Henry Weldon Collection.*

1. 18th Century Creamware Figures

The eighteenth century saw the introduction of English figure manufacture. The occasional individual piece may have been made earlier by an adventurous potter but figures had never before been produced on a commercial scale. By the middle of the century English porcelain makers not only reproduced figures from the Orient and from Europe but also devised new and popular subjects that would appeal to the wealthiest classes. The earthenware manufacturer, seizing the opportunity, produced a range of cheaper wares to fill a gap at the lower end of the market and as techniques and skills improved so the complexity of the figures increased.

Amongst the most charming and desirable of all figures are the earliest Staffordshire earthenware examples, often referred to as 'Astbury' type. The subject matter tends to be rather simple and unassuming, reflecting aspects of contemporary life. Occasionally a tradesman is found at his work — a cobbler being the most common — but more usually a variety of musicians were depicted engaged in playing both familiar and unfamiliar instruments.

Whilst the bases may be made from Staffordshire red clays, the bodies are usually of a light colour. White clays imported from Devon and Dorset were mixed with flint to produce a cream coloured earthenware, suitable for the production not only of the tablewares made famous by Josiah Wedgwood, but of the more humble images produced by the figure maker. The figures are made by a combination of hand modelling and press moulding. After making, the component moulded and hand modelled parts are dried and then assembled using slip (liquid clay) and left to dry again. The bodies and bases were moulded separately, and one can often see the seam line down the sides of the head and torso where the two halves meet, but many of the limbs are solid and may have hand modelled details. After drying, coloured slips were occasionally applied for decorative effect, perhaps brown to pick out the eyes or to ornament the costume, and white slip dots often enhance a red clay musical instrument. More usually the piece was fired to the biscuit state and coloured metal oxides were applied in streaks of manganese brown, copper green, iron yellow, or cobalt blue, before liquid lead glazing and a second firing.

The range and variety of this class of figure has led a number of leading authorities to suggest that more than one hand must have been at work and that the pieces could have been made over a period of twenty years. Despite this the name 'Astbury' has been introduced and although this is said to be a generic title and there is general acceptance amongst past authors of a prolonged production period, because of the name these figures are still closely associated with the personality of John Astbury and dated to the 1740s.

You may think it pedantic to resist the use of a generic title based on a potter's name, but here we have a good example of the name controlling our understanding of the wares. John Astbury, who is supposed to have made these figures, died in 1743; in consequence they have been dated to the early 1740s, when it is much more likely that they were made some time later. Several

Musician with typical underglaze oxide decoration, made in Staffordshire, mid-18th century, ht. 153mm. *Henry Weldon Collection.*

factors lead to the conclusion that the figures cannot be dated to 1740. First of all consider the moulds used to produce these figures: whilst primitive earthenware moulds had been used to make slipware plates and rough teawares in the seventeenth and early eighteenth centuries, the plaster of Paris moulds needed to make figures of this kind were not in general use in England until about 1740-5, when Ralph Daniel is credited with their introduction to North Staffordshire from France.[1] Secondly, we must consider the biscuit and glost double firing cycle combined with a liquid glaze which was used to produce these figures, this is also a post-1740 introduction; the earliest known pieces made in this way are two bowls dated 1743.[2] The example in the British Museum inscribed 'EB 1743' is attributed to Enoch Booth, the originator of the process. It may have been some years later that the double firing cycle was combined with the use of coloured oxides as a means of decoration and is not known on any piece which can be dated to the 1740s with any certainty.

It seems most unlikely, therefore, that John Astbury was responsible for the early figures, but as the attribution is said to be traditional and without wishing to overlook the slightest possibility that they could be Astbury's work, the past literature has been investigated. No catalogue or book of the nineteenth century credits Astbury with figure making and no relevant documentary evidence of the eighteenth century is known. The name was first introduced in the present century for the convenience of collectors and dealers. Another problem with this class of figure is that whilst casting round for a suitable eighteenth century manufacturer's name one also needs to consider twentieth century names.

In 1929 Herbert Read concluded his book on Staffordshire pottery figures by writing 'I am not acquainted by any forgeries of Astbury Whieldon type'.[3] However, there were plenty about at the time. If a potential forger is looking for suitable wares to reproduce, he must be delighted to find simple hand made pottery costing little to make, fetching high prices in the salerooms. Captain Price, in his book published in 1922, writes of 'Astbury' figures: 'They are very difficult to find, and it is a remarkable fact that from 1907-1917 not a single Astbury figure appeared at auction at Christie's but in November 1917 an equestrian figure came up for sale in the King Street rooms and realised 325gns'.[4] This was an exceptionally high price when compared with the salt-glazed man on a rhinoceros which fetched only 32gns just a couple of years before. Price goes on to tell us with some surprise that within three months at the same salerooms a pair of figures was knocked down at 130gns though badly damaged and another horseman for 320gns. In his preface to the book Price writes: 'The collection here catalogued was started in 1907 and more or less

1. *History of the Staffordshire Potteries*, S. Shaw 1829, reprinted David & Charles, 1970, pp.162-164.
2. City Museum & Art Gallery, Stoke-on-Trent. British Museum.
3. Read, H., *Staffordshire Pottery Figures*, Duckworth, 1929, p.23.
4. Price, R.K., *Astbury, Whieldon, and Ralph Wood Figures and Toby Jugs*, John Lane, 1922.

completed in 1917; as a matter of fact over eighty figures were bought in the latter year...I was stationed in Bedford in 1917 and was able to run up to London for a few hours once a week, and a lot of figures coming on the market during the year accounts for the number being bought'.[5] This signified the opening of the floodgates for 'Astbury' type figures and they became increasingly more easily available in many of the London auction houses. Mr. A.J.B. Kiddell of Sotheby's, who had seen this trade increase, eventually became suspicious and began to doubt the authenticity of some of the previously unrecorded models. The final flurry of fakes included a pew group impressed Wedgwood (now in the Victoria & Albert Museum) and a seated figure impressed 'Wood Burslem' (now in the City Museum & Art Gallery, Stoke-on-Trent). Possibly the forger had flooded the market with 'standard' models and so decided to spice up the scene with a few more desirable marked pieces, which were to be his undoing. I understand that many of the forgeries came from a workshop in Vauxhall, London, but details of this clandestine trade have never been published, only passed in whispers from one generation to the next. In 1933 The English Ceramic Circle reported: 'At the conclusion of the meeting Mr Wallace Elliot gave a word of warning to collectors as to the spurious Astbury figures which were being offered for sale in certain shops'.[6] Understandably, the market in early figures has never recovered the degree of buoyancy it enjoyed in the 1920s.

When studying mid-eighteenth century naïve figures one first needs to find a reliably authentic piece. This can be done with a little lateral thinking and a familiarity with well established collections. The Willett Collection, housed at Brighton Museum, is a very fine collection of pottery, including figures, which was gathered together to illustrate popular British History. The makers of the ware and its desirability in the collectors' market were not taken into consideration by Willett and an extremely catholic collection of almost 2,000 pieces was assembled. I believe the collection was completed by 1890 (at any rate a catalogue was produced in 1899), it therefore follows that anything in that catalogue must have been made before the forgeries were in production.

At the time I came to this conclusion I did not know that someone had arrived there before me. In fact in 1967 Ross E. Taggart, formerly Senior Curator of the William Rockhill Nelson Gallery of Art, Kansas City, Missouri, published an article in *The Art Quarterly* entitled 'John Astbury 1730 or 1930?'. Mr Taggart, Mr Kiddell and Mr Mountford (former Director of the City Museum & Art Gallery Stoke-on-Trent) often discussed the problems of identifying the figures and the forgeries. Their knowledge and expertise were passed to me by my Director, however, any errors in the distillation and retelling are all my own.

Despite the naïve modelling the early figures have a degree of detail in their

---

5. Ibid.

6. English Ceramic Circle, *Transactions No.1*, 1933, p.55.

Two figures of musicians sent for date testing: left, dating to the 18th century, right, dating to the 20th century. (See fakes, reproductions and mis-attributions, Chapter 7.)

execution which is lacking in the twentieth century fakes. Close examination of pieces in the Willett Collection showed consistent care in the depiction of dress — an emphasis on the neck cloth, the jacket cuffs, pleats and pockets and a general understanding of the fashion points of the day — which is totally neglected by the forger who little understood the importance of these details. Not only are these niceties not observed but the whole demeanour of the subject is wretchedly conceived. Perhaps it is because I think I know which is which that makes me so sure that the forgeries lack the liveliness and the vivacity of the originals and whilst the eighteenth century potters are unlikely to have thought they were creating small works of art, their unconscious interpretation of eighteenth century life has a unique quality which cannot be captured by a mere laboured copy.

In an effort to bring some scientific evidence to bear on my fairly subjective opinions, three figures were sent to the Oxford University Archaeology research laboratory for thermoluminescence testing and eventually positive results were achieved for two of the pieces. The conclusions confirmed that the theories concerning the relative merits of the modelling were correct and that the more detailed musician was indeed eighteenth century, whilst the sad little piece proved to be a twentieth century copy. Perhaps we can use the tested pieces as 'type specimens' to form the basis of a system of classification; certainly through comparison we should be able to distinguish the majority of the original figures from the copies.

A variety of figures was produced in the mid-eighteenth century. Without doubt the most well known are the musicians, which, as Reginald Haggar suggests, 'collectors delight to form into bands, in the same way as children marshal their toy lead soldiers'.[7] The most impressive of these bands is the military parade illustrated in Captain R.K. Price's book where seven horsemen lead twenty-four pipers and drummers.[8]

The base of the early creamware figure is usually modelled with a tree stump or pillar to support the subject in either a standing or seated position. The base may be either white or red clay and is occasionally decorated with rouletted bands around the circumference or with incised patterns on the rear of the pillar support. It is not difficult to tell that the same moulds were used time and again and we can see identical figures mounted on slightly different bases and given different musical instruments. The majority of the figures are engaged in musical pursuits, playing instruments, singing, or refreshing themselves with a drink. Many of the various moulds look as though they were prepared by the same hand and whilst there is an amazing variety to be found within this general class, there are several large sub-groups which are most commonly encountered.

The sub-groups are divided according to their common moulded features, the basic figure is the same in each category but may have additional details such as a hat or a variety of accoutrements, and it is suggested that the figures within each group were produced by the same source. We have no evidence to tell us whether a source may have made more than one of the groups.

The major sub-group groups are the most typical of the figures but there are many individual subjects and one or two strange categories, most notably a set of coarsely modelled subjects made from white clays and decorated with coloured glazes which would indicate a date of about 1780 and suggests that these figures may have been made over a long period.

7. Haggar, R.G., *English Country Pottery*, Phoenix, 1950, p.67.

8. Price, op.cit., pl.XVIII.

Man playing a zither, he holds the instrument in his hands and plays with his thumbs, made in Staffordshire, mid-18th century, ht. 124mm. *City Museum & Art Gallery, Stoke-on-Trent, 138.P.1949.*

Man reading, coarsely modelled, decorated with clear and coloured glazes, made in Staffordshire, 1750-75, ht. 145mm. *City Museum & Art Gallery, Stoke-on-Trent, 149.P.1949.*

Two figures from the Willett Collection, made in Staffordshire, mid-18th century, ht. 135mm. *Royal Pavilion Art Gallery & Museum, Brighton, HW888.*

Reverse of two figures from the Willett Collection showing details of their hair style and coats. *Royal Pavilion Art Gallery & Museum, Brighton HW888.*

The most commonly found group of early creamware figures is that represented by seated figures from the Willett Collection, Brighton (HW888) and from Stoke-on-Trent (138.P.1949). The subject is seated on a small column which may be intended to represent the base of a tree trunk. The seat and the base are moulded as one and are often made from red clay, occasionally the back of the seat has a design of incised lines forming a diamond pattern. The figures are of cream coloured earthenware, the heads are modelled with simple features, the eyes often picked out in brown slip, the wig styled away from the face with a centre parting and two rows of curls just above the collar. The suit of clothes includes knee breeches, which are marked just below the knee with two incised lines; a neck cloth is tied at the throat and although no shirt is visible, a buttoned waistcoat can be seen beneath the half open jacket. The jacket has buttoned pleats at the back, turned back buttoned cuffs displaying a handsome show of lace and buttoned pocket flaps. Occasionally a separately moulded tricorne hat completes the ensemble. The arms of the figure may vary as they are moulded and applied separately and can therefore be from different moulds and adapted to suit the activities of the subject. The most popular instruments are of the violin family and a curious form of bagpipe; others may be the flute, horn or zither. Their companions may raise a glass to the entertainers.

Another major sub-group of seated musicians shown opposite may be found with either red or cream coloured earthenware bases. The figures are somewhat simple in detail, lacking a neck cloth and wearing only a rudimentary waistcoat, however, the head is nicely finished with the wig having a rolled curl in a continuous circle framing the face and extending round the back of the head. The potter gave most of his attention to the jacket, with detailed pleating to the back and with wide, buttoned and frilled cuffs. This is the most versatile figure, who can be found at work or at play as a cobbler, horn player or bagpiper, or merely relaxing with a bottle and glass.

Seated man holding a bottle and a glass, made in Staffordshire, mid-18th century, ht. 124mm. *Royal Pavilion Art Gallery & Museum, Brighton, HW1485.*

Reverse of seated man holding a bottle and a glass showing details of the hair style and pleated jacket, made in Staffordshire, mid-18th century. *Royal Pavilion Art Gallery & Museum, Brighton, HW1485.*

A common form of standing figure shown over the page has a taller supporting 'tree stump'. The face is simply modelled but the wig has a rather fetching arrangement of curls about each ear and a short queue tied in a complex way; occasionally a separately modelled tricorne hat is set on top of the head between the side curls. The knee breeches have a side fastening at the knee, the partly opened jacket shows a button waistcoat and a neck cloth tied loosely at the throat. The jacket has two sets of pleats at the back and wide buttoned cuffs with falls of lace. The proportions of this model are somewhat eccentric, in that the separately moulded legs and body seem to have been modelled with little regard to their final assembly; the rather short legs do not appear to be attached to the body but dangle from the edges of the waistcoat.

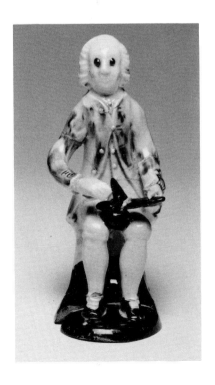

Figure of a cobbler, made in Staffordshire, mid-18th century, ht. 120mm. *Fitzwilliam Museum, Cambridge, Glaisher Collection, 817.*

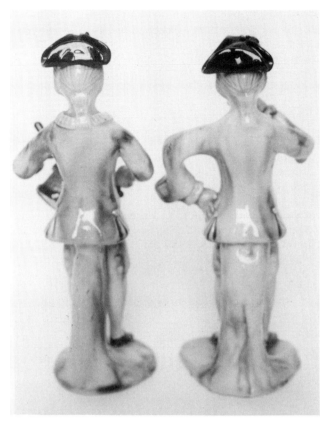

Two musicians with underglaze oxide decoration made in Staffordshire, mid-18th century, ht. 155mm. *Royal Pavilion Art Gallery & Museum, Brighton, HW888.*

Reverse of two musicians showing details of hair and jackets, made in Staffordshire, mid-18th century. *Royal Pavilion Art Gallery & Museum, Brighton, HW888.*

Two musicians with underglaze oxide decoration, made in Staffordshire, mid-18th century, ht. 150mm. *Wisbech & Fenland Museum, 1900. 44 & 45.*

Reverse of two musicians showing details of hair style and pleated jacket, made in Staffordshire, mid-18th century. *Wisbech & Fenland Museum, 1900. 44 & 45.*

Musician playing a violin, with rouletted base and streaks of colour highlighting the buttons, buttonholes and cuffs of the jacket, made in Staffordshire, mid-18th century. *City Museum & Art Gallery, Stoke-on-Trent, 145.P.1949.*

Another common form of standing figure is made entirely from cream coloured earthenware, of which the circular base, which is modelled with a supporting column, is often decorated with incised rouletted designs highlighted with an underglaze oxide colour. The face is simply modelled, the wig has a roll of curled hair framing the face and a long queue beautifully tied with a bow. The suit is distinguished by rows of well modelled buttons and buttonholes on the jacket, waistcoat and breeches; there are also elaborate cuffs with pleated lace and the whole is finished with a finely tied neck cloth. These figures are particularly well decorated with underglaze oxides, often with streaks of colour to highlight the rows of buttons and buttonholes on the jacket, or to draw attention to other fine details of modelling.

Musician with rouletted base and underglaze oxide decoration, made in Staffordshire, mid-18th century, ht. 150mm. *Royal Pavilion Art Gallery & Museum, Brighton, HW888I.*

Reverse of musician showing decorated support, made in Staffordshire, mid-18th century. *Royal Pavilion Art Gallery & Museum, Brighton, HW888I.*

Two figures of bagpipers wearing kilts, both stand on red earthenware bases, the creamware body is decorated with underglaze oxides, made in Staffordshire, mid-18th century, ht. 160mm. *Royal Pavilion Art Gallery & Museum, Brighton, HW888.*

Reverse of the two bagpipers showing the short queue wigs and the jackets with three sets of pleats, made in Staffordshire, mid-18th century. *Royal Pavilion Art Gallery and Museum, Brighton, HW888.*

The final major sub-group is that of standing musicians distinguished by the wearing of kilts. The figure stands on a red clay base with supporting column and is made of cream coloured earthenware. The face is simply modelled with a short queue topped with a small round cap. The details of the neck cloth, jacket buttons, buttonholes and cuffs are well modelled. The kilt is a shortish garment, often modelled with a diced pattern perhaps to simulate a design, more rarely the knee length socks are given the same treatment. Across the body is worn a baldric and the musician plays a set of bagpipes.

1. Group of musicians, cream coloured earthenware (two with red clay bases), with underglaze oxide decoration, made in Staffordshire, mid-18th century, ht. 155mm. *City Museum & Art Gallery, Stoke-on-Trent.*

Drummer, standing on red earthenware base and with red slip over the head, decorated with underglaze oxide colours, made in Staffordshire, mid-18th century, ht. 165mm. *Royal Pavilion Art Gallery & Museum, Brighton, HW888.*

Drummer with rouletted base and well modelled jacket but with a very stylised face, made in Staffordshire, mid-18th century, ht. 163mm. *Royal Pavilion Art Gallery & Museum, Brighton, HW888.*

Cymbal player with rouletted base, lively modelling with a stripe of green glaze down the centre front, made in Staffordshire, 1760-75, ht. 152mm. *City Museum & Art Gallery, Stoke-on-Trent, 151.P.1949.*

Women rarely occur as individual figures in the mid-eighteenth century and are usually seen as part of an elaborate assemblage, perhaps at a tea-table or sitting beside men on a bench. The latter, known as pew groups, are more commonly found (if the adjective common can ever be applied to these pieces) in saltglazed stoneware. The naïve modelling gives these figures a particular charm, evoking a spontaneous reaction in which enthusiasts and collectors find themselves responding to the unaffected depiction of eighteenth century life. If the musicians seem a little preoccupied and dull, the dancers whirl with abandon and who could resist speculating on the probable conversation between the occupants of the pew groups?

The lucky owners of the fortress figures have studied their two pieces very carefully, and after many entertaining suggestions have decided that one illustrates the fortress troops about to show their might, with all the soldiers involved in soldierly duties, whilst the other fortress shows what happens when the cannon are fired and the regiment rushes out to see the result — a sort of before and after piece.

A slightly more sophisticated product was available from the third quarter of the eighteenth century; my own favourites are the arbour groups. Within the confines of an arbour or garden pavilion sit gossiping ladies or young lovers, wearing the most fashionable garments and conveying with expressive gestures their desires, both honourable and otherwise. The more arboreal of these groups are encrusted with floral sprays and rosettes of the type normally associated with ornamented tewares of the 1750-70 period; certainly the reverse of the example in the Willett Collection, Brighton, looks like nothing

Pew group, in which a violinist plays whilst
a lady next to him takes tea from a tray
held by a black servant, creamware
decorated with coloured oxides, made in
Staffordshire, mid-18th century, ht. 136mm.
Colonial Williamsburg, 1963-335.

Figure group depicting a scene in a tavern,
where four men sit around a table bearing
a punch bowl and drinking vessels, a
young lady sits on the knee of one of the
revellers, the creamware body decorated
with coloured oxides, made in Staffordshire, mid-18th century, ht. 172mm.
Colonial Williamsburg, 1963-242.

2. Lady with a lap dog, mounted cavalry officer, cream coloured earthenware with underglaze oxide decoration, made in Staffordshire, c.1750-70, ht. 188mm. *City Museum & Art Gallery, Stoke-on-Trent, 3005, 135.P.1949*

3. Arbour group, cream coloured earthenware with underglaze oxide decoration, made in Staffordshire, c.1750-70, ht. 146mm. *City Museum & Art Gallery, Stoke-on-Trent, 129.P.1949.*

4. A group of cream coloured earthenware figures, with underglaze oxide decoration in a typical range of colours, made in Staffordshire, c.1760-80, ht. 193mm. *City Museum & Art Gallery, Stoke-on-Trent.*

Model of a fortress with soldiers and loaded cannon, the creamware body decorated with coloured oxides, made in Staffordshire, mid-18th century, ht. 175mm. *Henry Weldon Collection.*

Model of a fortress with soldiers and empty cannon, the creamware body decorated with coloured oxides, made in Staffordshire, mid-18th century, ht. 175mm. *Henry Weldon Collection.*

Arbour group, with a young lady and gentleman in the seclusion of a garden arbour, the creamware body decorated with coloured oxides, made in Staffordshire, c.1750-70, ht. 172mm. *Colonial Williamsburg, 1963-392.* A similar example may be found in the Glaisher Collection, Fitzwilliam Museum, Cambridge.

Reverse of arbour group showing the floral encrustations over a basic diaper pattern with stars and dots more typical of tablewares of the period. *Colonial Williamsburg, 1963-392.*

Figure of a woman, wearing an open robe displaying tiered petticoats over wide panniers, the creamware body decorated with coloured oxides, made in Staffordshire, c.1750-70, ht. 124mm. *Colonial Williamsburg, 1963-590.*
This model can also be found in groups such as the floral encrusted arbour group and a similar example is in the Glaisher Collection, Fitzwilliam Museum, Cambridge.

Figure of a woman seated in an ornately modelled chair holding a lap dog, the creamware body decorated with coloured oxides, made in Staffordshire, c.1750-70, ht. 140mm. *City Museum & Art Gallery, Stoke-on-Trent, 3005.*
This is possibly the most common female model of the period and examples can be found in many museum collections.

Equestrian figure, with the man sitting astride the horse carrying a woman side-saddle, the creamware body with coloured oxide decoration, made in Staffordshire, 1750-70, ht. 210mm. *Royal Pavilion Art Gallery & Museum, Brighton, HW1173.*
The figure of the woman appears to be the same model as the seated woman with a lap dog, with the addition of a hat.

A pair of lovers embracing, the creamware body with coloured oxide decoration, made in Staffordshire, c.1750-60, ht. 105mm. *Henry Weldon Collection.*
This group can also be found in white saltglazed stoneware and in a version with the woman's leg exposed to the knee.

Figure of a woman wearing a wide panniered skirt, the creamware body with coloured oxide decoration, made in Staffordshire, c.1750-60, ht. 111mm. Colonial Williamsburg, 1963-385.
This figure may also be found in white saltglazed stoneware.

so much as a dot and diaper moulded plate, which again one would normally associate with the 1750s to 1770s.

Many of the moulded figures appear singly, or in arbours and other figure groups. A moulded lady wearing a wide panniered dress is known as a single standing figure in a number of collections, and can be identified dancing with a gentleman in an arbour group in the Kansas City, Missouri, collection and seated in arbours in the collection at Colonial Williamsburg and in the Willett Collection, Brighton. One of the most common figures is that of a woman seated in a decorative, high backed chair holding a lap-dog; she may also be found within an arbour group in the collection of the British Museum and riding side-saddle in an equestrian group in the Willett Collection. A similar figure in the Colonial Williamsburg Collection has the impressed mark 'FELL' and is considered to be a twentieth century copy.

The use of moulds to create a variety of finished goods is sound economical practice and similar figures may be found singly or in groups, in both earthenware and stoneware. The seated lovers with hands resting on the woman's knee can also be found in white saltglazed stoneware, as can at least one of the panniered lady figures. Studying the links between these individual models and groups helps to isolate and classify categories of figures, which may one day find the appropriate maker's name.

The problem of attributing these wares seems to be illustrated by the terms 'Astbury-Whieldon' and 'Whieldon', used to describe a wider range of more

Three soldiers, one playing a fife, one a drum and the third holding a sword, the creamware body touched with underglaze oxides, standing on coloured glaze base, made in Staffordshire, 1770-80, ht. 150mm. *Courtesy of Earle P. Vandekar.*

Figure of a soldier holding a rifle with bayonet attached, made in Staffordshire, 1770-80, ht. 155mm. *Colonial Williamsburg, 1963-222.*

sophisticated models produced in the mid to late eighteenth century. There is a narrow division between these and the naïve models and it is difficult to know where one class ends and the next begins. As these figures are made and decorated in basically the same way, I prefer to call them eighteenth century creamware figures, a group term which is all encompassing. Like the naïve figures, the more sophisticated pieces were also made from cream coloured earthenware, again decorated at the biscuit stage with coloured oxides sponged or painted on to the body before glazing and re-firing, after the manner of tortoiseshell and similar wares. The range of subjects widens to include a greater number of contemporary figures and models of domestic and exotic animals. The moulds are usually simple with as few parts as possible (extended limbs and accoutrements are kept to a minimum as these need additional moulds and assembly processes). Because of the relatively cheap method of production, these figures would have been inexpensive compared with enamelled saltglaze and the even more costly porcelains available from the mid-eighteenth century.

Amongst the most popular subjects are models of men with guns and/or swords, some of whom are soldiers and others may be huntsmen. Certainly a number appear to be wearing uniform, and others wear the ordinary clothes of an eighteenth century man. A letter to the National Army Museum to solicit information about the military style figures produced some interesting information: the reply suggested that the figures were interpretive rather than

Equestrian figure, moulded with additional hand modelled details and standing on a high ornate base, the creamware body with coloured oxide decoration, made in Staffordshire 1760-80, ht. 253mm. *City Museum & Art Gallery, Stoke-on-Trent, 3007.*

'The figure with a cloak on a white horse bears much less resemblance to a soldier. The cap is superficially similar to that adopted by the Light Dragoons but the clothing details are purely decorative. The figure has a rather continental look, and it may have been devised from illustrations of foreign troops.' *(Letter from the National Army Museum, August 1988.)*

Equestrian figure, moulded with additional hand modelled details, the creamware body sponged with coloured oxides, made in Staffordshire, 1760-80, ht. 253mm. *Royal Pavilion Art Gallery & Museum, Brighton, HW240.*

This figure appears to be the same model as that in Stoke-on-Trent and is occasionally found paired with another soldierly equestrian; the model illustrated here is known in a number of museum collections with different decorative treatments.

Mounted soldier, the creamware body with coloured oxide decoration, made in Staffordshire, 1760-80, ht. 191mm. *City Museum & Art Gallery, Stoke-on-Trent, 135.P.1949.*

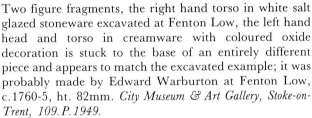

Two figure fragments, the right hand torso in white salt glazed stoneware excavated at Fenton Low, the left hand head and torso in creamware with coloured oxide decoration is stuck to the base of an entirely different piece and appears to match the excavated example; it was probably made by Edward Warburton at Fenton Low, c.1760-5, ht. 82mm. *City Museum & Art Gallery, Stoke-on-Trent, 109.P.1949.*
A complete example decorated with a green glaze can be found in the Museum of London, 3197/12.

Figure of Admiral Rodney, titled vertically by the side of his right leg, the creamware body with coloured oxide decoration, made in Staffordshire, probably to commemorate his success in naval battles, 1780-2, ht. 146mm. *City Museum & Art Gallery, Stoke-on-Trent, 164.P.1949.*

exact representations of military subjects, but that there was no doubt they were originally based on British military uniforms. The individual figures of soldiers were considered to be quite good, but the cut of the coats and waistcoats suggested a period later than that normally accepted for pottery figures of this kind. Military clothing of the mid-eighteenth century was loose and voluminous: these figures wear the closer fitting uniforms of the 1770s.

The most impressive figures of this period are the equestrian models. Whilst a number of the equestrian figures are made from red clay, the majority of them are of white clay and flint, the basic ingredients of cream coloured earthenware which became one of Staffordshire's staple products from the mid-eighteenth century. The complex, mounted soldiers deserve particular mention, certain subjects were obviously popular and occur in many collections. The elaborate high bases of a number of figures first drew my attention to one particular model, in which the range of decorative techniques produces such a variation in the finished product that it is not immediately obvious that they are from the same mould. Examples in the Willett Collection, Brighton, have been sponged and painted with coloured oxides at the biscuit stage, producing a strong tortoiseshell effect under the lead glaze. A similar piece from the City Museum & Art Gallery, Stoke-on-Trent, made from the same mould, has a more restrained use of coloured pigments resulting in a more sophisticated looking product.

In a very few cases it is possible to link figures with a particular manufacturer, e.g. Whieldon, Warburton or Greatbatch, but the great majority of figures will remain anonymous until further studies are carried out. The use of any generic title based on a person's name is likely to hinder future research with a confusing terminology and inaccurate dating. For example on page 39, if we call the figure on the left Astbury-Whieldon we consciously or subconsciously further classify it as made about 1750, after saltglaze and before more sophisticated models. None of these things are true about this piece or necessarily about any other naïve figure. A generic title based on a potter's name also makes us complacent, because we don't have to discover the right name, we don't have to consider a date as late as 1765 and we have a tidy sequence of figure development from saltglazed to pearlware.

The saltglazed torso on the right was excavated at Fenton Low, a potworks owned by Thomas Whieldon, but as far as we can tell, never occupied by him. A green glazed example of this figure is in the collection of the Museum of London (3197/12). Green glaze was a technical development introduced and popularised by Josiah Wedgwood about 1759.[9] This evidence suggests that the figure must post-date 1759, at which time the Fenton Low site was occupied by the Warburton family; therefore we can say that figures of this type were produced by Edward Warburton at Fenton Low about 1760-5.

Another problem which is often encountered is that all simply conceived figures are assumed to be early, when in fact they were merely made for the cheaper end of the market and were produced over a very long period. Many of the simpler figures are attributed to Thomas Whieldon and as such are frequently dated to the mid-eighteenth century. The figure of Admiral Rodney on page 39 is titled vertically down the left-hand side of the plinth and the earliest this item could possibly be is 1768, when Rodney contested the seat in the Northampton election, and a few tin-glazed plates are known from this period. It could have been produced when Rodney was appointed Rear-Admiral of Great Britain in 1771, however, as portrait figures were so rarely made, it seems unlikely that these two events of localised interest should have been immortalised in clay. It is far more reasonable to suppose that the figure was made about 1780-2, when Rodney's success in naval battles made him a national hero and when many other commemoratives were issued. A model of this type would more usually be dated to 1750-60 and it is hoped that this example serves to justify a wider date range than has hitherto been accepted. Perhaps this group could be called creamware figures of 1750-80?

I believe that oxide decorated figures must have been produced well into the 1770s, otherwise we lose continuation of production. If, as is commonly held,

9. Wedgwood's *Experiment Book No.1*, MSS E26.19117, courtesy Trustees of the Wedgwood Museum.

5. Figures of an elephant and a lion, cream coloured earthenware, the bases with underglaze manganese oxide decoration, made in Staffordshire, c.1750-70, ht. 130mm. *City Museum & Art Gallery, Stoke-on-Trent, 212, 213.*
These figures have no decoration on their bodies and show clearly the cream colour produced by the iron contamination in the glaze.

6. Group of birds, cream coloured earthenware with underglaze oxide decoration, made in Staffordshire, c.1750-70, ht. 270mm. *City Museum & Art Gallery, Stoke-on-Trent, 210, 2956, 211.*
The pair of parrots are decorated with applied grape and vine sprays, the centre bird stands on a tall base with applied leaves and rosettes; similar decorations may be found on contemporary tablewares.

the early naïve figures were made in the 1740s and the more sophisticated tortoiseshell figures were 1750-60, what was made from 1760 to the late 1770-80 period when coloured glazes were introduced?

The foregoing arguments were laid out in some detail in order to illustrate the problems associated with generic title. However, I do not wish to be entirely negative on the subject of figures and their makers and I would like to introduce one or two new names as well give as some basic facts about one of our most famous potters.

Thomas Whieldon is arguably the best known Staffordshire potter of the mid-eighteenth century. He was baptised at Stoke-upon-Trent in 1719. Many of the earliest writers on ceramics have suggested that Whieldon began potting in Fenton Low, basing this on the evidence of Simeon Shaw who wrote: 'In 1740 Thomas Whieldon's manufactory at Little Fenton consisted of a small range of low buildings, all thatched'.[10] For some reason earlier researchers took Little Fenton to be Fenton Low, when in fact they are two distinct and separate areas of Fenton, about half a mile apart.[11] Perhaps these researchers were not conversant with the problematic topography of the Potteries, but Little Fenton, also correctly known as Fenton Vivian (a name which I shall continue to use to avoid further misunderstanding), was a manorial district with Fenton Low lying outside its boundary on rising ground to the north-east.

There is no direct evidence that Thomas Whieldon ever potted at Fenton Low, but it is known that he owned land and a pottery there which he rented to others. Pottery from this site has been recovered and attributed to Whieldon, when it should have been more correctly attributed to his tenants. It is possible that Whieldon occupied the site at Fenton Low before becoming established at Fenton Vivian, but there is no evidence to support this view and he was certainly occupying Fenton Vivian before 1747, when a document concerning the owner of the site describes the pottery in terms which indicate that Whieldon was undertaking a substantial business. Thomas Whieldon bought the Fenton Vivian property in 1748 and made further purchases of land and buildings in 1749, including the large house called Fenton Hall and a flint mill.[12] When Thomas was married to Anne Shaw in 1744, he eschewed the cheaper marriage by banns and entered into a marriage by licence; his marriage bond lists him as a potter and his bondsmen were bound in the sum of £100. Within four years his wife and daughter Anne had died; his daughter Mary died ten years later. Thomas's second marriage, in 1758, was to Alice Parrot, a member of an eminent family in nearby Newcastle under Lyme. Again he married by licence and his marriage bonds called him Gentleman rather than potter, indicating his elevated status as a successful business man.

---

10. Shaw, op.cit., p.155.

11. Mountford, A.R., 'Thomas Whieldon's Manufactory at Fenton Vivian', English Ceramic Circle, *Transactions Vol.8 Part 2,* 1972.

12. Staffordshire County Record Office, mss.D239/M 2393-2402.

Alice died childless in October 1772.

Thomas Whieldon's third marriage took place four years later in 1776; again he entered into a marriage bond, standing as his own bondsman, together with Charles Garland Greenwollers of New Inn, London, and secured a licence to marry Sarah Turner of London. This appears to have been a happy and successful union and about 1780 Thomas gave up the potting business, razed the factory to the ground and converted the lands into pleasure grounds around his family home.

In 1968, following the discovery of some key documents, the Archaeological Society attached to the City Museum & Art Gallery, Stoke-on-Trent, began excavating the Whieldon site and uncovered some thousands of fragments, which led to the discovery of several figure models which we now know were produced at Thomas Whieldon's pottery in Fenton Vivian. Fairly extensive excavations on this site revealed a wide range of pottery from slipwares to sophisticated enamelled creamware. Amongst the thousands of fragments recovered were pieces from ten figure models, hardly the quantity one would expect from the man who is credited with making almost every mid-eighteenth century figure we see. We have to remind ourselves that by 1750 about 150 potworks were in operation in North Staffordshire and many may have made figures alongside their main tableware productions. We must also remember that Whieldon does not necessarily mean 1750-60. Thomas Whieldon continued in business until about 1780, making tortoiseshell, creamwares and saltglazed stonewares, apparently not moving with his illustrious contemporaries into jasper, basalt or other neo-classical stonewares.

Few of the figures found on the Whieldon site are of particularly outstanding quality; indeed the small bird on a stump is one of the least remarkable of its type. It is a tiny piece less than two inches high and its two-part moulded construction is of the simplest and cheapest kind. The decoration is a brown manganese oxide sponged on to the biscuit body, the lead glaze applied over the top fills in the few details of modelling, leaving a smooth stylised form; the whole is only redeemed by its charm and the warm silky feel it has when held in the hand. Pieces like this emphasise the tactile qualities which mean so much to a lover of English pottery. Much more difficult to identify was the fragment which turned out to be the leg of a buffalo from a boy on a buffalo figure. The legs of buffalo figures can be quite different from each other and this piece tells us only that this particular style of buffalo was produced by Whieldon, not that all buffalo figures were his work. Two other glazed fragments were very small parts of arms, one bent at the elbow the other with a frilled cuff, but the complete figures have yet to be identified.

All the other fragments which have been recovered are of cream coloured earthenware fired to biscuit temperature and then discarded for some reason or another. There are pieces from six other figures or groups, but none of the pieces are very substantial and a great deal of detective work is needed to match them with extant pieces.

Figure of a bird, the creamware body with coloured oxide decoration, together with a fragment of a bird excavated on the site of Thomas Whieldon's pottery, Fenton Vivian, the complete example made in Staffordshire, probably by Thomas Whieldon, 1750-70, ht. 55mm. *City Museum & Art Gallery, Stoke-on-Trent, 110.P.1949.*

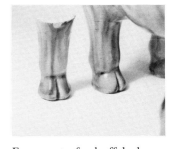

Fragment of a buffalo leg, the creamware body with coloured oxide decoration, seen here with part of a complete figure *(City Museum & Art Gallery, Stoke-on-Trent, 3044)*. The fragment was excavated on the site of Thomas Whieldon's pottery, Fenton Vivian.

7. Water buffalo and rider, cream coloured earthenware, with underglaze oxide decoration, made in Staffordshire, c.1750-70, l. 230mm. *Sotheby's, London.*
The rider is unusual and is often found as a free-standing figure, said to be a shepherd based on a 17th century bronze. Fragments of this figure, together with the leg of a buffalo, were found on the site of Thomas Whieldon's pottery at Fenton Vivian.

8. Pair of spill vases with figures of goats, cream coloured earthenware with underglaze oxide and coloured glaze decoration, made in Staffordshire, c.1760-80, ht. 200mm. *City Museum & Art Gallery, Stoke-on-Trent, 3065, 3066.*

Boy on a buffalo, the creamware body with coloured oxide decoration, the boy painted with dark red slip, made in Staffordshire, possibly by Thomas Whieldon, 1750-70, ht. 161mm. *City Museum & Art Gallery, Stoke-on-Trent, 3044.*

Boy on a buffalo, the creamware body with coloured oxide decoration, made in Staffordshire, 1750-70, ht. 172mm. *City Museum & Art Gallery, Stoke-on-Trent, 158.P.1949.*

Biscuit earthenware fragments of a pair of shepherd and shepherdess figures were found on the site of Thomas Whieldon's pottery, Fenton Vivian. Figures of this type are said to be based on early bronze originals, but the sources are not known to the author. The models are known in various types of pottery including red stoneware and white saltglaze.

Biscuit earthenware fragment of a dog sitting on a plinth, probably part of a figure of a shepherd. Excavated on the site of Thomas Whieldon's pottery, Fenton Vivian.

Figure of a shepherdess, undecorated creamware, made in Staffordshire, possibly by Thomas Whieldon, 1750-60, ht. 203mm. *Temple Newsam House, Leeds, 1/42.*

The figure of the dog on a plinth is usually accompanied by his master; unfortunately the master has become dislodged in this case and we are left to find the complete piece with very little evidence to assist us. The figure is probably that of a shepherd, said to have a bronze prototype, which is better known in saltglazed stoneware and also occurs in red stoneware. The head of

Biscuit earthenware fragment of the head of a figure, probably that of a shepherd (see complete example). Excavated on the site of Thomas Whieldon's pottery, Fenton Vivian.

Figure of a shepherd, the creamware body with coloured oxide decoration, made in Staffordshire possibly by Thomas Whieldon, 1750-60, ht. 140mm. *Colonial Williamsburg, 1963-348.*

Figure of a shepherdess, the creamware body with coloured oxide decoration, made in Staffordshire possibly by Thomas Whieldon, 1750-60, ht. 133mm. *Colonial Williamsburg, 1963-349.*

Biscuit earthenware fragment of the torso of a female figure holding a staff in the right hand and a stylised flower in the left, similar to that of a figure of a shepherdess. Excavated on the site of Thomas Whieldon's pottery, Fenton Vivian.

Three figure fragments, creamware body unglazed; left, the legs of a man possibly a soldier; centre, figure possibly representing Autumn from the Seasons; right, reverse of a female figure showing a sac-back dress. Excavated on the site of Thomas Whieldon's pottery, Fenton Vivian.

Seated pug dog, the creamware body with coloured oxide decoration, made in Staffordshire, 1755-65, ht. 76mm. *Rosalind Pretzfelder Collection.*
The face of the dog appears to match exactly fragments excavated on the site of Thomas Whieldon's pottery, Fenton Vivian.

such a shepherd was found on the site and is a further clue to the identification of true Whieldon productions. Part of a female figure from the site appears to be a shepherdess (probably the companion to the aforementioned shepherd), which is also found in white saltglazed stoneware (Northampton Museum 1920-1-dl-172). One would not have associated the shepherds with the buffalo figure mentioned above, until a buffalo carrying a shepherd was sold recently in a London saleroom; however incongruous the subject, at least one would have reasonable grounds for associating the piece with Thomas Whieldon.

Part of the head of a pug dog, excavated from the site of Thomas Whieldon's pottery, Fenton Vivian.

Other Whieldon figure fragments include the bodice of a female figure, the back view showing a fashionable sac-back dress. A complete version of this lady appears in Captain Price's catalogue (no. 48), where she is of undecorated cream coloured earthenware, and another example in the Metropolitan Museum has underglaze oxide colouring. Another female figure is a badly worn but recognisable figure of Summer, from a set of Seasons, holding a basket of seasonal produce under her right arm. The most difficult piece to match is a pair of male legs which I do not recognise. One of the most exciting fragments is a small piece of the shoulder and back of a male figure, with the hair tied in a queue very like that of the musician figures. As yet I have to find an example with an exactly similar hair style. Finally there are two small fragments which appear to be the head and neck of a dog wearing a collar. The face seems to match a number of extant examples. Unfortunately, many of the excavated fragments are badly worn and do not reproduce well in photographs.

Thomas Whieldon had purchased the site of Fenton Low pot works by 1750, when he was consolidating his land holdings in the Fenton area. In that year he received from William Meir, £14.10s. for the annual rent of 'a house & potworks & 3 small clowses'.[13] The parish registers seem to indicate that

13. Thomas Whieldon's notebook, City Museum & Art Gallery, Stoke-on-Trent.

Group of fragments from the William Greatbatch site, Fenton; left, a green glazed wing; centre, a biscuit earthenware swan; right, the head of a bird. *City Museum & Art Gallery, Stoke-on-Trent.*

Cybele, the creamware body with coloured oxide decoration, made in Staffordshire, c.1775-80, ht. 136mm. *Colonial Williamsburg, 1963-413.*
The figure appears to match the fragments from William Greatbatch's site in Fenton.

Fragments of the feet of Cybele, creamware with overglaze painted decoration, excavated from the site of William Greatbatch's factory, Fenton, Staffordshire, c.1775-82.

William Poulson had occupied the site until his death in 1746, thus William Meir had a very short tenancy, for by 1751 the potworks was in the hands of the Warburton family. William Warburton died in 1754 and he was succeeded by his son Edward, who continued to pay rent for Fenton Low throughout the period covered by Thomas Whieldon's note book, that is until 1761. It is likely he continued to occupy the premises until his death in 1767. Because of lack of post-medieval excavation experience the fragments from Fenton Low were recovered in a somewhat haphazard way. The owners of the site collected the surface pieces over a number of years during the 1920s and they were dispersed amongst Museums and interested antiquarians of the day. It is impossible to tell if we have access to all the fragments. Collections are known in Liverpool, Norwich, London and Stoke, but information about other caches may greatly assist future research. Apart from the simple white saltglazed gentleman discussed above, there is a small cream coloured earthenware fragment from the head of a figure of a Chinese Immortal, decorated in underglaze oxides. This can be seen in the Victoria & Albert Museum and appears to match a complete example decorated in a similar manner in the Schreiber Collection at the Museum. No other figures from this manufacturer are known at this time.

William Greatbatch is one of Staffordshire's rising stars, brought to prominence through the excavations and writings of David Barker of the Archaeology Department of the City Museum & Art Gallery, Stoke-on-Trent. William Greatbatch also had a potworks in Fenton, which was in operation between 1762 and 1782. Many tons of ceramic waste testify to the range and quality of Greatbatch's work, but once again figures seem to have been a very small part of the production output. The most interesting fragments were those that on reconstruction formed the base of a female figure with a lion at her feet and a cornucopia spilling out on the ground in front of her. The fairly early date and simplicity of construction of this figure gives it affinities with the Whieldon examples. Several complete examples have been recorded in both English and American collections and whilst the two bases recovered from the site are of cream coloured earthenware decorated over the glaze with enamel painting, coloured glazed examples are also known.

Other models found on the Greatbatch site include the head of a finch-like bird in biscuit creamware, of simple form, but with nicely modelled feathers, so easy to see in the unglazed fragment, but which are likely to be obscured by glaze in any extant specimen we are lucky enough to find. Another avian figure is that of a swan, again a simple model with nicely detailed feathers and wonderful arching neck; this model occurs in both biscuit and glost cream coloured earthenware. A dramatic wing of cream coloured earthenware with green overglaze enamel painted tips testifies to a more exotic bird, which we have yet to identify. The only other human figure to be found was represented by a leg exposed from a draped garment, not a lot to go on but perhaps a collector with an eye for legs will recognise it.

No other figures from this mid to late eighteenth century creamware class can be positively identified as the work of a specific manufacturer, however, the unknown pieces include some of the best and most interesting items.

The source of inspiration for the Staffordshire manufacturer at this date can only be speculated upon. Many of the subjects are obviously of Chinese origin, but whether they were copies of Chinese pieces, of Continental or English porcelain models, or from some other source, we do not know. One of the most popular figures is the buffalo carrying a variety of Chinese and other less appropriate passengers, as discussed above. The most usual rider is a small Chinese boy, occasionally painted beneath the glaze with a dark slip which fires to a brownish black. The Chinese Immortals occur in various models, including the type suggested as the work of the Warburtons of Fenton Low. A particularly fine pair of Lohans are those copied from a pair of blanc-de-chine figures of Fujian porcelain, which are also known in white saltglazed stoneware.

It seems that at this time manufacturers rarely specialised in one particular class of pottery and it is necessary to look at all the ceramic materials to build up a picture of the whole range of possible figure productions. This is true of a fine pair of saltglazed stoneware busts of Maria Theresa and her husband Francis I in the Victoria & Albert Museum's Schreiber Collection (1187 & A),

Pair of portrait busts identified as Francis I of Germany (1708-1765) and his wife Maria Theresa, the parents of Marie Antoinette. The creamware body with coloured oxide decoration, made in Staffordshire, c.1760, ht. 222mm. *Royal Pavilion Art Gallery & Museum, Brighton, HW367.*

Figure of a bird, creamware body with underglaze oxide decoration, made in Staffordshire, 1760-80, ht. 197mm. *City Museum & Art Gallery, Stoke-on-Trent, 171.P.1949.*
The bird appears to be based on Chinese Kangxi porcelain models which were widely copied by European porcelain makers.

Recumbent horse, the creamware body with coloured oxide decoration, made in Staffordshire, 1755-65, ht. 210mm. *City Museum & Art Gallery, Stoke-on-Trent, 155.P.1949.*
This model is also known in Longton Hall porcelain and white saltglazed stoneware.

which appear to come from the same mould as a cream coloured earthenware pair decorated with underglaze oxides in the Willett Collection at Brighton (Willett 367). Again in the Victoria & Albert Museum is a Longton Hall porcelain figure of a horse lying in front of a tree stump, a figure which is also known in cream coloured earthenware decorated with underglaze oxide colours.

Portrait bust, the creamware body with coloured oxide decoration, made in Staffordshire, 1760-70, ht. 216mm. *City Museum & Art Gallery, Stoke-on-Trent, 214.*

Portrait busts of Augustus, Duke of Cumberland, who was a patron of the Chelsea porcelain factory, on the right is a Chelsea porcelain bust and on the left a creamware example, the body with coloured oxide decoration, made in Staffordshire, 1750-70, ht. 114mm. *Royal Pavilion Art Gallery & Museum, Brighton, HW111 & 112.*

A number of busts and standing figures were made which may have been intended to represent a particular person, either real or literary, but none were titled and it is often difficult to identify the subject after such a long period. One portrait bust which can be identified is the model of the Duke of Cumberland, which appears to have first been produced in Chelsea porcelain before being copied by Staffordshire figure makers.

Squirrel eating a nut, the creamware body with coloured oxide decoration, made in Staffordshire, 1760-70, ht. 191mm. *City Museum & Art Gallery, Stoke-on-Trent, 3060.*
The figure of a squirrel eating a nut is based on a Meissen original and porcelain copies were made at Chelsea and Derby.

Model of a dovecot, the creamware body with coloured oxide decoration, made in Staffordshire, 1760-70, ht. 228mm. *Sotheby's London.*

Figure of a bear, the creamware body with coloured oxide decoration, made in Staffordshire, c.1760-70, ht. 140mm. *City Museum & Art Gallery, Stoke-on-Trent, 3043.*

Amongst the most popular figures with collectors are those depicting animals. Within this category are found domesticated cows and bulls, wild deer, exotic bears and lions and an ornithological confusion. It was difficult for the potter to give an anatomically accurate rendering of the more exotic species as the opportunities to view at first hand were limited and the printed sources were not always reliable. However, those figures which are fairly recognisable are not nearly so endearing as the naïvely conceived pieces, the species of which can only be guessed at. Birds are amongst the most ambitious pieces and include both Oriental and European subjects; the potters may have used printed books or porcelain originals for sources of inspiration.

Fragment of a face recovered with fragments of draperies from the site of the Warburton pottery, Cobridge.

Impressed mark 'P & F WARBURTON'.

Figures of Summer and Autumn, cream coloured earthenware, impressed on the reverse 'P & F WARBURTON', c.1800, ht. 180mm. *City Museum & Art Gallery, Stoke-on-Trent, 33.P.1958.*

A creamware cruet stand with the male figure forming the handle may be seen in the collection of Temple Newsam House, Leeds, cat. no.440, acc.no.1901.7.

It is difficult to suggest a terminal date for creamware figures. The newly introduced pearlware seemingly offered the manufacturers a more satisfactory medium for their work and very few sophisticated creamware figures are recorded. From Staffordshire only the work of Peter and Francis Warburton is known. A pair of figures from a set of Seasons is known marked 'P & F WARBURTON'. These may have been dual purpose models which were sold free standing, or which formed the ornamental finial of a creamware dinner service cruet stand or centrepiece in the style of a grand plat ménage.[14] A second figure has recently come to light during the excavations in Cobridge of a site occupied by the Warburtons, and fragments of a classical subject, which promised to be of the finest quality, were recovered from a layer with marked Warburton shards. As yet no match has been found to suggest the form of the complete figure. The Warburton family occupied potworks in Cobridge for many years; in 1796 Jacob Warburton's name occurs in the trade directories, but it is known that shortly after that time Peter and Francis were in a partnership which was dissolved and the business was continued by Peter alone until his death in 1813, when the site was then occupied by Ralph and James Clews. Excavations on the upper Clews' levels, have not revealed any evidence of continued figure making.

14. Walton, P., *Creamware and other English Pottery at Temple Newsam House Leeds,* Leeds Art Collection Fund, pp.114-5, cat. no.440.

Recumbent deer, the creamware body with overglaze painted decoration, impressed 'BRAMELD 5', made at Swinton, Yorkshire, c.1820, ht. 82mm. *Rotherham Museum, R585.*

Other creamware figures which are recorded are from potteries in Yorkshire; the best known of which is the factory built in Jack Lane, Leeds, in 1770. Many figures produced in this works were of pearlware; others which purport to be Leeds Pottery creamware were produced during the 1890s to the early twentieth century by J.W. and G.W. Senior, marketed by W.W. Slee. Of the known creamware the busts emblematic of the elements are best known, and the model of 'Air' was amongst those reproduced by Senior.

The work of a Yorkshire pottery which is becoming increasingly well known is that of Swinton. A great range of wares was produced on the site from slipwares to porcelain. There were no earthenware figure fragments excavated from the site but two marked examples are recorded: a pair of Jobson & Nell impressed 'BRAMELD 4'[15] and a recumbent hind impressed 'BRAMELD 5'. The hind appears to be based on a Derby original and has small square holes to take antlers, presumably to be made of metal. The pieces date to about 1820 and these creamware figures appear to be the last examples of their kind produced by the English potteries.

The vast majority of creamware figures were decorated with the limited range of colours that would withstand the temperatures of a glost firing; they were economical to produce and therefore probably cheap to buy. The creamware glaze was exactly that — cream — and the rising demands were for whiter wares emulating the expensive porcelains. In order to respond to the taste for whiter wares the potters developed a new glaze which they called china glaze; its bluish, pearly sheen finally dominated the industry and new classes of figures were introduced.

15. Cox, A. & A., *Rockingham Pottery & Porcelain 1745-1842,* Faber & Faber, 1983, pl.31.

2. Coloured Glazed Figures

During the late eighteenth century a more sophisticated taste in pottery evolved in the home market. Imports of Continental and European porcelain had stimulated the development of English china and a demand for whiter wares of modest price was answered by the Staffordshire potters with the introduction of pearlware.

Possibly the earliest pearlware figures are those decorated with coloured glazes and for many years this particular class of figure has caught the interest of the collector. The subtle colouring and charming subjects combine to offer the highest aesthetic standards and the soft, silky lead glaze has tactile qualities unrivalled in the field of ceramics.

As these figures are indeed pearlware they must post-date the development of this particular glaze technique (the contemporary name was china glaze). Recent research into pearlware has been unable to pin-point the introduction of this process but it seems unlikely to have been before 1775 and possibly some years later.[1]

Many of the figures of this class are hand pressed in simple two-part moulds, but an increasing number have limbs and accessories modelled separately from the body, requiring extra moulds and necessitating an extra assembly process. The completed figures were fired to the biscuit stage ready for painting with glaze.

The plain pearl glaze is translucent with a bluish tint, produced by the addition of a small amount of cobalt to the standard lead glaze used for creamware. It was thought that the resulting blue tint made the finished pieces look whiter than cream coloured earthenware and more like the imported Oriental porcelains. In the original documents pearlware may be referred to as 'china glaze' or 'white', sometimes abbreviated to 'wt'. These simple china glaze pieces would be the cheapest of all to make as the biscuit (once fired) earthenware body could be quickly dipped into the liquid glaze, drained, dried and fired. The resultant figure would have a simple, bluey-white finish, with the exact shade depending on the quantity of cobalt blue in the glaze.

Other metal oxides used to tint the glaze are copper for green, iron for yellow, manganese for brown or purple and extra cobalt for a stronger blue. The subdued shades derived from these metal oxides were the only colours able to withstand the temperature of a glaze firing. The documentary sources refer to these wares as 'coloured' or in abbreviated forms 'colour'd', 'coul'd', 'col'd' or 'cold'.[2] These figures were more expensive than the plain china glaze examples, as the coloured glazes had to be individually hand painted on to the biscuit earthenware body. In the haste to complete the work little nooks and crannies were left unpainted and therefore bare of glaze. This is a point to look for when the decorating method is in doubt: look under arms, at the

1. Lockett, T.A., 'The Later Creamwares and Pearlwares', *Creamware & Pearlware*, City Museum & Art Gallery, Stoke-on-Trent/Northern Ceramic Society, 1986.

2. John Wood's account books, City Museum & Art Gallery, Stoke-on-Trent.

Two earthenware figures decorated with coloured glazes. The example on the left entitled 'ROMAN CHARITY', is a complex group made up from numerous press moulded parts stuck together with slip. The lion on the right is from a simple two-part press-mould. Roman Charity with impressed numeral 92, ht. 197mm. *City Museum & Art Gallery, Stoke-on-Trent, 2207, 170.P.1949.*

Apollo, earthenware china glaze undecorated, made in Staffordshire 1780-1800, ht. 230mm. *Wisbech & Fenland Museum, 1900.59.*
The figure of Apollo occurs several times in John Wood's account book, including 18 March 1786 to Mr James Ewer '1 Appollo colour'd 1/3d'. The figure also occurs in orders purchased from the Enoch and Ralph Wood partnership including 8 February 1787 'Bought of Ralph Wood...1 pr Diana & Apollo white & gold 3.6d'.

junction of one figure and another, or around bases where additional animals or children are applied and often dry patches of unglazed, uncoloured body will be found. Another helpful point in checking whether or not a coloured glaze has been used is to look into the deep folds of the drapery and if the glaze is coloured you will notice that the deeper the pool the deeper the colour. This particular characteristic is used to great advantage by the modellers, whose range of subjects included many with flowing and draped garments which gave better expression to this medium.

Both china glaze and coloured glaze pieces were decorated with gilding, but unfortunately, the techniques of gilding were not thoroughly understood by the Staffordshire potters, and as very few extant figures have any extensive gilding, the remaining traces only hint at former richness. There is very little evidence relating to decorating techniques used during the eighteenth century, however, *Handmaid to the Arts,* a volume published by Dossie in 1758 (revised in 1764), gives us some idea of the state of knowledge during the middle of the century. Gold leaf was used to decorate the glazed pottery surface and it could be applied in one of two ways. The least likely way was to paint the required decoration in a glue or size and to press a small sheet of thin gold leaf on to the sticky surface: when the sheet was removed the gold leaf adhered to the pot in the required pattern. The more likely method was to grind the gold leaf into a powder, which was done using honey as a binding medium. Once the gold was ground fine enough, water was added to the mixture, and as the honey dissolved the heavier particles of gold sank to the bottom, the honeyed water was then poured away and the rinsing continued until all the gold was clean. The design was then painted on to the wares in glue or size and the gold powder dusted on to the sticky surface with a squirrel-tail brush. (I know of no way of telling whether the honey process was used and some confusion has arisen from the belief that honey was the adhesive medium, but there is no evidence to suggest that honey was used for anything other than the grinding process.) The London porcelain painters certainly knew the method of successful gilding and Josiah Wedgwood suggested to his brother in 1765, that he might indulge in a little industrial espionage, by inducing one of the girls from the Chelsea factory to part with the secret.[3] The main problem for the Staffordshire potters was that they had not realised that a special material needed to be mixed with the gold so that during firing it became fused on to the surface of the pot. The special material known as a flux is usually a glassy substance which fuses at low temperatures. Gilding needs a separate firing from glaze or enamels, as it has a very low maturing temperature of about 700°C.

All references to the Wedgwood MSS refer to the Wedgwood papers held at the University of Keele, North Staffordhire, and are quoted by kind permission of the Trustees of the Wedgwood Museum.

3. Wedgwood MSS. 18083-25.

Pair of Haymakers, earthenware decorated with coloured glazes, made in Staffordshire 1780-1800, ht. 184mm. *City Museum & Art Gallery, Stoke-on-Trent, 186 & 188.P.1949.*

The Haymaker subject occurs frequently in John Wood's accounts: one entry gives a little detail of the models, 14 September 1786 to Mr Wm Mortlock '1 pair Mower & Haymaker with Scythe & rake 1.6d'.

Enoch and Ralph Wood also supplied this subject, 25 January 1787 'Bought of Ralph Wood...1 pr Mower & Haymaker wt & Gold 2.6d'.

Bull baiting group, earthenware decorated with coloured glazes, made in Staffordshire 1780-1800, ht. 162mm. *City Museum & Art Gallery, Stoke-on-Trent, 61.P.1962.*

John Wood's account book records 11 February to Mr Saml. Ward '2 coloured bulls with dogs 1.8d'.

Existing documents give details of prices charged by figure manufacturers to retailers, known as chinamen, and the structure of charges reflects the amount of work involved in production.[4] A very rough average price for a figure such as Apollo or the Haymaker was about 10d. for a china glazed finish, 1s.3d. for coloured glaze, 1s.9d. for china glaze and gilt, 2s.3d. for coloured glaze and gilt and 2s.6d. for enamel painted. Obviously the cheapest were the easiest to make, as china glaze requires only a swift dip into the glaze mixture before its final firing; coloured glaze requires a little more attention with hand painted glazes before a final firing; the addition of gold involves extra cost, not only for the material and labour in decorating, but also for the fuel and labour costs incurred by a third firing. Enamel painted pieces are even more costly, because, depending upon the range of colours used, several more firings may be necessary.

The potters continued to produce models showing contemporary figures going about their daily work. Country people such as haymakers, gamekeepers, shepherds and gardeners were particularly popular, and a

4. John Wood, op.cit.

Elephant spill vase, earthenware decorated with coloured glazes, made in Staffordshire 1780-1800, ht. 203mm. *City Museum & Art Gallery, Stoke-on-Trent, 198.P.1944.*
John Wood's account book records 6 October 1783 to Mr Tho. Dickins '1 Elephant 1.3d'.

Minerva, earthenware decorated with coloured glazes, made in Staffordshire 1780-1800, ht. 318mm. *City Museum & Art Gallery, Stoke-on-Trent, 2974.*
John Wood's account book records 11 May 1786 to Mr James Ewer '1 Minerva white & Gold 3.0d'. Enoch and Ralph Wood also supplied this subject 8 February 1787 'Bought of Ralph Wood...1 Minerva white & Gold 3.0d'.

romantic interpretation of the rural life was depicted through a host of young men and women, whiling away their time leaning on scythes, resting on grassy mounds or displaying their musical accomplishments. Animal figures continued to be produced and a range of stags, hinds, sheep, and goats vied with the ever popular models of dogs of various breeds and the more exotic subjects, such as elephants and buffaloes. The various farm, game and

9. Group of earthenware figures, decorated with coloured glazes, made in Staffordshire, c.1780-1800, ht. 271mm. *City Museum & Art Gallery, Stoke-on-Trent.*
This group illustrates the variety of subjects available in this type of figure and shows the limited range of colours derived from metal oxides which would withstand the glaze firing temperature.

Figure of Hudibras, earthenware decorated with coloured glazes, made in Staffordshire 1780-1800, ht. 285mm. *City Museum & Art Gallery, Stoke-on-Trent, 306.*
Some models are known with the impressed numeral 42, this figure also occurs with overglaze enamel painted decoration. John Wood's account book lists 11 February 1786 to Mr Saml. Ward '1 Hudibras on Horse 2.0d'.

King David, earthenware decorated with coloured glazes, made in Staffordshire 1780-1800, ht. 298mm. *City Museum & Art Gallery, Stoke-on-Trent, 176.P.1949.*
John Wood's account book lists 8 March 1786 to Mr John Edwards '1 King David with Harp coloured 1.9d'. Enoch and Ralph Wood also supplied this subject 8 February 1787 'Bought of Ralph Wood... 1 King David white & gold 3.0d'.

domestic animals would have been familiar subjects to maker and customer, but one wonders what sources inspired the Staffordshire potters to produce the fantastic beasts of the East. How these came to the potters' attention we can only begin to guess, however, it indicates that life in eighteenth century Staffordshire was perhaps not so isolated as is sometimes imagined.

New themes reflected the classical revival which dominated the arts in the late eighteenth century, and amongst the most commonly found figures are pairs of Apollo and Diana. Venus seems to have been a flexible sort of goddess and can be found allied with Neptune or Bacchus. Minerva and Jupiter were among the individual figures which could be sold singly or in any desired combination of sets. An order of 11 February 1786, supplied by John Wood to Mr. Saml. Ward, included:

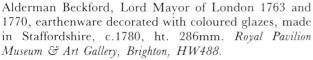

Alderman Beckford, Lord Mayor of London 1763 and 1770, earthenware decorated with coloured glazes, made in Staffordshire, c.1780, ht. 286mm. *Royal Pavilion Museum & Art Gallery, Brighton, HW488.*
The figure is based on John Francis Moore's monument to William Beckford in the Guildhall, London, erected in 1772 after the death of Beckford.

Admiral Van Tromp, a Dutch Admiral, earthenware decorated with coloured glazes, made in Staffordshire, c.1780-1800, ht. 261mm. *Henry Weldon Collection.*
Some models are known with the impressed numerals 37 or 38, and overglaze enamel painted versions also occur. John Wood's account book lists 9 December 1785 to Mr John Edwards '2 Van Tromps 1/3d 2/6d'.

One set White & Gold		
1 Minerva	3/6)	
1 Pair Bacchus & Venus	4/-)	10/-
1 Pair Mower & Haymaker	2/6)	

This combination of five figures may seem unusual today but it emphasises the problems of trying to understand the eighteenth century from a twentieth century standpoint.

As well as figures from classical literature there were also models from contemporary writings, the most famous being that of Hudibras from Samuel Butler's satirical burlesque on the Puritans.

Religious subjects included humorous depictions of the clergy, sometimes asleep at their work as in 'The Vicar and Moses'; biblical themes came from

10. Figures of Apollo in china glaze and coloured glaze decoration, made in Staffordshire, c.1780-1800, ht. 220mm. *City Museum & Art Gallery, Stoke-on-Trent, 3016, 184. P. 1949.*
The figure on the left shows the grey-blue sheen of the pearl or china glaze figure, and some traces of gilding can be seen on the laurel wreath in his hair and on his lyre. The coloured glaze example shows a more lively version of the same piece. China glaze examples would normally be less expensive than coloured glaze pieces, but the additional costs of gilding and the extra firing would make a china glaze and gilt piece more expensive than the coloured glaze.

11. Two figures depicting the 'Lost Piece', with coloured glaze decoration, made in Staffordshire, c.1780-1800, ht. 228mm. *City Museum & Art Gallery, Stoke-on-Trent, 180. P. 1949, 183. P. 1949.*
The figure on the left has traces of gilding to the neckline of the bodice, the girdle at the waist and the lining of the overskirt. The subject depicts the parable of the widow searching for her lost coin, symbolising God's concern for the lost sinner and his rejoicing when the sinner repents and returns. These are two of at least three different models of this title and they illustrate the problem of attributing specific figures to a manufacturer merely on the evidence of the subject.

12. Charity, with coloured glaze decoration, made in Staffordshire, c.1780-1800, ht. 203mm. *City Museum & Art Gallery, Stoke-on-Trent, 182.P.1949.*

13. Detail of the bodice showing how the glaze lies in pools within the folds of drapery: the deeper the pool the deeper the colour. This characteristic feature of coloured glazes is used to great effect by modellers of classical figures.

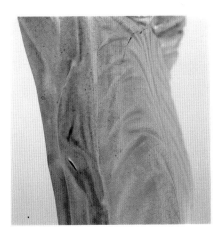

14. Detail showing a bare patch where the worker has not paid attention to detail and the glaze is not painted all over. This characteristic feature can be observed on many examples at the junction of two colours or in nooks and crannies.

both the Old Testament, with models of King David, and from the New, with illustrations of the parables such as 'The Lost Piece'. The majority of Staffordshire potters were of Nonconformist religious persuasion, some attended the Unitarian chapel in Newcastle under Lyme, many others followed the teachings of John Wesley, the father of the Methodist movement. The Anglican church was the stronghold of the landed classes and the manufacturers and workers alike felt much more at home in the less hierarchical chapels and meeting houses which became established in the manufacturing areas of Great Britain.

Amongst the least common subjects are those that depict well-known public figures. The portrait of Alderman Beckford, Lord Mayor of London 1763 and 1770, appears to have derived from a statue in the Guildhall in London which was erected in 1772. The sources for Benjamin Franklin and his popularity in both England and America guaranteed wide sales, but who bought the figures of Admiral Van Tromp? There were two Admirals Van Tromp, a Dutch father and son who both fought in the Anglo-Dutch wars of the seventeenth century: both were dead by 1691. There are no traceable sources for the figure and no obvious reason for its production so long after their period of activity and a more than passing resemblance to the figure of Hudibras only serves to add to the confusion.

There appears to be a number of styles of modelling and it is possible to observe certain common characteristics which help to classify the figures into separate groups. I cannot yet draw any conclusions from these groupings but without some effort to organise the vast range of subjects no headway in classification can be made.

One group of figures has very coarse features and forms and despite their rarity and the sophisticated subtle glaze colours they remain peculiarly unattractive to me. In this class I would place the large pair of figures depicting the Vicar and the Farmer's Wife from the tithe-pig group, Plate XXXII in the catalogue of Captain R.K. Price's collection[5] and also the farmer and his wife illustrated in the Frank Partridge Catalogue, fig.205.[6] More commonly found figures in this class include a pair of figures depicting old age with the impressed number '55', the old lady feeding birds, of which examples are known marked 'Ra. Wood Burslem', and similarly marked 'Dutch boy and girl' with baskets of fruit and flowers. Because of their rarity it is not possible to see all of these figures in one collection and to compare them in the hand, but from illustrations and random access to one or two pieces it seems that common features are apparent which must suggest that they come from a common source. Whether that source is one particular factory, such as that of Ralph Wood, is difficult to determine, perhaps they are the work of one

5. Price, R.K., *Astbury Whieldon and Ralph Wood Figures and Toby Jugs,* John Lane, 1922.

6. Partridge, F., *Ralph Wood Pottery,* private print, c.1923.

Old woman feeding a bird, earthenware decorated with coloured glazes, made in Staffordshire, c.1780-1800, ht. 194mm. *Henry Weldon Collection.*
This figure is also known with two birds, and with the impressed mark '70' and 'Ra. Wood Burslem'. This unmarked version may date to the Enoch and Ralph Wood partnership period, 1783-90.

Figure of Winter, earthenware decorated with coloured glazes, made in Staffordshire 1780-1800, ht. 177mm. *City Museum & Art Gallery, Stoke-on-Trent, 190.P.1949.*
Based on a model by Paul Louis Cyfflé, who worked at Luneville in France.

modeller who supplied a number of factories or most likely they are copied from a common source by more than one workman.

My apologies to all who have these figures, for they are indeed fine examples of their type and are often modelled in great detail, but they are not to my taste, a taste which you may consider distinctly suspect when I tell you that the figure which I like least is that depicting Winter, also known as the Sweep or the Clown, and which appears to be based on a model by Paul Louis Cyfflé, produced for the Luneville factory in France.

The figures I particularly like are those which are modelled with a degree

Dutch boy and girl, earthenware decorated with coloured glazes, made in Staffordshire, c.1780-1800, ht. 172mm. *Henry Weldon Collection.*

These figures are known with the impressed numeral '49' and the impressed mark 'Ra. Wood Burslem', the girl also with 'R. WOOD'. John Wood's account book lists a number of sales of Dutch boy and girl including 11 May 1786 to Mr James Ewer '2 Pair Dutch Boy & Girl White & Gold 3.4d'.

Enoch and Ralph Wood also supplied these figures 8 February 1787 to Mr Swann 'Bought of Ralph Wood 1pr Dutch Boy & Girl with Basket of Fruit 1.8d'.

of sensitivity and which have little details that lend added charm. The sportsman with game hanging from his belt is well observed and one feels that the hares, etc., are a bonus from the potter who often just presents the sportsman as simply a figure with a gun. I also enjoy the figures which tell us something of their period and here I would particularly like to commend to you the sailor who wears wide legged trousers and a sorrowful face, together with his lass who clasps a tear stained handkerchief as she bids him goodbye.

Coloured glazed figures with makers' marks are quite rare, but a number of marked Ralph Wood figures are known. A lack of technical knowledge in past authors has meant that the significance of the pearl glaze was overlooked by authors and under the pressure to date pieces as early as possible the wares were attributed to the wrong generation of Ralph Woods. This in turn resulted in half a century of mis-attribution and deterred serious research into this class of figures.

Gamekeeper, earthenware decorated with coloured glazes, made in Staffordshire, c.1780-1800, ht. 219mm. *Henry Weldon Collection.*
This figure is known with the impressed 'Ra. Wood' and '36'. John Wood's account book lists 11 February to Mr. Saml. Ward '4 Gamekeepers with Hare & Dog 1/3d 5/-.'

Sailor and his lass, pearlware or china glaze, made in Staffordshire 1780-1800, ht. 200mm. *Wisbech & Fenland Museum, 1900. 57&58.*
John Wood's account book records 6 October to Mr Tho. Dickins '3 pair Sailor & Lasses coloured 2.6d'.

Ralph Wood I (1715-1772) was married to Mary Wedgwood, daughter of Aaron and niece to Thomas and John Wedgwood, master potters of the Big House, Burslem. They were married in the parish of Stoke-upon-Trent on 5 August 1738 and eight children were born before Mary died in 1756.[7] The responsibility for caring for the surviving children, who ranged in age from two to seventeen years, appears to have been a difficult task for Ralph, who was often in debt. John Wedgwood rented a house to the family at £1.18s. per annum.[8] For some years John Wedgwood contributed to the rent himself, his rent book records 'said would give no Earnest for 1757 however allow £1.0.0.' and the difference was made up from small cash sums paid, by Ralph, at infrequent intervals. In 1760 Ralph Wood I was arrested at Burslem Wakes

---

7. Burslem parish registers.
8. John Wedgwood's rent account book, City Museum & Art Gallery, Stoke-on-Trent.

for owing Thomas Malkin £14.0.0d; these and other debts were settled by John Wedgwood.[9] After 1760 Ralph seems to have pulled himself together. He moved to another of Thomas and John Wedgwood's houses in 1764, 'the House at the Red Workhouse', the rent was £3.0.0. per annum. (The Red Workhouse itself was let to Josiah Wedgwood from 1766 to 1772 at an annual rent of £10.0.0.) Ralph paid his rent quite regularly for a few years up to 1770 when again he was allowed earnest and had his wages stopped to defray rent debts.

Ralph Wood I, like his brother Aaron, was a modeller in the North Staffordshire pottery industry; there is no evidence that he was ever a Master Potter. John and Thomas Wedgwood's hiring accounts indicate that Ralph Wood was in their employ for many years.[10] A number of hand modelled blocks for making moulds for saltglazed stoneware are in existence with the initials 'RW' or the name 'Ralph Wood' in full and are dated between 1748 and 1770.[11] The last reference in the hiring book reads: 'Ralph Wood left off work in the Spring of 1772 and Died the latter end of the year and his daughter Sarah died a little before him and his son John and Ralph left off that year . . .'

The incomplete hiring and account books lead us to conclude that at various periods between 1756 and 1772, and probably for the whole of that time, Ralph Wood I was employed by John and Thomas Wedgwood, of the Big House in Burslem, and could not have been working in his own manufactory at those times. There is no evidence that Ralph Wood I ever modelled anything other than tablewares. He died in 1772, some years before the introduction of pearl glazing and therefore it would be impossible for him to have made the coloured glazed figures which belong to this class of ware.

What is known of Ralph Wood's sons? The eldest surviving son, Josiah, married Mary Wedgwood, daughter of Thomas Wedgwood of the Overhouse, Burslem. He is recorded in *Bailey's British Directory* of 1784 as a potter in Burslem. The entry reads 'Wood Josiah, Manufacturer of fine Black glazed, variegated and cream coloured ware and Blue'. Josiah Wood died in 1789 at the age of forty-nine and nothing more is known of his pottery productions.

Two of Ralph Wood I's younger sons, John and Ralph II, left more evidence of their activities. John Wedgwood notes in his hiring book 'Hired young Ralph Wood for 6/6 no Earnest for the year 1769'. So Ralph Wood II had his early training in the works of the Big House Wedgwoods. Ralph's older brother John received a training in the London warehouse/salerooms of Josiah Wedgwood; a clerk of that name wrote to the Etruria Works from 1769 to 1772 and correspondence at a later date confirms this clerk to be the same John, brother of Ralph Wood II.[12]

9. John Wedgwood's MSS, City Museum & Art Gallery, Stoke-on-Trent.

10. John and Thomas Wedgwood's hiring book, City Museum & Art Gallery, Stoke-on-Trent.

11. Mountford, A.R., *Staffordshire Salt-glazed Stoneware,* Barrie & Jenkins, 1971.

12. Wedgwood MSS. 22788-30.

When Ralph Wood I died in 1772, it appears he left no will, and it is unlikely that he had anything of value to leave his sons. From John Wedgwood's account book it is noted that between August 1772 and March 1773 their great-uncles advanced over £65 to John and Ralph II to assist them in establishing a pottery making business. It was, however, an unsuccessful venture, as Josiah Wedgwood records in a letter to Thomas Bentley of 3 April 1773:

'I am afraid John & R Wood must give over Potting in a week or two — They have laid out all their money, and are near £200 in debt! and their frds. do not think they are in a way of retrieving. Ralph minds his spiritual affairs too much to do any good with Temporals — He is become a capital Preacher — and poor John for whom we are very much concerned is too mild, and too full of nonexertion to manage a Pottery with any prospect of success. I have given them cash for the enclos'd which I suppose must be their last card. We (their uncles and me) have had several meetings on their account, the conclusion of which has been, that the sooner they stop the better. I have been rash enough to offer 50 or 100 more among with their uncles, to give them another tryal, but have been over ruled, and I believe they are right as far as prudence rules in these matters, but my feelings for the Lads carries me farther than prudence could justify, for I am fully persuaded that they are not made for Master Potters.'[13]

With the failure of their business John tried to sort out the aftermath whilst Ralph Wood II left Burslem for pastures new. Transcripts of the register for the Parish of St. James, Broadmead, Bristol record:

'Ralph Wood of the parish of St. Stephen and Sophia Lambert of this Parish were married in this Church by Licence this Twenty fifth day of June 1774 by me James Roquet. This marriage was solemnized between us Ralph Wood Sophia Lambert in the presence of Nicholas Ellis, William Daniel.' Through this marriage, in the same year Ralph became a freeman of Bristol and a *Bristol Directory* for 1775 lists 'Wood, Ralph, Earthenware and glass seller, 32 on the key'.

The parish register of St. Stephen's in Bristol records the following baptisms for the children of Ralph and Sophia Wood:

19th May 1775, Ralph (2 weeks old)
24th July 1776, Sophia
1st Oct. 1777, Susannah (16 months)
   Anna Maria

In the City rate books Ralph is still listed in 1780 as at the Quay, but the 1781 assessment has the entry 'Wood now Pritchard'. Ralph II had carried on his china dealing business in Bristol from his marriage in 1774 to 1781. There

---

13. Ibid., 18453-25.

are letters from Ralph II to his brother John, and to Thomas and Josiah Wedgwood, concerning the retail business and from these we learn that by 1780 Ralph was having problems paying for the goods he received. He wrote to Thomas Wedgwood at Etruria asking for more crates to be sent, saying he would remit the money as soon as it was in his power to do so.[14] In a later letter to Thomas Wedgwood we learn of the disturbing events which brought the Bristol business to an end. The letter which tells the story is a copy made by Thomas Wedgwood of Ralph's original to him, which Thomas sent to Josiah I at Greek Street. It includes a list of Wood's creditors and has a note from Thomas to Josiah telling him what is being done to get Wood's stock secured in Bristol. Ralph Wood II wrote to Thomas: '...thro' a most melancholy stroke I am secreted and intend to live somewhere a while unknown, a man from the most trivial and innocent circumstances has scandalized me with and sworn to an attempt of sodomy upon him and thereby ruined my family and me for my life perhaps'.[15]

With his business and reputation in ruins Ralph II intended 'to live somewhere awhile unknown'; the letter to Thomas Wedgwood continued in a later paragraph: 'I hope you will look upon me with some compassion and as an injured man, what to do I know not nor where to go at present — please to direct for me this time as usual, if you when you are together can give me any advice I shall heartily thank you. I would much rather settle in my own country.' He was obviously asking his family whether he would be made welcome and by 1783 Ralph had returned to Burslem where he settled with his family. The parish registers show that his last child, Josiah, was baptised there in 1783, but within a few months had died.

During 1783 Ralph must have been preparing for his new business for he bought 500 bricks and a load of clay from his brother John.[16] The account was settled by Enoch Wood and in *Bailey's Directory* 1784, we find: 'Wood Enoch and Ralph, Manufacturers of all kinds of useful and ornamental Earthen Ware, Egyptian Black, Cane and various other Colours also Black Figures, Seals & Cyphers Burslem'. In view of his impending bankruptcy and personal problems I cannot believe that Ralph had anything to bring to the partnership unless he was assisted financially by his uncles or brothers. Enoch had practical experience of a first rate pottery company and access to a substantial sum of money. Ralph is rarely referred to in any documentary sources of the period and is completely omitted from Enoch's own account of his establishment as a potter.[17] Ralph must have been a fairly insignificant member of the partnership and possibly was responsible for sales, as he had

---

14. Ibid., 11493-12.
15. Ibid., 11494-12.
16. John Wood, op.cit.
17. Falkner, F., *The Wood Family of Burslem*, Chapman & Hall, 1912.

15. Group of figures, with coloured glaze decoration, made in Staffordshire, c.1780-1800, ht. 242mm. *City Museum & Art Gallery, Stoke-on-Trent.*
These subjects are typical of those made by members of the Wood family of Burslem (see Appendices 1 & 2).
Documentary references do not have sufficient detail to identify specific models and none of these pieces can be attributed to a particular Wood with any confidence.

16. Group of figures, with coloured glaze decoration, made in Staffordshire, c.1780-1800, ht. 245mm. *City Museum & Art Gallery, Stoke-on-Trent.*

specialised in that side of the business in Bristol.

It is difficult to ascertain where the cousins set up their works. Within five years they had separated. A map of 1802 shows Ralph Wood's potworks at site number 27;[18] this site was later acquired and rebuilt by John and Richard Riley who named it Hill Manufactory. The Hill Manufactory was later renamed Royal Victoria Works sometime around the middle of the nineteenth century.

The same map of 1802 shows Enoch Wood further up the road on a site which was developed as Fountain Place. Confusion arises after the death of Enoch in 1840, when his factory was put up for sale under the name Hill Works. Presumably there was no contemporary confusion because the other site had, by that time, been renamed Royal Victoria Works. Whilst the situation may have been perfectly clear in 1840, subsequent historians have had to struggle with conflicting evidence as to the original site of the Enoch and Ralph Wood partnership.

On balance I think that they began at site 27 on the 1802 map and that when Enoch left, Ralph continued to make the same wares and to expand the range, at last able to mark pieces with his own name. This would explain the existence of many unmarked Ralph Wood type figures which may have been produced earlier, during the cousins' partnership about 1783-9. It may also mean that if Enoch continued to make the same kind of wares his productions may be indistinguishable from those of Ralph during the early years after their partnership ended.

Very little is known of the work produced during the partnership except for one or two orders dated between 1783 and 1787. The orders are in Ralph's name but as I believe he was responsible for the sales side of the business this does not conflict with my opinion that these early orders are from the Enoch and Ralph partnership.

The first record is the famous order of 16 November 1783 from Messrs Josiah and Thomas Wedgwood, which is preserved in the Wedgwood Archives at Keele University.[19]

The order lists:

12 George & Dragons	@ 2/- a piece	£1.4.0
6 Venuses purple lining	15d	7.6
6 Neptunes do	15d	7.6
6 do blue lining	18d	9.0
12 Shephards	6d	6.0
12 Apollos	10d	10.0
12 Men with lost sheep	9d	9.0

18. *A View of the Staffordshire Potteries,* T. Allbut, 1802. The text of the directory appears to be a reprint of his 1800 edition with new title/contents page and map, perhaps the map was compiled 1800-1, as Ralph Wood, who appears on the map, died in 1801.

19. Wedgwood MSS, 11496-12.

St. George and the Dragon, earthenware with coloured glaze decoration made in Staffordshire 1780-1800, ht. 280mm. *City Museum & Art Gallery, Stoke-on-Trent, 2979.*

John Wood's account books record 30 March 1784 to Mr Robt Dickinson '1 George & Dragon 1/9'd. Enoch and Ralph Wood also made this subject: Wedgwood MSS 11496-12 of 16 November 1783 lists 'Bought of Ralph Wood...12 George & Dragons 2/- a pair'. A similar model is also known of the post-Enoch and Ralph Wood period partnership marked 'Ra Wood Burslem 23'. The example illustrated may be of the Enoch and Ralph Wood partnership period, 1783-90.

Figure of a stag with light spots, earthenware decorated with coloured glazes, base impressed 94, made in Staffordshire 1780-1800, ht. 221mm.
Colonial Williamsburg, 63-460.

Stags occur frequently in the John Wood accounts and the Wedgwood MSS 11496-12 of 16 November 1783 lists 'Bought of Ralph Wood...12 Stags white spotted 9d a pair'. Other models of stags with white spots are known.

12 Charities	5d	5.0
12 Apollos gilt	15d	15.0
12 Sailors lasses	5d	5.0
12 Stags white spotted	9d	9.0
12 Hinds do do	9d	9.0
12 Hinds spotted black	9d	9.0
12 Stags do do	9d	9.0
12 Goats	10d	10.0
12 Sheep & rams	10d	10.0
1 pair Venus & Neptune Gilt		3.6
1 elephant		1.3
Man with boy sitting on a rock		1.0
do with a boy in his Hand standing		1.0
6 Doz small colour'd figures 18d a doz		9.0

17. Group of classical subjects, with coloured glaze decoration, made in Staffordshire, c.1780-1800, ht. 268mm. *City Museum & Art Gallery, Stoke-on-Trent, 200.P.1949, 178.P.1949, 181.P.1949.*
The cupid on a panther is impressed '46' on the reverse and has traces of gilding.

18. Goat and sheep, with coloured glaze decoration, made in Staffordshire, c.1780-1800, ht. 180mm. *City Museum & Art Gallery, Stoke-on-Trent, 2214, 2215.*

Man with boy sitting on a rock, earthenware decorated with coloured glazes, made in Staffordshire, possibly by Enoch and Ralph Wood, 1783-90, ht. 210mm. *Private Collection.*
Enoch and Ralph Wood made this subject, Wedgwood MSS 11496-12 of 16 November 1783 lists 'Bought of Ralph Wood...Man with boy sitting on a rock 1.0d'.

Man with a boy in his hand, standing, earthenware with coloured glaze decoration, made in Staffordshire, possibly by Enoch and Ralph Wood, 1783-90, ht. 292mm. *Henry Weldon Collection.*
Enoch and Ralph Wood made this subject, Wedgwood MSS 11496-12 of 16 November 1783 lists 'Bought of Ralph Wood...Man with boy in His hand standing 1.0d'.

From comparisons made with prices in other more detailed figure orders it seems likely that all these figures were decorated with coloured glazes with the addition of gilding where specified.

It is very difficult to identify the exact figure models made by Enoch and Ralph Wood from this order as there are so many variations to be found of most of the subjects, for example there are many models of shepherds, sailors, deer, sheep, etc. However, I do think that 'Man with a boy in his hand standing' and 'Man with boy sitting on a rock' are excellent descriptions of the pieces shown here and I know of no other versions of these subjects.

In 1784 there is a brief reference in John Wood's account book to 'Toys from Brother Ralph £1.17.1.', which may refer to figures.

On 25 January 1787 in John Wood's sales ledger is found a more detailed account appended to an order:

Gasconian with hurdy-gurdy and Galigo or Spanish woman with water jars, earthenware decorated with coloured glazes, made in Staffordshire, c.1780-1800, ht. 228mm. *Private Collection.*

The Spanish woman is also known in china glaze and with impressed '67' and 'Ra. Wood Burslem'. John Wood's account book lists 18 January 1787 to Mr Ebenezer Nevil '1 Pair Gasconian & Galigo wt & gold 3.6d'. Enoch and Ralph Wood also made this subject, 8 February to Mr Swann 'Bought of Ralph Wood...1pr Spanish Gasconian with music & Galego Woman with Water Jars White & gold 3.6d'.

This example may date to the Enoch and Ralph Wood partnership, 1783-90.

Bought of Ralph Wood for Andrew Barr

1 pr Neptune & Venus	wt & gold	4sh-
1 pr Shepd & Shepherdess	Do	3-
1 pr Spanish figures suppose dancing	Do	3-
1 pr Do small do with music	Do	1.9
1 pr Mower & Haymaker	Do	2.6
1 Spanish Woman with Water Pitchers	Do	1.9
1 pr Man with lost sheep & Woman with lost piece cold.		2-
2 Spanish peasants worshipping		1.8
1 Spanish woman spinning		1.3
1 pr Old Age with Crutches		2.-
1 Spanish Shepherd with Sheep under his arm		10
1 pr Do Figures suppose dancing		2.6
1 pr Stag & hind		1.6

The 'wt & gold' pieces are pearl or china glaze and gilt. Many of the pieces which exist today have very little gilding left and one can only imagine how sophisticated they would have looked with the rich, deep honey tones of early gilding emphasising the sweep of drapes, highlighting the hair or ornamenting the base.

On 1 February 1787 John Wood's sales ledger refers to a bill for Mr Isaac Swan including 'Images as per Bror. Ralphs Bill £2.11.9'. Images are another name for figures, but unfortunately the bill is not itemised.

Finally, an order sent by John Wood to Mr Swann on 8 February 1787 included:

Buslem 25th Jan.y 1787

Bou.t of Ralph Wood for Mr Andrew Barr —

1 P.r Neptune & Venus W.t & Gold —	4 —
1 P.r Shep.d & Shep.ss — D.o —	3 —
1 P.r Spanish Figures suppose Dancing D.o —	3
1 P.r D.o small D.o with Music —	2 — 1..9
1 P.r Woman Chapmaker — D.o —	2..6
1 Spanish Woman with Water Pitchas — D.o —	1..9
1 P.r Man with lost Sheep & Woman with lost Piece coin.t —	2..9
2 Spanish Peasants worshiping —	1..8
1 D.o Woman spinning —	1..3
1 P.r Old Age with Crutches —	2
1 Spanish Shephard with Sheep under his arm —	— 10
1 P.r D.o Figures suppose Dancing —	2
1 P.r Stag & hind —	1..6

1. 7.. 3

Sent to Mr Swan   Buslem 8th Feb.y 1787

John Wood

Bought of Ralph Wood

1 King David White & Gold —	3
1 Minerva D.o —	3
1 P.r Spanish Garconian with Music & Galego Woman with Water Jars —	3. 6
1 P.r Spanish Dancers with Music —	3
1 P.r Diana & Apollo —	3. 6
1 P.r Bacus & Venus —	3. 6
1 P.r Sportsman & Lady —	2..4
2 P.r Boy & Girl play with Cat & blowing charcoal —	3.. 4
1 P.r Small Spanish Figures with Music —	1.. 9
1 P.r Dutch Boy & Girl with Basket of Fruit —	1..8
1 P.r Surly Boy & Girl —	1.. 2
1 P.r Shep.d & Shep.ss on a Rock coul.t —	8
1 P.r Large Obelisks Pebble Gilt —	10 —
1 P.r Old Ages W.t & Gold —	3.

2. 10.. 9

Pebble Gilt Japand &c 7/6

Two orders from John Wood's sales ledger 25 January and 8 February 1787, referring
to goods bought from Ralph Wood to be sent with John's orders to his retailers. At
this time Ralph was in partnership with his cousin Enoch Wood and appears to have
been in charge of sales.

Shepherd and shepherdess on a rock, earthenware decorated with coloured glazes, made in Staffordhire, c.1780-1800, ht. 241mm. City Museum & Art Gallery, Stoke-on-Trent, 191.P.1949.

John Wood's account book lists 14 September 1786 to Mr Wm Mortlock '2 Shepherd & Shepherdess on Rock candlestick 8.-.' Enoch and Ralph Wood also made this subject; John Wood's account book lists 8 February 1787 'Bought of Ralph Wood . . . 1 pr. Shepherd & Shepherdess on a rock cold. 8.0d'.

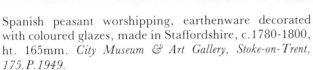

Spanish peasant worshipping, earthenware decorated with coloured glazes, made in Staffordshire, c.1780-1800, ht. 165mm. *City Museum & Art Gallery, Stoke-on-Trent, 175.P.1949.*
Enoch and Ralph Wood made this subject; John Wood's account book lists 25 January 1787 to Andrew Barr 'Bought of Ralph Wood...2 Spanish peasants worshipping cold. 1.8d'.

Shepherd and shepherdess on a rock, china glaze undecorated, impressed beneath 'Ra. Wood Burslem 89', c.1789-1801, ht. 292mm. *Private Collection.*
The subject is based on porcelain originals and may also be allegorical of courtship and marriage.

Bought of Ralph Wood

1 King David	white & gold	3.-
1 Minerva	Do	3.-
1 pr Spanish Gasconian with Music)		
& Galego Woman with Water Jars)		3.6
1 pr Spanish dancers with Music		3.-
1 pr Diana & Apollo		3.6
1 pr Baccus & Venus		3.6
1 pr Sportsman & Lady		2.4
1 pr Boy & Girl playing with Cat & blowing charcoal		3.4
1 pr Small Spanish figures with Music		1.9
1 pr Dutch Boy & Girl with basket of fruit		1.8
1 pr Derby Boy & Girl		1.2
1 pr Shepherd & Shepherdess on a rock cold.		8.0
1 pr Large obelisks pebble gilt		10.-
1 pr Old Ages wt & Gold		3.-
1 Pebble gilt teapot 24 @ 1/-		

I would like to emphasise the difficulty in identifying the products of the Enoch and Ralph Wood partnership from the titles of their figure productions, however, I have made some suggestions as to the wares possibly referred to in the illustrations accompanying this text. It is suggested that tentative attributions may be made for unmarked figures of this period by comparison with those which subsequently turn up marked Ralph Wood, which are of post partnership date, that is about 1789-1801.

It is not known how long the Enoch and Ralph Wood partnership lasted. The company appears in William Tunnicliffe's *Survey of the County of Stafford 1787* but the next known trade directory, *Universal British Directory,* 1793, lists Enoch Wood and James Caldwell as partners and for the first time there is an entry for Ralph Wood alone in business as a potter. Sometime between 1787 and 1793 Ralph and Enoch went their separate ways. Traditionally a date of 1790 is accepted as the beginning of Enoch Wood's partnership with James Caldwell and it would therefore seem logical to assume that the partnership between Enoch and Ralph ceased a little before this time. It is also reasonable to suppose that Ralph would have continued to make, and go on to expand, the range of figure models produced during the partnership.

From John Wood's sales ledger it is seen that in 1789 he continued his business dealings with Ralph, supplying some goods but mainly advancing cash and by 1793 the debit reached £123.18.9d. with only £15.10.6d. paid on account. The balance of probabilities is that Ralph began as a Master Potter in about 1789 and that he had limited financial success. In 1795, when Ralph Wood II died, there was no report of his death in the *Staffordshire Advertiser* and no trace of a will. Ralph Wood III continued the business but survived his father by only six years and at the age of twenty-six he died. This, the last Ralph Wood, received a mention in the local newspaper and left a will with a modest estate of less than £500 which was left to his mother. The last reference to this branch of the Wood family was in the *Staffordshire Advertiser,* 5 September 1801; 'TO BE LET FOR a Term of Years, and entered upon at Martinmas next. ALL that old established and commodious Set of POTWORKS, called the Hill, in Burslem, and late in the occupation of Mr Ralph Wood, Potter, deceased...' The potworks, which had never belonged to the Wood family but was leased from Mr. Byerley, was at this point in a very poor state of repair and a temporary tenant was found; when it was eventually sold to

Impressed mark of Ralph Wood, Burslem, the form 'R. WOOD' is also known. Ralph Wood II and III tenanted the Hill Pottery in Burslem from c.1789-1801, but it is not possible in the light of present knowledge to assign each mark to a distinct period within the twelve years of operation.

Charity, earthenware with china glaze, undecorated, impressed on the reverse 'R. WOOD', c.1789-1801, ht. 222mm. *Private Collection.*

Charity back view, showing impressed mark 'R. WOOD'.

John and Richard Riley they had to undertake complete rebuilding to make the premises commercially viable.

Figures made by the Ralph Woods are occasionally marked with the impressed name 'R. WOOD', 'R. Wood' or 'Ra. Wood Burslem'. With a scant twelve years of production, 1789-1801, it has so far not been possible to attribute the individual marks to any particular period within those years. Much of the marked work is of excellent quality and occasionally models are found with either coloured glazes or with the more expensive overglaze enamel painted decoration. (Ralph Wood enamel figures are discussed in more detail in Chapter 4.)

Pair of Spanish musicians, the man with castanets, the woman with friction drum, earthenware decorated with coloured glazes, man impressed 'Ra. Wood Burslem 71', c.1789-1801, ht. 210mm. *Glaisher Collection, 861, courtesy Syndics of the Fitzwilliam Museum, Cambridge.*

Top left:
Vicar and Moses, earthenware decorated with coloured glazes, impressed on base 'Ra. Wood Burslem', c.1789-1801, ht. 245mm. *City Museum & Art Gallery, Stoke-on-Trent, 2959.*
This subject is also listed a number of times in John Wood's account book.

St. George and the Dragon, earthenware decorated with coloured glazes, impressed 'Ra. Wood Burslem 23', c.1789-1801, ht. 285mm. *Sotheby's London.*

Diana and Apollo, biscuit earthenware, impressed 'R. Wood', c.1789-1801, ht. 219mm. *Colonial Williamsburg, 1960. 419-1&2.*

Marked subjects are known to include examples with impressed numbers, which are assumed to be related to the models or moulds. As the same number occurs on entirely different, otherwise unmarked, subjects, either the number has some other, as yet unidentified, significance or, more likely, there was more than one potter using impressed numbers. Obvious candidates for a similar system of marking would include Enoch and John Wood. A complete list of figures found with impressed numbers will be found in Appendix 1.

The John Wood side of the family was much more successful in business than the Ralph Woods, but John Wood sen. also had a tragic personal life. We have already established that John sen. and his brother Ralph II were briefly in partnership after their father's death. After their venture failed in 1773 John was offered his old situation at Josiah Wedgwood's Newport Street Warehouse. Initially he declined on the advice of his uncles John and Richard Wedgwood, who suggested that John and Ralph should see their business affairs settled before embarking on anything further.[20] Ralph eventually went

20. Ibid., 22788-30.

Girl feeding a bird, earthenware china glaze undecorated, impressed 'Ra. Wood Burslem 87', c.1789-1801, ht. 179mm.
Colonial Williamsburg, 1963.332.
A pair to this figure is a boy feeding birds impressed 'Ra. Wood Burslem 86'.

Boy with pipe, girl with lamb, earthenware china glaze undecorated, both impressed 'Ra. Wood Burslem', boy also with '78', c.1789-1801, ht. 156mm. *Southport Museum, 109.*

off to Bristol and John seems to have joined him for a brief time. In 1775 John wrote from Bristol to Josiah Wedgwood, giving details of business he was pursuing on Wedgwood's behalf, but the letter does not imply that John was in Wedgwood's employ. On 30 June 1775 the marriage register of St. Swithin's, Walcot, records that John Wood of the parish of St. Stephen's in the City of Bristol, bachelor, was married to Mary Price of St. Swithin's, by licence. The marriage bond gives Ralph Wood as bondsman, also of St. Stephen's, Bristol.[21] Perhaps John was working with his younger brother Ralph for a short time, but by the end of that year he had returned to Burslem. From December 1775 John Wood paid rent to John Wedgwood for a house

---

21. I am grateful to Mr. Wynn Hamilton-Foyn for drawing these records to my attention.

Brownhills Hall built by John Wood sen., c.1782-83, enlarged by John Wood jun., c.1830. In the early 20th century the house was converted to form part of a grammar school complex (rooms to the right and left of the main entrance were classrooms used by the author). The house was demolished in recent years. From John Ward's *History of the Borough of Stoke-upon-Trent*, 1843.

in Burslem and from March 1776 they entered into a pottery making partnership. From surviving papers it seems that John Wood ran the business, drawing a salary, whilst John Wedgwood was a sort of sleeping partner;[22] they shared any profit. There is no evidence of what they made nor if they were successful. In John Wedgwood's will it states: 'Also I give and bequeath to my said son Thomas Wedgwood all the household furniture in the house in which I dwell and all the Potting Utensils also the stock in trade that I may have in Partnership with Mr John Wood Also...all that household furniture belonging to me in the house in which Mr. John Wood dwells...' The will was made on 8 April 1779 and John Wedgwood died in 1780.

Perhaps John Wood had found the money for his partnership from his wife's dowry, for Mary was the eventual heir of Nicholas Price of Pont y Pandy. On John Wedgwood's death John Wood continued potting on his own behalf and the first trade directory recording the Staffordshire area, Bailey's *Northern Directory*, 1781, lists 'Wood John, potter, Burslem'. Whether John Wood's

22. John Wedgwood's account book, City Museum & Art Gallery, Stoke-on-Trent.

'nonexertion', as recorded by Josiah Wedgwood, had been replaced by a more mature business acumen or whether his wife's money enabled him to employ good managers, will never be known, but John Wood thrived. In about 1782 he negotiated the purchase of the Brownhills estate on the outskirts of Burslem, where he built a handsome house and manufactory adjacent. Within the Wood family papers is what must be one from a set of sales ledgers from Brownhills, dating from 1783 to 1787 and one of a set of crate books dating from 1770 to 1800.[23] From the sales ledger we know that John Wood was a successful producer of white stoneware, creamware, Egyptian black, black-glazed wares, redwares glazed and unglazed, blue glaze, new china, blue printed ware and of course, figures.

The very first reference to figures occurs on page 2 of the sales ledger, when on 30 May 1783 the goods sent to Mr Joseph Tidmarsh included:

	sh	d
6 Shepherds &c	3	-
6 Gardener &c	2	6
6 Sailor &c	2	6
2 Sets Faith Hope &c	3	-
2 Pipers		9
2 Man with lost sheep	1	6
2 Clowns		7
6 Stags & Hinds	4	6
1 Sheep & Goat	1	8
1 Lord Chattam	1	9

From the sales ledger it is obvious that figures were just a small part of John Wood's total output. The few orders which include figures may cause some readers to wonder if the trade was economical, or at worst whether such relatively few pieces may have been bought in by John Wood from another manufacturer. However, the ledger indicates very clearly the three occasions when figures were supplied by Ralph Wood; none of the other thirteen orders give any indication that the pieces were not supplied from John Wood's factory.

It is interesting to note that many of the subjects in John's orders also occur in lists of Ralph Wood productions and in marked Ralph Wood pieces, however, there is no evidence identifying the exact models produced by John and although the subjects may be the same, the interpretation or the details may differ from those made by Ralph.

---

23. John Wood, op.cit. Sales ledger gives details of individual items supplied to retailers. Crate book gives details of crate loads supplied to retailers.

[handwritten sales ledger — John Wood's accounts]

3 Doz Jugs 3, 4 & 6 ———————— 1.—

5 Doz small Ware ———————— 6.—8

No 10 Figures & Toys &c Viz

P Land 1 pair Stag & Hind coloured ——————— — 1.—6

4 D° Mower & Haymaker 1/3 ——————— 6.—8

4 D° Sportsman & Lady 1/2 ——————— 4.—8

4 D° Boy & Girl with Basket & Fruit 10 ——— 3.—4

4 Gamekeepers with Hare & Dog 1/3 ——— 5.—

1 Hudibras on Horse ——————— — 2.—

1 Set Faith Hope & Charity ——————— — 1.—6

6 Dianas & Appolos 1/3 ——————— — 7.—6

6 Bagpipers 6 ——————— — 3.—

3 Pair Gardeners & Mates 1/ ——————— — 3.—

1 Pair Neptune & Venus ——————— — 2.—6

1 Pair Fox & Greyhound ——————— — 1.—6

1 Pair Mower & Haymaker Enam'd ——————— — 4.—

1 Pair Sportsman & Lady D° ——————— — 4.—

1 Pair Diana & Appolo ——————— — 5.—

One Set White & Gold

1 Appollo 1/9 ——————— }

1 Pair Sportsman & Lady 2/4 } — 5.—9

1 Pair Boy & Girl 1/8 }

One Set D°

1 Minerva 3/6 ——————— }

1 Pair Bacchus & Venus 4/ — } — 10.—

1 Pair Mower & Haymaker 2/6 }

1 Pair Dolphin Flower pots ——————— — 1.—6

1 Doz French grey Balloon &c 19/3 ——— — 3.—9

—————

14 11 0

Bill sent Car'd to Wharf 1/ }

Cash 2/8 } 15 —

From John Wood's sales ledger, part of an order supplied to Mr. Saml. Ward, 11 February 1786.

The figures listed in John's own thirteen orders include:

Apollo
Bacchus
Bacchus with grapes
Bagpiper
Boy & girl

Hope
Hudibras on horse
King David with harp
Lord Chattam
Lyon & panther

Bacchus and Venus, earthenware china glaze with traces of gilding, made in Staffordshire, 1780-1800, ht. 235mm. Private Collection.

John Wood's account book lists a number of sales of Bacchus and Venus including 18 March 1786 to Mr James Ewer '1 Pair Bacchus & Venus white & gold 3.6d'. Enoch and Ralph Wood also supplied this subject; John Wood lists 8 February 1787 'Bought of Ralph Wood...1pr Bacchus & Venus white & gold 3.6d'.

Venus was one of the most popular subjects in John Wood's account book, and appears alone and with Neptune and Apollo.

Spaniel, earthenware decorated with coloured glazes, c.1780-1800, ht. 172mm. *City Museum and Art Gallery, Stoke-on-Trent, 196.P.1949.*

John Wood's account book lists 30 March 1785 to Mr Robt Dickinson '1 pair Spaniel & pointer Dog 1/6d'.

Pair of lion and panther with winged cupids, earthenware decorated with coloured glazes, made in Staffordshire, c.1780-1800, ht. 213mm. *City Museum & Art Gallery, Stoke-on-Trent, 2210, 2211.*

A similar panther is known with impressed numeral '46'. John Wood's account book lists 9 December 1785 to Mr John Edwards '1 pair Lyon & Panther with cupids coloured & Gilt 4.6d'. Examples of coloured glazed lions and panthers with traces of gilding are known.

Boy & girl with fruit
Boy & girl with basket & fruit
Boy & girl, Derby
Boy & girl, Dutch
Boy & girl, Dutch, fruit baskets
Boy & girl, small
Bull with dog
Charity
Clown
Diana
Elephant
Faith
Figures with music, small
Fox
Gamekeeper
Gamekeeper with hare & dog
Gardener & Mate
Gardener & wife
Gasconian & Galigo
George & Dragon
Goat
Gunner

Man with lost sheep
Minerva
Mower & Haymaker, rakes for women
Mower & Haymaker, scythe & rake
Neptune
Piper
Pointer
Sailor & lass
Sheep
Shepherd & shepherdess
Shepherd & shepherdess on a rock,
  candlestick
Spaniel
Spanish dancer
Spanish figure carrying jugs
Spanish figure carrying music
Sportsman & lady
Stag & hind
Van Tromp
Venus
Venus with dove
Vicar & Moses
Woman with lost piece

Piper, earthenware decorated with coloured glazes, made in Staffordshire, c.1780-1800, ht. 203mm. *City Museum & Art Gallery, Stoke-on-Trent, 189.P.1949.*

John Wood's account book lists several bagpipers including 30 May 1783 to Mr Joseph Tidmarsh '2 Pipers 9d', and 16 June 1786 to Mr Stephen Mundy '2 Bagpipers 1.0d'. The difference in price may be accounted for by the fact that the piper and the bagpiper may be two different models.

Apollo, earthenware decorated with coloured glazes, to the left of the base can be seen the rebus or symbol of a stand of trees said to represent Wood, made in Staffordshire, c.1780-1800, ht. 216mm. *City Museum & Art Gallery, Stoke-on-Trent, 146.P.1949.*

The decorative finish of many of the figures is unspecified, but a number have qualifying descriptions, such as 'coloured', 'white & gold' or 'enamelled'. Comparing prices of unspecified with specified decoration gives an indication of the production ratios. Coloured appear to be by far the most common type, white and gold less common and only three pairs of figures specify enamelled decoration. Possibly the years covered by the sales ledger, 1783-7, constitute the transitional period in John Wood's manufactory when enamel painted figures were becoming established.

John Wood's business and personal life seemed to be a notable success, but fate seemed to hold a tragedy in store for each of the Wood brothers. John and Mary Wood had five children, the first born, a son, died in infancy. John jun. survived, as did three sisters. The eldest of these sisters, Ann Maria, was the object of the affections of the family physician, a Dr. Thomas Millward Oliver. John refused permission for Dr. Oliver to pay his addresses to Ann Maria and Dr. Oliver shot him, inflicting a mortal wound resulting in the death of John

Wood three days later. It was 1797 and John jun. was left to continue his father's business. In 1800 *Allbut's Directory* recorded:

'Brownhills

The principal part of this place is the seat and manufactory late belonging to Mr John Wood deceased; a man possessed of true religion, which shone with lustre in his public and private walks his death was regretted by all who knew him, but especially by those with whom he was more intimately acquainted. The manufactory is now carried on by his son Mr John Wood.'[24]

John followed in his father's footsteps and found himself a wealthy bride. He married Mary Baddeley in 1807 and it was through her that the Bignall End properties in North Staffordshire came to the Wood family of Brownhills. John diversified his business interests, becoming involved in banking, so that by 1830 he no longer needed the manufactory which lay in the grounds of his house. The works were demolished, the house enlarged and the gardens were laid out so that by 1840 the house and estate was one of the finest in the borough.[25]

There are many conclusions that can be drawn from this research, not the least being that John Wood was a far more important potter than Ralph Wood II or III. His neglect is likely to be the result of an over-emphasis of the number of marked R. and Ra. Wood pieces, and the lack of identified wares from John Wood's manufactory. From the sales ledger it seems likely that many of the figures attributed to Ralph may also have been made by John. The sales ledger also gives conclusive evidence that coloured glaze, china glaze and enamelled figures were produced concurrently in the 1780s and that the date of production of coloured glazed figures is much later than generally supposed. The evidence points to Ralph Wood productions dating from 1789 to 1801 and there is little to assist in differentiating between the various impressed marks within that twelve year period. A further mark attributed to Ralph is the rebus, a moulded stand of trees symbolic of Wood, so far only recorded on figures of Apollo, which could just as easily be the mark of John, Josiah or Enoch Wood.

Whilst it may appear from marked pieces and from the available documentary sources that the Wood family of Burslem were the sole makers of coloured glazed figures, this is not the case. The work of William Greatbatch and Edward Warburton has been discussed in Chapter 1 and both these men made coloured glazed figures; Warburton in the 1760s used a green glaze on a creamware body, whereas Greatbatch's work is more akin to that of the Wood's and dates from 1775 to 1780.

Perhaps the most unusual coloured glaze piece recorded is a rather abraded example of a woman making a wreath of flowers; she has a sheep at her feet

---

24. *A View of the Staffordshire Potteries,* T. Allbut, 1800.

25. Ward, J., *History of the Borough of Stoke-upon-Trent,* Lewis, 1843, reprinted Webberley, 1984.

Cybele, earthenware decorated with coloured glazes, fragments from the William Greatbatch site, Fenton, match this model, c.1780, ht. 150mm. *City Museum & Art Gallery, Stoke-on-Trent, 146.P.1988.* (See also Chapter 1, page 48).

Woman making a floral wreath, pearlglazed earthenware decorated with coloured glazes, impressed on broken footring 'EALE & CO', for James Neale & Co, c.1785-90, ht. 162mm. *Private Collection.* The pedestal behind is broken and probably supported a vase.

Impressed mark 'S BOURNE'.

Stag, earthenware decorated with coloured glazes, base impressed 'S. BOURNE', made by Samuel Bourne, c.1803-8, ht. 140mm. *City Museum & Art Gallery, Stoke-on-Trent, 2941.*

Ram, pearlware with underglaze colour on the body and coloured glaze base, impressed 'FELL', made by Thomas Fell of Newcastle upon Tyne, c.1817-25, ht. 110mm. *Wisbech & Fenland Museum, 1901.80.*

Ewe, pearlware with underglaze colour on the body and coloured glazed base, exactly similar to an example in the Victoria & Albert Museum, impressed 'FELL', made by Thomas Fell of Newcastle upon Tyne, c.1817-25, ht. 116mm. *City Museum & Art Gallery, Stoke-on-Trent, 603.*

Impressed mark 'FELL'.

and a pedestal at her back, from which a piece is broken. This was probably a vase, as complete examples of this kind are recorded with enamel painted decoration. The figure is impressed on the broken footring 'EALE & Co', the missing front letter is probably 'N'. Neale is best known for his enamel pieces and his work is considered in detail in Chapter 4.

Amongst the very few other marked pieces is a reclining stag impressed 'S. BOURNE', which is believed to be the work of Samuel Bourne, whose partnership with John Bourne was dissolved on 23 April 1803; the business continued as Samuel Bourne and was included in the local rate records until 1808. Samuel Bourne worked in Shelton and a witness to his partnership dissolution was Charles Tittensor, whose name is also associated with figure making.[26] The one identifiable example of S. Bourne's work is not unlike other coloured glazed pieces normally associated with the Wood family of Burslem. Did he acquire Ralph's moulds after his death in 1801? Was he previously employed in one of the Woods' potworks? It is unlikely that an unmarked Bourne piece will be identified on the basis of the surviving evidence, but it serves as a salutory reminder of our incomplete understanding of the pottery industry.

One other manufacturer of coloured glazed figures, usually accompanied by some underglaze oxide colour, was Fell of Newcastle upon Tyne. The company was established at St. Peter's Quay by Thomas Fell and Co. in 1817 and remained in business until 1890. They manufactured all kinds of cream and whiteware, sponged, printed, coloured underglaze, coloured and enamelled wares. The mark found on a ewe in the Victoria & Albert Museum

26. *Staffordshire Advertiser*, 29 October 1803.

St. George and the Dragon, earthenware decorated with coloured glazes, made in Staffordshire, c.1780-1800, ht. 299mm. *City Museum & Art Gallery, Stoke-on-Trent, 2213.* This is a third version of the subject and emphasises the difficulty of identifying individual figures to specific manufacturers without marked examples as type specimens.

Jupiter holding a thunderbolt aloft and accompanied by an eagle, earthenware decorated with coloured glazes, made in Staffordshire, c.1780-1800, ht. 267mm. *City Museum & Art Gallery, Stoke-on-Trent, 177.P.1949.*
This model is known with the impressed mark 'Ra. Wood Burslem 29'; another model of Jupiter, in which he carries the thunderbolt like a sceptre in his right hand, is known impressed '79'.

Lion, earthenware decorated with coloured glazes, made in Staffordshire, c.1780-8, length 1.302mm. *Henry Weldon Collection.*
The base has a paper label which reads 'J'ay achettez ceci le 27 Janvie 1789'.

Old Age, earthenware chinaglaze undecorated, made in Staffordshire, c.1780-1800, ht. 235mm. *Southport Museum, 128.*

Bagpiper, earthenware decorated with coloured glazes, made in Staffordshire, c.1780-1800, ht. 193mm. *Royal Pavilion Art Gallery & Museum, Brighton, HW888F.*

A small group of figures is known mounted on square plinths with moulded swags of flowers. The majority of recorded examples appear to be decorated with coloured glazes, but examples are known with underglaze and overglaze painted decoration.

Detail of base.

Boy with apron full of fruit, earthenware decorated with coloured glazes, made in Staffordshire, c.1775-85, ht. 153mm. *Royal Pavilion Art Gallery & Museum, Brighton, HW1194.*

Figure of a man holding a small animal, earthenware decorated with coloured glazes, made in Staffordshire, c.1775-85, ht. 153mm. *City Museum & Art Gallery, Stoke-on-Trent, 167.P.1949.*

(3657. 1901) and on a ram in the Wisbech & Fenland Museum is 'FELL' impressed, a mark used between 1817 and 1830. This would normally be considered a late date for coloured glazed ware, but as the company did not exist before 1817 the date cannot be earlier. On close examination of the piece it must be said that the potting is somewhat heavier than would normally be expected from a late eighteenth century Staffordshire example and the addition of the underglaze oxide may also be considered a later feature.

Examples of Fell's work are more usually discussed with underglaze painted wares and further examples may be found in Chapter 3. However, these pieces serve to remind us that the cheaper production methods associated with coloured glazed figures made them economical to make and that some factories kept popular lines in production for a long time, leading to the conclusion that

Figure of a girl with a basket of fruit, earthenware decorated with coloured glazes, made in Staffordshire, c.1775-85, ht. 140mm. *Colonial Williamsburg, 1963-411.*

Venus, earthenware decorated with coloured glazes, made in Staffordshire, c.1775-85, ht. 143mm. *Colonial Williamsburg, 1963-412.*

coloured glazed figures were made over a much wider time scale than has hitherto been suggested.

It is inevitable that the vast majority of figures produced will remain anonymous, although more evidence may yet be found through documentary and excavated sources which will assist in future classification. The lack of marks, however, does not detract from our interest; pieces which are finely modelled, well produced and skilfully decorated may give greater pleasure than a poorly conceived attributable example. For those who are uncertain as to the qualities of coloured glazed figures I urge you to handle pieces. If you do not have easy access to a collection, visit antique fairs, view at auction houses or make an appointment at a museum; familiarity will not breed contempt, but further a deeper appreciation of one of Staffordshire's finest products.

3. Underglaze painted figures

In the last decade of the eighteenth century a development in pottery making occurred, which allowed manufacturers to produce cheap and colourful pearlware figures decorated with high temperature underglaze colours. This development offered a new range of figures which superseded those with coloured glazes at the cheaper end of the market. This class of pottery is often called Pratt ware by contemporary collectors, although only two marked jugs can be identified from this factory and there is no evidence that Pratt ever produced figures. A monograph has recently been published on this subject which is recommended for a more detailed discussion of these wares.[1] In order to avoid confusion between the hollow wares produced by Pratt and the multicoloured transfer printed wares also called Pratt ware by collectors, it is proposed to call this class underglaze painted figures.

Figures of this type were made from the white clays of Devon and Dorset, which were first moulded and fired to biscuit temperature, then painted or sponged with a limited range of colours before glazing and refiring. The

---

1. Lewis, John & Griselda, *Pratt Ware 1780-1840*, Antique Collectors' Club, Woodbridge, 1984.

Simple two-part moulded figure group of children in an arbour, earthenware with painted decoration under a pearl glaze, made in Staffordshire, early 19th century, ht. 95mm. *City Museum & Art Gallery, Stoke-on-Trent, 89.P.1962.*

Three earthenware figures of Autumn, the left with underglaze painted decoration, the centre with underglaze painting and green glaze base, the right with overglaze enamel painted decoration, c.1790-1810, ht. 197mm. *Private Collection.*
Although the same subject, these pieces are all from slightly different moulds and cannot be considered the production of one factory.

Complex multi-part moulded figure of St. George and the Dragon, earthenware with painted decoration under a pearl glaze, made in Staffordshire, c.1790-1800, ht. 267mm. *Private Collection.*

colours are all derived from metal oxides: yellow, green, blue, brown, black and purple are the only shades which would stand the temperature of the glaze firing. There are no reds or pinks, no delicate lemon yellows, apple greens or pale blues. There are only strong, bold, earthy colours with little subtlety but a redeeming charm and naïvety.

The colours may have been painted on to the biscuit earthenware body using an oily, binding medium such as linseed, which would have required a light firing to evaporate the oil before applying the glaze, but it is much more likely that the colours were mixed with water which evaporated naturally and therefore kept production costs to a minimum. After the colour had been applied, either by brush (known in the trade as a pencil) or by sponge and the piece had dried, it was dipped into a liquid pearlglaze and fired to seal in the painted colours. The simple processes employed made these figures cheap in comparison to enamelled pieces which required two firings before the decorating stages were even begun. The cheapest examples were the simplest two-part moulded pieces. There were also complex assemblies, some of them from the same moulds as figures with other decorative finishes; a number of models may be found with either underglaze or enamel painted decoration and if they are exactly similar presumably may have come from the same manufacturer.

There is a noticeably wider range of modelling qualities employed in the making of these pieces than in most figure types. Moulds which were also used for more expensively decorated subjects produced good, well-defined models

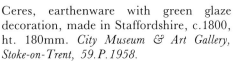

Ceres, earthenware with green glaze decoration, made in Staffordshire, c.1800, ht. 180mm. *City Museum & Art Gallery, Stoke-on-Trent, 59.P.1958.*

Simple green glazed pieces would have been the cheapest of all figures to produce and must have offered underglaze painted pieces some competition at the bottom of the market.

Sportsman and companion, earthenware with painted decoration under a pearl glaze, c.1790-1810, ht. 184mm. *City Museum & Art Gallery, Stoke-on-Trent, 394 & 395.P.1949.*

'SUMMER' and 'WINTER' from a set of the Seasons, titled on the front, earthenware with painted decoration under a pearl glaze, c.1800-1815, ht. 219mm. *Private Collection.*

These figures may also be found with overglaze enamel painted decoration.

Bull baiting group, earthenware with painted decoration under a pearl glaze, c.1800-15, ht. 215mm. *Royal Pavilion Art Gallery and Museum, Brighton, HW1020.*

Cat sitting on a cushion, earthenware with underglaze painted decoration, c.1810-20, ht. 66mm. *City Museum & Art Gallery, Stoke-on-Trent, 51.P.1962.*

Fallen rider, earthenware with painted and sponged decoration under a pearl glaze, c.1790-1810, ht. 210mm. *Royal Pavilion Art Gallery and Museum, Brighton, HW1057.*

and there exist some fairly sophisticated multi-part moulded examples, but there is also a range of small unsophisticated figures which appears to have been produced exclusively in underglaze painting. These simpler inexpensive figures are made from two-part moulds which were produced to cater for the cheapest end of the market. This latter class may often be so lacking in detail and so carelessly decorated that the subject is difficult to decipher; occasionally they received no underglaze colouring but are covered in a green glaze, making production costs even cheaper, and their naïvety often leads collectors into confusing cheap productions with earlier pieces, where simplicity was a product of technical rather than economic constraints.

The subject matter of the models produced with underglaze painting is very diverse and gathered from various sources. There are the usual contemporary figures depicting rural pastimes and occupations. The musicians, sportsmen, birdnesters and cockfighters were derived from everyday life and these subjects would have had a wide appeal for the intended customer, who would be familiar with country pursuits. Still popular were classical and allegorical subjects such as the Seasons, and Faith, Hope and Charity. Figures of Venus are particularly numerous, whereas Apollo and Neptune are less commonly found. It may be that the lowest end of the market was less aware of the significance of the classical allusions and purchases were made purely on visual appeal.

The large number of animal figures which have survived indicates that they were popular subjects and include domestic, circus and wild beasts. The range of domestic animals would not be complete without that most popular of subjects, the cat, but there are also dogs and birds; cows are sometimes accompanied by diminutive milkmaids or calves, there are bulls occasionally being baited and pastoral sheep and lambs. The figures of horses include racehorses; also hacking or hunting animals, often with riders. What appears to be a peculiarly vicious looking horse about to trample his poor owner under hoof is believed to be a model of a trained horse from Philip Astley's famous troop, performing one of its astonishing tricks. The animals that are particularly endearing are the wild species which were often exhibited in travelling shows; here the potter manages to tame the King of Beasts and depicts him as a lovable pet. Amongst the most popular of all birds is the owl, said to be symbolic of wisdom, where the figure stares back at the viewer with large, unblinking eyes and captures the heart of many a collector.

It is very difficult to judge when many of the underglaze painted pieces were made and the occasional issue of a commemorative bust or portrait model is particularly useful in providing dating evidence.

An interesting group of pieces, which may emanate from the same factory, can be found on square pedestal bases with moulded swags of flowers. The subjects include classical and contemporary figures, neatly potted and of modest size, and pieces occur in both coloured glazes and underglaze painted colours.

Lion, earthenware with painted decoration under a pearl glaze, made in Staffordshire, c.1790-1810, ht. 133mm. *City Museum & Art Gallery, Stoke-on-Trent, 1399.*

Owl, earthenware with painted and sponged decoration under a pearl glaze, made in Staffordshire, c.1790-1810, ht. 140mm. *City Museum & Art Gallery, Stoke-on-Trent, 3056.*

Sir Frances Burdett, titled and inscribed 'S + F BURDETT BRITAINS + FRIEND', earthenware with painted decoration under a pearl glaze, c.1810-20, ht. 102mm. *Royal Pavilion Art Gallery & Museum, Brighton, HW502.*

Sir Francis Burdett (1770-1844), was an M.P. from 1807-37 and was attacked for his radical views. He was imprisoned twice, once in 1810 and again in 1820, for speaking out against war with France, political corruption and flogging in the army.

A sailor, earthenware with painted decoration under a pearl glaze, the base with coloured glazes, c.1790-1800, ht. 152mm. *Royal Pavilion Art Gallery & Museum, Brighton, HW1194.*

Figures with this distinctively moulded base also occur in coloured glazes (see page 97) and overglaze painted decoration (see page 138).

Group of earthenware 'toys', with painted decoration under a pearl glaze, c.1800-20, ht. tallest 120mm. *Private Collection.*

Figure often found with the impressed title 'SIMON' and a pair to Iphigenia, impressed on the reverse 'WEDGWOOD', c.1790-7, ht. 163mm. *Sotheby's, London.* It is difficult to trace the origins of this model, which is certainly known at an earlier date in Strasbourg porcelain.

The subject matter of a large number of small figures can barely be discerned and often the blobs of colour obscure detail rather than enhance it; these tiny pieces must have been the cheapest of all figures and must surely have been toys, trifles or gewgaws.

Underglaze painted pottery was made in many potting centres, including Staffordshire, Shropshire, Liverpool, Yorkshire, Sunderland and Bovey Tracey, but not apparently in Wales or Bristol.[2] Many of the potters who made underglaze painted wares would have chiefly produced crockery for the kitchen and table but may have undertaken additional novelty lines to catch the eye and tempt the pocket. In common with all other late eighteenth to early nineteenth century figures, documentary evidence as to specific manufacturers hardly exists. There is a small number of marked examples, but no written evidence is known and very little archaeological evidence exists to assist in attributing the majority of these figures.

2. Ibid., p.22.

Farmyard group, earthenware with underglaze painted decoration and coloured glazes, impressed 'TITTENSOR', c.1810-25, length 1.365mm. *William F. Hull Collection, Atlanta Historical Society.* This large group is composed of several independent figures assembled on a large base; the individual elements may occur separately and this marked group would be a good basis for attribution.

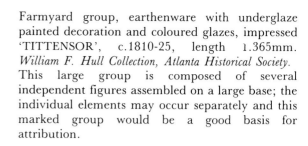

Impressed mark 'TITTENSOR'.

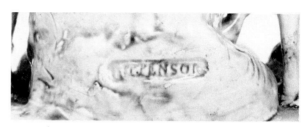

Reverse of farmyard group.

Perhaps it would be most useful to begin with a discussion of those wares which can be identified and which may assist in the tentative attribution of unmarked wares and to close with illustrations of the great variety of pieces which are never likely to be traced to their maker.

The earliest marked pieces which may be dated are those impressed 'WEDGWOOD', which I believe to be the work of Ralph Wedgwood in Burslem, 1790-7 (see page 107). The Wedgwood marked figures are usually enamel painted pieces; the background to this attribution and details of Ralph Wedgwood will be found in Chapter 4. Ralph appears to have used good quality moulds and careful decorators to produce the finest range of underglaze painted figures from a single manufacturer. The subjects produced are dominated by the prevailing taste for romantic, neo-classical models and offered the cheaper end of the market a tasteful, inexpensive alternative to the enamel painted productions.

The most prolific range of marked underglaze painted figures bear the impressed mark 'TITTENSOR'. This family name is not uncommon in North

9. Group of figures, with underglaze painted decoration, made in England, late 18th-early 19th century, ht. 230mm. *City Museum & Art Gallery, Stoke-on-Trent.*
These show the typical range of colours available for underglaze painted decoration. The palette was limited to colours derived from metal oxides which would withstand the heat of the glaze firing.

Pair of shepherd and shepherdess, earthenware with painted decoration under a pearl glaze and with green glazed base, impressed on the reverse 'TITTENSOR', c.1810-25, ht. 165mm. *Sotheby's London.*

This small group is composed of several independent figures assembled on a large base; similar models can be seen in other large compositions by Tittensor and as individual figures.

There are two distinctive bocages used on underglaze painted Tittensor pieces, which may have details unique to this manufacturer and may be useful in attributing unmarked pieces. Another noticeable feature of the figures is the heavily scored bases which have not been seen on marked examples from any other manufacturer.

Figure of a boy dressed as a soldier, earthenware with painted decoration a under pearl glaze, impressed on the reverse 'TITTENSOR', c.1810-25, ht. 101mm. *Tyne & Wear Museum Service, D1509.*

Boy reading, earthenware with painted decoration under a pearl glaze, impressed on reverse 'TITTENSOR', c.1810-25, ht. 180mm. *Peter Manheim, London.*

Girl reading, earthenware with painted decoration under a pearl glaze, impressed on the reverse 'TITTENSOR', c.1810-25, ht. 178mm. *Private Collection.*

Dog, earthenware with painted decoration under a pearl glaze, impressed on the reverse 'TITTENSOR', c.1810-25, ht. 86mm. *Private Collection.*

Equestrian, earthenware with painted decoration under a pearl glaze, unmarked, c.1810-25, ht. 190mm. *Royal Pavilion Art Gallery & Museum, Brighton, HW1058.*
This figure exhibits many features associated with the marked Tittensor figures; the bocage appears to be the same and the base is scored around the back.

Staffordshire and therefore it is not possible to be absolutely certain who produced these wares. However, the most obvious candidate is Charles Tittensor, first recorded as a potter in the *Staffordshire Advertiser,* 27 February, 1802, when a notice of Robert Pope's dissolution of partnership with John Brown was followed by the announcement that the business in Hanley was to be continued on the same premises by Robert Pope and Charles Tittensor. In little over a year the *Staffordshire Advertiser* of 15 October 1803, announced that the partnership between Robert Pope and Charles Tittensor had been dissolved on 1 July by mutual consent and that the business was to be carried on from the same premises by Charles and John Tittensor. The local rate books, which exist from 1807, indicate that by that date the company was carried on under the name of Tittensor and Simpson and that this partnership continued until 1813. The first trade directory entry concerning this figure maker appears in *Parson & Bradshaw's Directory* of 1818, as 'Tittensor Charles, potter, Queen Street Shelton'. His name does not occur under earthenware manufacturers but under the alphabetical lists of occupants for Hanley and Shelton. Whilst this may indicate that he was not in business for himself it is more likely to suggest that his potworks was a very small concern. A similar entry can be found in the alphabetical list for Hanley in *Allbut's Directory* of 1822-3; there are no entries in succeeding directories and in 1834, under China & Earthenware Toy Manufacturers, is listed 'Jackson Joseph, Queen Street, Shelton'. As there are no other known earthenware toy manufacturers in

20. Group of figures showing people in contemporary costume, with underglaze painted decoration, made in England, late 18th-early 19th century, ht. 232mm. *City Museum & Art Gallery, Stoke-on-Trent.*

21. Group of figures showing the classical influence, underglaze painted decoration, made in England, late 18th-early 19th century, ht. 265mm. *City Museum & Art Gallery, Stoke-on-Trent.*

22. Group of animal figures, with underglaze painted decoration, made in England, late 18th-early 19th century, ht. 190mm. *City Museum & Art Gallery, Stoke-on-Trent.*

23. Group of small figures typical of the inexpensive 'toys' produced in this class of ware, with underglaze painted decoration, made in England, late 18th-early 19th century, ht. 135mm. *City Museum & Art Gallery, Stoke-on-Trent.*

Queen Street, Hanley, it may be deduced that Tittensor had relinquished his pottery sometime between 1822 and 1834 and that Joseph Jackson had taken over the premises.

The problems of dating Tittensor's marked work are obviously complicated by his many changes of partnership. Would Pope or Simpson have allowed the one simple name 'TITTENSOR' to be impressed on their joint productions? It is unlikely this question will ever be answered, therefore alternative means must be found of deciding a date range. I imagine most collectors would be unhappy with their figures being given the general date range 1803-30 and therefore I have tried to narrow the field. I give you my reasoning here in order that you may understand why I have come to certain conclusions. It appears to me, having examined a number of marked Tittensor pieces, that the marks were consistent with the production of pieces in a reasonably self-contained period, that is I do not believe that a few were produced in 1803 and some in 1815 and others in 1830! I think the mark would have changed more over a prolonged period of production. Many of the figures are in traditional or classical costumes and attitudes, which offer no guidelines to dating, but there are many bocage pieces, and as I believe bocage was introduced some time around 1810-15, it seems likely that most of this work is of the 1810-25 period.

Some of the most impressive pieces of work from Tittensor are the large composite groups. These are usually formed from a large base and built up with figures taken from his standard production range. A particularly fine example is that from the Atlanta Historical Society, where the two figures overlook a range of animals, including a deer, sheep, goat, and horse and with a tiny milkmaid almost hidden beneath a contented looking cow. Elements from this large figure group can be found singly or in smaller groups and are important links towards identifying unmarked wares. This use of smaller figures appearing in groups of various sizes enabled Tittensor to make a wide range of wares and it is surprising that this economically sound system was not adopted by other makers.

A noticeable feature of Tittensor figures is the distinctive scoring often found on the bases, where it seems that some kind of combing tool was used for decoration, possibly to disguise the junction between the base and the figure itself. Many of the figures stand in front of bocage or branching tree devices and whilst details of various bocage models are discussed in some depth in Chapter 6, I believe the bocages that appear on Tittensor marked figures are peculiar to his manufacture. No evidence is known to suggest that any other maker used Tittensor bocage and if exactly similar bocage occurs on an unmarked figure there could be reason to suspect a Tittensor attribution.

Whilst most of his wares appear to be decorated with underglaze colours there are a few examples of enamel painted pieces marked 'TITTENSOR' and reference is made to them in Chapter 6. From known pieces of Tittensor's work it can be seen that he did not specialise in particularly high quality productions; in this respect he was probably typical of the growing number of

Fish seller, possibly representing the element Water, earthenware with painted decoration under a pearl glaze, inscribed in underglaze blue on the base 'Jacob Marsh', made early 19th century, ht. 135mm. *Private Collection.*

small specialist figure makers who operated on a small scale, producing wares for a small sector of the cheaper market. As a specialist maker he was able to make his mark with a range of pieces whose naïve charm belies their lowly position in the nineteenth century market place.

It is unfortunate that many of the other known marked figures decorated with underglaze painting are single examples from a factory which must have had a fairly significant output. One such figure is that of a woman holding a basket of fish, which may have been sold as either a fish seller or as part of a set of Elements in which she represented Water. The base is signed in underglaze blue with a cursive 'Jacob Marsh'. Many pieces of pottery, including figures, have names inscribed on the bases and it is thought that these usually indicate the workman involved in making the pieces rather than the factory owner, however, it is generally accepted that this piece came from the manufactory of Jacob Marsh.

Jacob Marsh was first known in 1793, trading as a specialist enameller; by 1803 he was insuring his potworks, stock and utensils for £500 and in 1805 was listed as an earthenware manufacturer of Burslem. In 1806 he left Burslem and moved to Fenton (Lane Delph) where he rented a potworks. In 1818 Marsh purchased land and built a new factory on the boundary between Fenton (Lane Delph) and Longton (Lane End); the pediment on the building reads 'Boundary Works 1819'.

24. Deer hunter, with underglaze painted decoration impressed 'TITTENSOR' on reverse, made by Charles Tittensor, Shelton, c.1810-25, ht. 152mm. *Private Collection; photograph by Gavin Ashworth, New York.*

25. Charity, inscribed 'Charity' on the base in brown, with underglaze painted decoration, made in Staffordshire, c.1800, ht. 230mm. *City Museum & Art Gallery, Stoke-on-Trent, 50.P.1970.*

26. Sportsman and companion, with underglaze painted decoration, made in Staffordshire, c.1790-1800, ht. 178mm. *City Museum & Art Gallery, Stoke-on-Trent, 394 & 395.P.1949.*

27. Watch stand with removable pottery watch, with underglaze painted decoration, impressed on the top of the base at the foot of the clock 'DIXON AUSTIN & Co.', made by Dixon Austin & Co., Garrison Pottery, Sunderland, c.1820-6, ht. 270mm. *City Museum & Art Gallery, Stoke-on-Trent, 21.P.1956.*

28. Lost sheep, with underglaze painted decoration, impressed on the base 'HAWLEY', made in Yorkshire at either Thomas Hawley's Kilnhurst Old Pottery or William Hawley's Top Pottery, c.1795-1810, ht. 222mm. *Yorkshire Museum, 4472.*

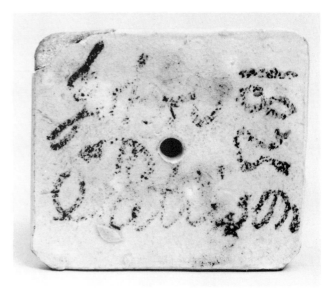

Inscription 'John Pattison 1825' on base of Venus.

Venus, earthenware with painted decoration under a pearl glaze, inscribed and dated 'John Pattison 1825', ht. 146mm. *Private Collection.*

Whilst there is no evidence to indicate the type of wares made by Marsh throughout his manufacturing period, I think it unlikely that he specialised in figures. His entries in *Pigot's Directories* of 1828-9 and 1830 do not carry the symbol which indicates makers of 'Toys only'. The one known marked figure has no distinctive features which enable any accurate date to be ascribed, nor does it help to identify unmarked pieces from this factory. Stylistically, taking into account the style of base, the subject and the quality of modelling, an early nineteenth century date can be suggested, and it may be that the piece was signed by Jacob Marsh to commemorate his change over from enameller to potter at the turn of the century, or his removal to one of his subsequent factories in Lane Delph.

One of the most frustrating signed figures is that of Venus with a barely distinguishable 'John Pattison 1825' painted in brown. No John Pattison can be found in the records of pottery makers; only a James Pattison is listed as an earthenware and toy manufacturer in Longton, between 1818 and 1830. The date of this piece is quite startling and again confirms that popular models are likely to have been made over a long period of time and that a wide date range should be offered when no specific evidence for attribution is available.

There were large centres of pottery production outside Staffordshire and a number of factories in the North of England used underglaze painting to decorate a range of figures, particularly animal models. Cow cream jugs cannot be seriously considered as table wares even though they purport to be jugs and I know certain collectors claim to use them. Their claims to ornamental or figure status are equally uncertain, but, as I have access to a number of marked examples in the legendary herd at the City Museum & Art

Horse, earthenware with sponged decoration under a pearl glaze, impressed on the base 'S^TANTHONY 2', c.1800, ht. 140mm. *City Museum & Art Gallery, Stoke-on-Trent, 47.P.1963.*

Goat, earthenware with sponged and painted decoration under a pearl glaze, impressed on the base 'S^TANTHONY 2', c.1800, ht. 139mm. *City Museum & Art Gallery, Stoke-on-Trent, 46.P.1963.*

Cow cream jug, earthenware with sponged decoration under a pearl glaze, impressed on the base 'S^TANTHONY 2', c.1800, ht. 137mm. *City Museum & Art Gallery, Stoke-on-Trent, 50.P.1963.*

Cow cream jug with recumbent calf, earthenware with sponged decoration under a pearl glaze, impressed on the base 'SEWELL 4', c.1805-15, ht. 130mm. *City Museum & Art Gallery, Stoke-on-Trent, 294.P.1963.*

Gallery, Stoke-on-Trent, and as such examples may be of use in classifying other figures they are included here in my discussion.

In the Tyneside area of north-east England a number of factories existed which occasionally marked their wares. The St. Anthony pottery in Newcastle upon Tyne was established in the late eighteenth century and in 1800 the factory was sold by William Huntley to Foster & Cutter, who in 1804 sold it to Joseph Sewell who continued the business until 1819 when the company became Sewell & Donkin. Figures known from this factory include a particularly dapper type of pony, a benign looking goat and two cow cream

Cow cream jug with milkmaid, earthenware with sponged and painted decoration under a pearl glaze, impressed on the base 'Taylor & Co', c.1821-3, ht. 130mm. *City Museum & Art Gallery, Stoke-on-Trent. 189.P.1963.*

Cow cream jug, earthenware with sponged decoration under a pearl glaze, impressed on the base 'FELL'. c.1820, ht. 120mm. *City Museum & Art Gallery, Stoke-on Trent, 47.P.1967.*
For impressed Fell ram see page 95

jugs, all with the impressed mark 'ST ANTHONY 2'. The animals stand on thin, flat, green glazed bases. The sides of the bases are painted dark brown and the edges do not form straight lines but curve in towards the centre and have canted corners.

For a brief time it seems that the St. Anthony pottery used the owner's name Sewell as a mark which may have run concurrently with the St. Anthony mark during the relevant period 1804-19. Only three marked figures are recorded, two of which are cow cream jugs with recumbent calves, marked on the base 'SEWELL 4'. The other is accompanied by a milkmaid and is impressed 'SEWELL' with the figure 1 above it.

Another little known pottery which included figures in its wares was that established at St. Peter's Quay in Newcastle upon Tyne by Thomas Fell & Co. in 1817. The impressed mark 'FELL' appears on cow cream jugs and figures of sheep. The sheep offer a particularly salutory example of the extended tradition of naïve figure making. Unmarked examples could easily be confused with the so-called Wood family pieces and dated to the eighteenth century, when the evidence of the mark tells us that these pieces are indeed nearer to 1820, the date range being 1817-30. The sheep have green glazed bases with a distinctive pattern of moulded leaves, and the body of the animal has patches of ochre yellow applied under the glaze. The cows stand on flat, green glazed bases and have sponged patches of a peculiar yellow tint which runs through shades of lemon to brown.

Cows are also recorded with the mark of 'TAYLOR' and 'TAYLOR & Co. Whilst there are records of a George Taylor in business in Hanley in the Staffordshire Potteries from about 1780 to 1820 and subsequently continued by his descendants until about 1830, there is a more compelling case to be made for the mark being that of another Newcastle upon Tyne pottery. The Tyne Pottery was occupied by Taylor & Co. from about 1821 to 1823. When

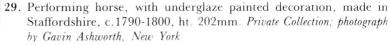

29. Performing horse, with underglaze painted decoration, made in Staffordshire, c.1790-1800, ht. 202mm. *Private Collection; photograph by Gavin Ashworth, New York*

30. Cock fighting, with underglaze painted decoration, made in Staffordshire, early 19th century, ht. 210mm. *City Museum & Art Gallery, Stoke-on-Trent, 243.P.1949.*

31. Lion, with underglaze painted decoration, made in Staffordshire, c.1795-1800, ht. 159mm. *City Museum & Art Gallery, Stoke-on-Trent, 3874*

Cow cream jug with calf, earthenware with underglaze sponging and overglaze painted decoration on the moulded base, impressed 'I MOLE', c.1815-25, ht. 120mm. *City Museum & Art Gallery, Stoke-on-Trent, 28.P.1963.*

Two cow cream jugs from very similar moulds; left, with sponged and painted decoration over the glaze; right, with sponged and painted decoration under a pearl glaze; left impressed on base 'E BROWN', right impressed 'P&C', c.1810-20, ht. 120mm. *City Museum & Art Gallery, Stoke-on-Trent, 41 & 38.P.1963.*
(The mark P&C is not distinct and could read P&O).

the partnership was dissolved one of the Taylors set up at the nearby Newcastle Pottery trading as Taylor & Son.[3]

Other marked cow cream jugs exist, but none of their makers have yet been identified. One has 'I Mole' impressed in large letters on the base of a particularly handsome beast standing with her calf on a lively moulded base. Two very similar models have slight differences in their bases and are impressed 'E. BROWN' and 'P & C'. Neither of these manufacturers appear in Staffordshire records so perhaps are from potteries elsewhere in England. The E. Brown example is in overglaze enamel colours, but could easily have been produced with underglaze painted decoration.

---

3. R.C. Bell, in his book *Tyneside Pottery,* suggests the firm began as Tyler & Co.; Trade Directories confirm that this is a transcription error and that the company was indeed Taylor & Co. (I am grateful to Dr. Katherine Ross for checking this point on my behalf.)

Set of Seasons, earthenware with painted decoration, under a pearl glaze, titled and impressed 'DIXON AUSTIN & Co', c.1820-6, ht. 222mm. *Private Collection.*

Watch stand, earthenware with painted decoration under a pearl glaze, impressed 'DIXON AUSTIN & CO', c.1820-6, ht. 280mm. *City Museum & Art Gallery, Stoke-on-Trent, 21.P.1956.*
The watch stand has a ceramic pocket watch to replace the real one during use.

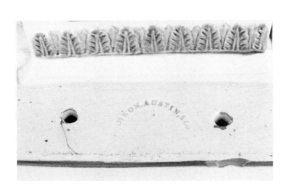

Impressed mark 'DIXON AUSTIN & CO'.

Bust of Nelson, buff coloured stoneware, impressed 'HERCULANEUM', c.1805, ht. 216mm. *Williamson Art Gallery, Birkenhead.*

Bust of Napoleon, earthenware with painted decoration under a pearl glaze, c.1805, ht. 222mm. *City Museum & Art Gallery, Stoke-on-Trent, 3317.*

The best known of the north-eastern potteries is probably that of Dixon, Austin & Co., who occupied the Sunderland or Garrison Pottery. The factory dated to the early years of the nineteenth century and from about 1820 to 1826 Robert Dixon and Thomas Austin were partners in the concern, using the title Dixon, Austin & Co. This factory was one of the few figure makers known to include tablewares in their production and novelty or fancy goods, including black printed and pink lustre souvenirs and frog mugs. Their best known figures are those of the Four Seasons, of which at least two full marked sets are known and several individual unmarked models have been noted. The watchstands in the form of a longcase clock are supported by two small figures which occur in other unmarked groups and might be key features in widening the field of attributable Sunderland Pottery figures.

On the opposite coast of England at the port of Liverpool, the pottery industry had long been established and it is not surprising to find that at least one factory was producing underglaze painted wares. The success of the Staffordshire Potteries was keenly felt by the Liverpool merchants who saw crate loads of ware shipped abroad. To join this lucrative trade Samuel

Loyal Volunteer,
earthenware with painted
decoration under a pearl
glaze, c.1800-10,
ht. 216mm. *City Museum
& Art Gallery, Stoke-on-Trent,
236.P.1949.*
Loyal Volunteer regiments
were established all over
Great Britain in order to
train men to repel any
French invasion. Figures of
this type come in a variety
of models and on many
different bases; there is no
evidence to support a
traditional Liverpool
attribution.

Worthington recruited experienced Staffordshire work people and moved them to Toxteth, where the Herculaneum Pottery was established in 1796. A wide range of pottery was produced there, including creamware, pearlware, stoneware and porcelain. A number of figure models has been attributed to this company but the only marked pieces are portrait busts, mainly of military and naval heroes made in various stoneware bodies. Identical earthenware examples with underglaze painting appear to come from the same moulds and there may be some justification for their attribution to Herculaneum, but there is no evidence to support any other models being necessarily of Liverpool manufacture. A tantalising advertisement was placed in the *North Staffordshire Mercury* of 23 January, 1841, when Herculaneum's closure sale offered stock including 'superior Figure MOULDS'. Whether the figures were exclusively confined to commemorative busts is not yet known, but that the moulds were sold and used again seems to be indicated by the record of a Copeland & Garrett bust of Lord Duncan, which appears to come from the same mould as the earlier Herculaneum piece.

Horse, earthenware with sponged and painted decoration under a pearl glaze, attributed to Leeds Pottery, c.1810, ht. 406mm. *Sotheby's London.*

Horses of this kind were reputed to have been used for window displays by saddlers and dealers in horse medicine. This model was reproduced in creamware during the late 19th- early 20th century by the Senior family and sold through W.W. Slee of Leeds.

A longcase clock money box, earthenware with painted decoration under a pearl glaze, inscribed on reverse 'J Emery Mexbro' 1838', ht. 229mm. *Private Collection.*

Figure group centred around a longcase clock money box, earthenware with painted decoration under a pearl glaze, unmarked but identical to a group inscribed by James Emery of Mexborough Pottery, c.1838, ht. 229mm. *Sotheby's London.*

The history of the numerous potteries of Yorkshire has been well researched; besides Heather Lawrence's standard work of reference,[4] there are several monographs on individual factories. The cities and towns of Leeds, Doncaster and Swinton are the most well-known pottery centres but dozens of small factories were scattered throughout Yorkshire, many of them must have produced underglaze painted wares for the local and national markets.

The Leeds Pottery is perhaps the best known of these factories and its history is detailed in Chapter 4. Marked ornamental wares with underglaze painted decoration are recorded and figures have been attributed to the pottery, based on comparisons with marked examples in other decorative finishes. The Leeds horses are amongst the most striking figures ever made: their level gaze dares the viewer to doubt their authenticity, but it is known that they were reproduced in quantity by the Senior family using the original moulds at their factory in Hunslet, Leeds.[5]

4. Lawrence, H., *Yorkshire Pots and Potteries,* David & Charles, Newton Abbot, 1974.
5. Ibid.

Performing animals, earthenware with coloured slip and painted decoration under a pearl glaze, c.1810-20, ht. 140mm. *City Museum & Art Gallery, Stoke-on-Trent, 426.P.1949.*

The buff coloured earthenware used to produce this piece is not of the type used in Staffordshire; possibly this piece comes from one of the Yorkshire or Tyneside potteries.

Group with bird's nest, earthenware with painted decoration under a pearl glaze, c.1810-20, ht. 117mm. *City Museum & Art Gallery, Stoke-on-Trent, 62.P.1962.*

Candlestick figure, earthenware with painted decoration under a pearl glaze, c.1800-10, ht. 254mm. *City Museum & Art Gallery, Stoke-on-Trent, 244.P.1949.*

Man and woman in Turkish costume, earthenware with painted decoration under a pearl glaze, c.1810-20, ht. 121mm. *City Museum & Art Gallery, Stoke-on-Trent, 75.P.1962.*

Tiger, earthenware with painted decoration under a pearl glaze, c.1805-15, ht. 152mm. *Private Collection.*

The Hawley family, which has connections with Staffordshire, established the Kilnhurst Old Pottery, which was worked by Thomas Hawley from 1783 to 1808 and the Top Pottery, Rawmarsh, which William Hawley began in 1790. Pieces marked 'HAWLEY' include underglaze painted wares in strong distinctive shades of blue, ochre and olive green, and black is extensively used to outline features such as eyes. Only one marked figure is recorded which is unremarkable in subject, being a standard shepherd with lost sheep, but the coloration conforms to that noted on other Hawley wares. Whilst the palette of a piece should not generally be taken as a guide to identification, the peculiar qualities of the Hawley colours may be the exception that proves the rule.

Another of the small potteries which produced underglaze painted pieces was that of James Emery, who worked through the middle years of the nineteenth century. An interesting figure group inscribed and dated 'J. Emery Mexbro' 1838' demonstrates how long the popularity of this type of pottery continued. The group is made from an assortment of individual figures on bases assembled on to a larger moulded base with a longcase clock money box in the centre. The money box is known to have been made as a separate item and there is no reason why the man and woman or their dogs may not also be found as independent figures.

It is impossible to estimate accurately the number of potteries which made underglaze painted wares and therefore could have included this type of figure in their output. There must have been many more than fifty establishments, perhaps even one hundred, however, it is known that less than fifteen left any record of their work. It is not surprising to discover that the vast majority of these figures remain unattributed. Future archaeological and documentary discoveries are awaited to reveal more of the history of pottery production and to see if those cherished orphan pieces will ever have a family to call their own.

4. Enamel painted figures : the first phase

The earliest period of enamel painted decoration produced some of the most technically accomplished earthenware figures ever made. These have often been rejected by the collector, in favour of coloured glazed examples, merely because it was believed that their sophisticated appearance reflected a later date. I hope I may have convinced some readers that, for a number of years, both types of figures were produced and that the type of decorative treatment may indicate the price range and not necessarily the date range of a figure.

During the early eighteenth century the only easily available enamel painted ceramics in England were those from the Orient. Enamel painting was a costly process and involved a degree of scientific knowledge not available to the early Staffordshire potters.[1] I believe that the earliest decorators were independent artists, who in the mid-eighteenth century advertised their talents as miniature painters on gold and copper, or who painted in enamels on panels or plaques

---

1. Pitt, W.A., *Topographical History of Staffordshire,* 1817, pp.419-20.

'Painting and Gilding China or Earthenware' from Enoch Wood's Manufactory, 1827.

for the 'toy' industry, which produced boxes or scent bottles for people of taste and fortune; they enamelled dial plates for watches and clocks and painted on pottery and glass supplied by the customer. It has been recorded that more than 300 painters of all kinds are known to have been in practice in London at some time between 1745 and 1770, and at least sixty-seven painted in enamel colours on metal, pottery, porcelain or glass.[2]

By 1758 Robert Dossie had published his *Handmaid to the Arts,* in which he recorded in detail 'the nature, composition, glazing, painting and gilding of porcelain or china ware'. The section on overglaze ceramic painting states: 'there is not the slightest difference between this and other enamel painting with respect to the choice or treatment of the colours'. The revised edition of 1764 has almost one hundred pages devoted to 'the nature, preparation and use of the several substances employed in enamel painting' and fifty pages are given over to the preparation of gold and the gilding of various surfaces.

The process being expensive and its secrets not widely known in mid-eighteenth century Staffordshire, enamel painting was first confined to the more costly wares such as porcelain and white saltglazed stoneware. Whilst some of these pieces may have been painted in London, skilled artists were soon tempted to work nearer the source of production. As earthenware improved and the decorating techniques became more widely understood, their use spread to creamware and naturally to the newly developed pearlware. By the last quarter of the eighteenth century many manufacturers must have had decorating establishments within their factories, for by 1784 seventy-five potteries in Staffordshire are listed in *Bailey's British Directory* along with the names of only three specialist decorators who, between them, could scarcely have accommodated all the pottery production requiring enamel painting.

During the late eighteenth century, the potters were fortunate to have a wide variety of subject matter which interested potential purchasers. The fashionable artistic styles dominated the markets from top to bottom. It was a century in which a great deal of building took place and from the mid-eighteenth century the Classical revival prevailed. The main sources of inspiration were the antiquities of Italy and Greece, dominated by the collections, galleries and museums in Rome. This was the age of the Grand Tour, a European trip which was conducted over several years. In 1757 *Instructions for Travellers* commented, 'Persons who propose to themselves a Scheme for Travelling generally do it with a view to obtain one or more of the following ends; viz First to make Curious Collections, as Natural Philosophers, Virtuosos or Antiquarians. Secondly to improve in Painting, Statuary, Architecture and Music. Thirdly to obtain the reputation of being Men of Vertu and of an elegant Taste'. The works of art which these tasteful young travellers collected made England one of the treasure houses of Europe.

---

2. Benton, E., 'The London Enamellers', English Ceramic Circle, *Transactions,* Vol.8, Pt.2, 1972.

Many of the new great houses that were built had casts and copies of famous antique statues, exteriors had stone copies on the skyline, lead copies in niches on the facade, whilst plasters, bronzes and marbles were used indoors. The demand exceeded that which could be supplied from Rome, leaving opportunities for enterprising workmen at home. The best known of these was John Cheere, the leading producer, in mid-eighteenth century England, of lead garden statuary, plaster casts, bronzed plaster statuettes and plaster library busts.[3] He sent casts and copies to all parts of the country and exported his work to Europe. It also seems that his work yards at Hyde Park Corner were much visited; Hogarth, who made an engraving of John Cheere's yard to use in his *Analysis of Beauty,* remarked that it was through visiting Cheere's yards that the most admired antique statues were more widely known than any of the equally good modern works.

John Cheere was only one of many plaster makers; evidence exists of several others including Peter Vanina, Charles Harris, Hoskins and Grant and Richard Parker. The plaster reproductions were available for anyone to buy. It is obviously much quicker and cheaper for a pottery modeller to copy a three-dimensional source than to conceive the whole piece from the beginning and plasters were one easy way to obtain popular subjects. Certain types of earthenware figures share common characteristics, which may lead one to suppose that they came from a single pottery factory, when it is equally possible that the only thing they have in common is that the originals came from the same source of plaster makers or modellers. John Cheere's plasters were widely available and although he died in 1787, his moulds obviously remained in existence for some time, for in 1792 a number were acquired by John Flaxman's father.[4]

The acquisition of models from plaster makers has been remarked upon by art historians in the past, but the ceramic historian seems to have neglected this useful avenue of research. Whilst it has been acknowledged that a number of Josiah Wedgwood's models were purchased from specialist suppliers, similar practices by other potters have been overlooked; admittedly it is not so easy when so few wares are marked, but it will be demonstrated later in this chapter that some of the well-known classical earthenware models have a traceable source.

Plasters were not the only source of subjects for the Staffordshire figure maker, but it has proved impossible to find the origins of a great number of the pieces seen today. One might imagine that prints would have offered as much inspiration to the Staffordshire modellers as to the engravers, but most of the printed sources seem to have been made first into figures and groups by the Continental and English porcelain manufacturers, whose work again

---

3. Friedman, T., and Clifford, T., *The Man at Hyde Park Corner: Sculpture by John Cheere,* catalogue of an exhibition, Leeds, 1974.

4. Haskell, F. & Penny, N., *Taste and the Antique,* Yale University Press, 1982, p.80.

offered a three-dimensional model to copy. Many Staffordshire earthenware figures can be seen to reflect earlier porcelain originals. That direct copying was undertaken is indicated by a letter of 2 May 1785 to Mr. Swift of Etruria, which reads:

> Sir,
>
> Today Mr Isaac Warburton told me, if I would apply to Mr Swift he believed he could help me to a small foreign china enamelled Figure about 4 inches high which he gave Mr Wedgwood to see & has been kind enough to favour me with it as a pattern to model. Should be much oblig'd Sir could you procure & send it by Uncle Moses Wood
>
> Ralph Wood[5]

It is fortunate that the Wedgwood correspondence has been preserved and is generously made available to researchers, but this surely was not the only time that such a piece was used as a model; it must have been a regular occurrence, but unfortunately other sources of evidence are woefully inadequate.

It is highly unlikely that pottery manufacturers like Ralph or Enoch Wood sat in a workshop designing and modelling figures themselves. There is no evidence to suppose that Ralph had any talent in that direction and Enoch Wood wrote in a letter of 1830 that 'he had done very little in the way of modelling for 47 years',[6] that meant since 1783 when he first became self-employed. Competent local hands must have been employed to supplement the London suppliers and the widest variety of sources would have been used.

In order to make the most economical use of their resources potters used the same models for a variety of decorative finishes. As long as a subject remained popular it was produced. The same model can be found treated with both coloured glazes and overglaze enamel painting. Hudibras, Admiral Van Tromp, Haymakers, Apollo and Diana are just a few which come to mind immediately, no doubt the list can be multiplied by those with a keen eye and good memory.

As the century drew to a close and the enamel painted pieces became more widely produced, their popularity spread and the coloured glazes were phased out. Many of the old favourite subjects continued in production, although new models based on old themes were also introduced. The bucolic subjects received a good deal of attention, with Mowers and Haymakers, Gardeners, Shepherds and Shepherdesses all depicting a romantic, idyllic life style.

A group of related figures which remained popular, consisted of Gasconians,

---

All references to Wedgwood MSS refer to the Wedgwood papers held at the University of Keele, North Staffordshire, and are quoted by kind permission of the Trustees of the Wedgwood Museum.

5. Wedgwood MSS, 11498-12.

6. Falkner, F., *The Wood Family of Burslem,* Chapman & Hall, 1912, p.50.

Group of bucolic subjects, depicting gardener and companions, pearl glazed earthenware with overglaze enamel painted decoration, small 'Gardener' and his companion impressed on reverse '1' and '2', made in Staffordshire, 1780-1800, ht. 215mm. *City Museum & Art Gallery, Stoke-on-Trent, 272, 273 and 688.P.1949.*

Spanish Dancers and Gasconian, pearl glazed earthenware with overglaze enamel painted decoration, made in Staffordshire, 1785-95, ht. 240mm. *City Museum & Art Gallery, Stoke-on-Trent, 262 & 326.P.1949.*
The figure entitled Spanish Dancers is actually playing a friction drum and can be found in coloured glazes, the Gasconian hurdy-gurdy player can be seen in coloured glazes on page 78.

Spanish Dancers and Flemish Music, which in coloured glazes lacked the titles which help to recognise the subject, but which in enamel painted versions proclaim their Continental origins. Where the potters came upon their sources for such themes remains a mystery. Continental and English porcelain figures of hurdy-gurdy players are not uncommon, but similar examples with friction drums and castanets are not known. A printed source may be the answer but as yet none has come to light.

The most fashionable subjects would undoubtedly have been the neo-classical models; some of the old examples such as Minerva, Juno and Jupiter, Neptune and Venus and Apollo and Diana were joined by Andromache, Charlotte, Europa and Anthony and Cleopatra. Many new allegorical subjects were introduced, including the Christian virtues of Faith, Hope and Charity, expressed in classical forms and joined by the four natural virtues, Justice, Fortitude, Prudence and Temperance. Some subjects such as the Seasons were produced in both classical and contemporary styles in order to offer the customer the widest possible choice.

Biblical subjects continued in production but new models were introduced; Elijah and the Ravens for instance, can be found with an interpretation of both biblical and classical costume. The Lost Piece and the Lost Sheep remained popular as did depictions of the Saints.

St. Peter, pearl glazed earthenware with overglaze enamel painted decoration, made in Staffordshire, late 18th century, ht. 368mm. *City Museum & Art Gallery, Stoke-on-Trent, 613.*

Jupiter, pearl glazed earthenware with overglaze enamel painted decoration, made in Staffordshire, late 18th century, ht. 216mm. *City Museum & Art Gallery, Stoke-on-Trent, 315.P.1949.*

St. Paul, pearl glazed earthenware with overglaze enamel painted decoration, made in Staffordshire, late 18th century, ht. 362mm. *City Museum & Art Gallery, Stoke-on-Trent, 616.*

Portrait bust of William Pitt the Younger, pearl glazed earthenware with overglaze enamel painted decoration, made in Staffordshire late 18th century, ht. 216mm. *Julian Critchley Collection.*

John Wilkes holding a scroll inscribed 'The Rights of the People', pearl glazed earthenware with overglaze enamel painted decoration, made in Staffordshire, late 18th century, ht. 254mm. *Royal Pavilion Museum & Art Gallery, Brighton, HW497.*
Possibly made at the time of Wilkes's death in 1797.

Amongst the least common subjects are portraits, many of which were confined to busts but a few full length figures were produced as well. It must have entailed a considerable financial risk to produce portraits of contemporary subjects, as the popularity of statesmen, politicians, etc., is notoriously unpredictable and very few received a ceramic accolade. The Staffordshire potter seemed content to wait awhile and confirm a long standing and widespread interest in a subject before committing his factory to production. The general popularity of John Wilkes for his championship of the rights of the people was celebrated by many an inscription on a creamware teapot of the 1760s, an inexpensive response to an immediate demand, but one can hardly put so early a date on the magnificent figure of Wilkes in the Willett Collection. The piece is pearlware, finely painted and perhaps more typical of the 1790s. John Wilkes died in 1797. Perhaps it was made at that time to commemorate his life and work? The most unusual subject portrayed is that

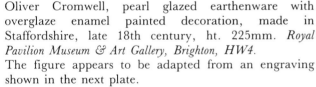

Oliver Cromwell, pearl glazed earthenware with overglaze enamel painted decoration, made in Staffordshire, late 18th century, ht. 225mm. *Royal Pavilion Museum & Art Gallery, Brighton, HW4.*
The figure appears to be adapted from an engraving shown in the next plate.

Engraving of Oliver Cromwell by Charles Grignion after a design by Samuel Wale. It is one of the illustrations from *A New Universal History of England* by George Frederick Raymond, published in 1787. *By permission of the British Library.*

of Oliver Cromwell; it is difficult to imagine why he should be so popular in the late eighteenth century, but the figure is based on an illustration from a contemporary volume which must have enjoyed some success. The use of one figure for two subjects was not a feature of the late eighteenth or the early nineteenth century but became a more common practice when makers of Victorian portrait figures were trying to produce at a most economical rate.

Subjects which declined in popularity included those in a Chinese style. The chinoiserie fripperies were totally overwhelmed by the fashionable neo-classical designs and never resumed their pre-eminent place in the Staffordshire figure makers' repertoire. Animal figures, which also lost favour, were not completely abandoned but were relegated to the cheaper classes of ware and many were produced with high temperature underglaze painting.

The earliest datable enamel painted figure known is that which William Greatbatch appears to have made. Fragments of an enamel painted Cybele were excavated on the site of Greatbatch's pottery in Fenton, which was in operation from 1762 until 1782; there is no evidence that the business was continued by anyone else after Greatbatch's bankruptcy, therefore fragments found during the excavation must pre-date 1782. The fragments clearly depict

Fragments of the feet of Cybele, pearl glazed earthenware with overglaze enamel painted decoration excavated from the site of William Greatbatch's factory, Fenton, Staffordshire Potteries, c.1775-82.

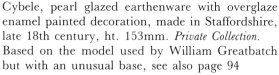

Cybele, pearl glazed earthenware with overglaze enamel painted decoration, made in Staffordshire, late 18th century, ht. 153mm. *Private Collection.* Based on the model used by William Greatbatch but with an unusual base, see also page 94

a grass and rock mound and a pair of bare feet, bounded on the right hand side by a cornucopia spilling its contents, and on the left by the head of a recumbent lion. The fragments are accompanied by pieces of a square base which has become detached from its figure. The details of the mound match in every particular the figure of Cybele standing holding a cornucopia in her left arm, with her right hand holding the draperies of her classical robes. This model has been found on a variety of bases and in a variety of decorative finishes which leads one to believe that, following Greatbatch's bankruptcy, his moulds may have been sold to recoup some monies and that some of his wares may have continued in production at other sites.

The earliest documentary reference to enamel painted figures is found in John Wood's account book,[7] where in 1786 he records that Saml. Ward was supplied with:

1 Pair Mower & Haymaker Enamd. 4/-
1 Pair Sportsman & Lady Do.   4/-
1 Pair Diana & Appolo   5/-

7. John Wood's account books City Museum & Art Gallery, Stoke-on-Trent.

Sportsman and Haymaker, earthenware with overglaze enamel painted decoration, Sportsman impressed '27' on base, made in Staffordshire late 18th century, ht. 185mm. *City Museum & Art Gallery, Stoke-on-Trent, 378.P.1949, 48.P.1970.*

Flemish Music, pearl glazed earthenware with overglaze enamel painted decoration, base impressed 'Ra. Wood Burslem', c.1785-1800, ht. 205mm. *City Museum & Art Gallery, Stoke-on-Trent, 285.P.1949.*

It is unfortunate that the City Museum has only one from the set of John Wood's account books and that this contains only a single reference to these three enamelled figures. As John does not appear to have marked his wares and it is likely that they are indistinguishable from those produced by Enoch and Ralph Wood, we can only speculate which pieces have come from his factory. Whilst many of the subjects illustrated here were certainly made by John Wood it cannot yet definitely be said that these were his models, as indeed they are merely typical productions of the period.

Inevitably Ralph Wood left just enough evidence of his enamel figure production for some of his work to be identified and thereby overshadow his illustrious brother and cousin. Ralph Wood II and his son Ralph III were in business from about 1789 to 1801;[8] the elder Ralph died in 1795 and left the younger man to continue until his early death in 1801, at the age of twenty-six. Although best known for their coloured glaze pieces, their output also included enamel painted figures which were often of outstanding quality.

Amongst the finest pieces are marked examples of Newton and Chaucer, on

8. See pp. 68-93, Chapter 2.

Elijah and the Ravens, pearl glazed earthenware with overglaze enamel painted decoration, base impressed 'Ra. Wood Burslem', c.1795-1800, ht. 260mm. *Private Collection.*

Isaac Newton, pearl glazed earthenware with overglaze enamel painted decoration, impressed 'Ra. Wood Burslem 137' c.1785-1800, ht. 310mm. *Royal Pavilion Art Gallery & Museum, Brighton, HW 970.*
For a similar figure from the Leeds Pottery see p.173.

which the superb enamel painting may be enhanced by rich gilding. Other marked subjects include Flemish Music, Elijah, and a fine bust of Zingaria, probably taken from a plaster after a popular Greek marble.

Perhaps the finest enamel painted figures of the last quarter of the eighteenth century are those marked Neale & Co. James Neale first became involved in the pottery trade as a retailer in London where he is recorded in 1763 selling wares for Wedgwood. By 1767 he had settled at premises in St. Paul's Churchyard and an alliance was established with Humphrey Palmer, a potter of the Church Works, Hanley, in the Staffordshire Potteries. Whilst James Neale was an acute business man, it appears that Humphrey Palmer lacked this skill, and Neale took over the Church Works in 1778, when Palmer's financial affairs were in turmoil.[9]

From at least 1781 the company traded as James Neale & Co., when it is likely that Neale took Robert Wilson as a partner to manage the manufacturing business and returned to London to join other partners in the

9. Edwards, D., *Neale Pottery and Porcelain,* Barrie & Jenkins. 1987.

32. Group of figures, with overglaze enamel painted decoration, made in Staffordshire, c.1785-1810, ht. 353mm. *City Museum & Art Gallery, Stoke-on-Trent.*
This group is typical of the first phase of enamel painted figures. There is a wide range of subjects and the colours used are usually delicate and subtle. A number of manufacturers stood larger figures and groups on bases painted to resemble marble (compare with colour plate 46).

Actaeon the hunter, pearl glazed earthenware with enamel painted decoration, base impressed 'NEALE & Co', c.1785-90, ht. 126mm. *Private Collection.*

Venus, pearl glazed earthenware with enamel painted decoration, impressed 'NEALE & Co', c.1785-90, ht. 222mm. *Geoffrey Godden Collection.*

Impressed mark 'NEALE & Co'.

retail end of the trade. This, of course, meant that Neale knew just what the customer required and that he could produce it. He demanded the highest standards from his factory and there is undoubtedly no one to match the quality of the wares in which they specialised in the late eighteenth century.

The young Enoch Wood had, of course, worked for Palmer and it seems likely that he continued under the new ownership until he and Ralph Wood set up in business in 1783. Enoch's well-known portrait bust of John Wesley may have been modelled during the last year or two at Neale & Co., and while no marked examples of this subject from this period are known, a companion bust of the Rev. George Whitfield, impressed 'Neale & Co' on the base, appears to be identical with signed Enoch Wood examples.[10] It is just possible that Neale & Wilson took advantage of the talents of their young employee, or alternatively the models may have been produced in Enoch's own time and therefore his property to take with him and use at his own factory if he wished.

The largest recorded Neale figure is the reclining Cleopatra, who lies clasping the asp to her bosom awaiting the fatal strike. This popular model was made by a number of factories and occurs in various forms: a porcelain example from the Liverpool factory of Richard Chaffers may be found in the Victoria & Albert Museum dating to about 1755-60 and at least two similar later earthenware versions have been recorded, one of which is often said to be the work of Enoch Wood, but there is no evidence to sustain this attribution as the same model is known to have been made in Swansea. The second version is that known with the mark 'Neale & Co' impressed on the footring. The Neale piece has particularly delicate details which mark it as the work of a first rate factory. The subject itself is taken from an antique marble in the Galleria delle Statue in the Vatican and is likely to have reached the potters through a popularly produced bronze or plaster cast. It is interesting to note that a Neale & Co. black basalt version of Cleopatra is recorded, together with its pair Lucretia, rather than the more commonly found Anthony and that the two suicidal heroines were suggested as a pair in the late eighteenth century list of bronzes supplied in Rome to the Grand Tourists by Francesco Righetti.[11] The crisp detail of the dry bodied black basalt no doubt offered superior imitations of the bronze souvenirs, but the brightly painted versions would have appealed to the less purist customer.

Whilst large pieces are known, the majority of Neale & Wilson's figures are of modest size, are usually very finely modelled and the detail is quite marked in comparison to other enamelled figures. It seems that the moulds were replaced perhaps more frequently than in some establishments, where they were used long after their water absorbent surface had become worn and lost detail. The quality of the glaze is outstanding with a lovely pearly sheen, which is particularly suited to the depiction of skin tones in reproductions of classical figures. The enamel painting is always impeccably applied and the palette of colours very pleasing. The combination of a translucent turquoise and warm puce seems to have been used very frequently, particularly to highlight scrolling bases, but this is not a reliable guide to attribution.

The most commonly seen of Neale & Wilson figures are sets of the Seasons, modelled as small child-like figures and found with contemporary dress or classical costume. The pieces are occasionally marked and often have their

10. Victoria & Albert Museum, acc. no. 83-1874.

11. Haskell, F. & Penny, N., *Taste and the Antique*, Yale University Press, 1982, p.186.

33. Two bagpipers, on the left with overglaze enamel painted decoration, impressed '21' on reverse, on the right with coloured glaze decoration, made in Staffordshire, c.1780-800, ht. 220mm. *City Museum & Art Gallery, Stoke-on-Trent,. 329.P.1949. 184.P.1949.*

34. Group of classical and allegorical subjects, with overglaze enamel painted decoration, made in England, c.1790-1810, ht. 330mm. *City Museum & Art Gallery, Stoke-on-Trent.*

35. Group of porcelain figures made at Derby, 1765-1825, ht. 310mm. *Tullie House Museum, Carlisle, W387, W387, W40, W345, W192.*
All these figures have counterparts in earthenware. Staffordshire potters may have used the porcelain example for models and may have engaged the same modellers or used the same sources. There is little documentary evidence known about the origin of most English earthenware figures.

36. Two musicians, on the left an earthenware example, on the right a Derby porcelain piece, c.1825, ht. 144mm. *City Museum & Art Gallery, Stoke-on-Trent, 282.P.1949; Tullie House Museum, Carlisle, W387.*

Set of Seasons, Spring, Summer, Autumn, Winter, pearl glazed earthenware with overglaze painted decoration, bases titled and impressed 'NEALE & Co', c.1785-90, ht. 140mm. *Private Collection.*

Spring and Summer from a set of the Seasons, pearl glazed earthenware with overglaze enamel painted decoration, base of Spring impressed with crown over 'G', base of Summer impressed with crown over 'C', attributed to Wilson, c.1790-1800, ht. 137mm. *Private Collection.*

Minerva, pearl glazed earthenware with overglaze painted decoration, base impressed 'NEALE & Co', c.1785-90, ht. 150mm. *City Museum & Art Gallery, Stoke-on-Trent, 3163.*

Tambourine player, pearl glazed earthenware with overglaze enamel painted decoration, base impressed 'NEALE & Co', c.1785-90, ht. 216mm. *City Museum & Art Gallery, Stoke-on-Trent, 280.P.1949.*

Piper, pearl glazed earthenware with overglaze enamel painted decoration, impressed on base 'NEALE & Co', c.1785-90, ht. 210mm. *Wisbech & Fenland Museum, 1900.41.*

subject title impressed beneath the base. It may be that some workmen were careless or that subjects were thought interchangeable, for certainly one can find the young lady with flowers impressed 'SPRING' or 'SUMMER'.

Occasionally Neale & Wilson's finest figures have additional gilding which must have added considerably to the cost, but the finished item may have been thought superior enough to offer real competition to porcelain pieces which commanded a high price. A good example of this superior product can be seen in the figure of Minerva, whose gilded breastplate must have sparkled amid the ranks of more simply decorated pieces. Larger figures such as the tambourine player and piper are in a style more widely adopted by the Staffordshire potters; one could be forgiven for thinking that they were examples from the Wood family, except for very clear Neale & Co. marks.

It is possible that some of the Neale & Co. figures date from the earliest years of their partnership. The business was known as Neale & Co. at least as early as 1781, but generally the date of 1785-90 is accepted. In about 1790-1 James Neale gave up the ownership of the factory to his pottery business partner, Robert Wilson. It is possible that at this time the mysterious impressed mark

37. Cleopatra, with overglaze enamel painted decoration, impressed on base 'NEALE & Co', made at James Neale's Church Works, Hanley, c.1785-90, ht. 187mm. *Private Collection.* There are a number of different models of Cleopatra, some have rock-like bases, others have softer drapes, this Neale example has a heart shaped clasp on her sandal. All the models are based on a marble sculpture in the Galleria delle Statue in the Vatican, a popular subject reproduced in small size bronzes and plasters.

38. Bust entitled on the reverse 'SADNESS', with overglaze enamel painted decoration, impressed on reverse 'WEDGWOOD', made by Ralph Wedgwood, Burslem, c.1790-7, ht. 560mm. *City Museum & Art Gallery, Stoke-on-Trent, 1619.*

39. Portrait bust of George Washington, with overglaze enamel painted decoration, impressed on reverse with two separate marks, 'WASHINGTON' & 'Ra Wood, Burslem', made by Ralph Wood, Burslem, c.1785-1800, ht. 212mm. *Jackson-Mitchell Collection.*

40. Pair of spill vases with female figures, incised on the base 'WL 1804', with overglaze enamel painted decoration, made in Staffordshire, 1804, ht. 215mm. *City Museum & Art Gallery, Stoke-on-Trent, 95, 96. P. 1949.*

The figure on the right is Maria, sometimes called Poor Maria, taken from a description in *A Sentimental Journey Through France and Italy,* by Laurence Sterne, 1768. The subject was well known through paintings and earlier designs for jasper plaques. The figure on the left seems to symbolise grief inscribing a funerary urn and may be based on the classical figure of Antonia, who is usually depicted with an urn containing the ashes of her son Germanicus.

41. Group of figures on pedestal bases, with overglaze enamel painted decoration, made in Staffordshire, 1790-1800, ht. 375mm. *City Museum & Art Gallery, Stoke-on-Trent, 623, 614, 328. P. 1949.*

'King David' with additional gilding and impressed numeral on reverse '129'. 'St. Andrew', impressed numeral on the reverse '122'. 'Van Tromp', impressed numeral on reverse '38'.

The Assassination of Marat by Charlotte Corday, pearl glazed earthenware with overglaze enamel painted decoration, base impressed 'LAKIN & POOLE', c.1793-95, ht. 343mm. *City Museum & Art Gallery, Stoke-on-Trent, 3135.*

Rinaldo and Armida, pearl glazed earthenware with overglaze enamel painted decoration, base impressed 'LAKIN & POOLE', c.1791-95, ht. 254mm. *City Museum & Art Gallery, Stoke-on-Trent, 828.P.1963.*

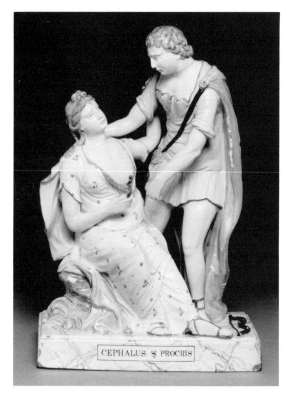

Cephalus and Procris, pearl glazed earthenware with overglaze enamel painted decoration, base impressed 'LAKIN & POOLE', c.1791-5, ht. 280mm. *Glaisher Collection, 940. Courtesy of Syndics, Fitzwilliam Museum, Cambridge.*

Ganymede, cup bearer to the Gods, pearl glazed earthenware with overglaze enamel painted decoration, base impressed 'LAKIN & POOLE', c.1791-5, ht. 324mm. *Julian Critchley Collection.*

Apollo, pearl glazed earthenware with enamel painted decoration, unmarked but possibly by Lakin & Poole in the same series as Ganymede, c.1791-5, ht. 317mm. *Julian Critchley Collection.*

Time Clipping the Wings of Cupid, pearl glazed earthenware with overglaze enamel painted decoration, base impressed 'LAKIN & POOLE', c.1791-5, ht. 310mm. *Southport Museum, 122.*

of a crown above 'G' or 'C' came into use for it is found together with the Neale & Co. mark on table wares and on pieces also marked 'Wilson'; the mark also occurs alone and is thought to be of the Wilson period. Under Robert's ownership the factory expanded and his son David was taken into the business, but their partnership was a short lived venture as Robert died in 1801. David continued taking his own son David jun. into partnership, but David jun. was not an asset to the company and their business terminated in 1820. In the early years Robert and David Wilson responded to changing demands of fashion, but their figure production, which had continued in the Neale & Co. neo-classical traditions, declined, and we have no records of pieces which can be dated to the later years of this company.

A relatively short lived business, which also operated during the late eighteenth century, was that of Lakin & Poole. Thomas Lakin had entered into partnership with John Ellison Poole in 1791. An insurance policy of 1st Dec. 1791 valued their Burslem potworks at £500, their stock of earthenware at £650, moulds and utensils at £200 and five dwelling houses occupied by labourers at £20 each. In February 1795, Poole's brother-in-law, Thomas Shrigley, became a co-partner; it is recorded that the pottery was managed at this time by a Thomas Heath and Lakin is described as a traveller. The new partnership arrangements did not seem to suit Thomas Lakin, who withdrew

42. Bacchus and Ariadne, based on an original marble (now known as Priapos and a Maenad), with overglaze enamel painted decoration, made in Staffordshire, c.1790-1810, ht. 635mm. *City Museum & Art Gallery, Stoke-on-Trent.*

Monumental figures of this type may have been modelled from plaster statues available from specialist makers in London. It is not possible to identify the maker of these large anonymous pieces because the reduced size plasters were available to any potter. Only two Staffordshire potters, Ralph Wedgwood and Enoch Wood, marked pieces of this kind; other anonymous makers may also have made them.

43. Purity, with overglaze enamel painted decoration, made in Staffordshire, c.1790-1810, ht. 715mm. *City Museum & Art Gallery, Stoke-on-Trent, 1618.*

44. Group of figures on similar bases, with overglaze enamel painted decoration, made in Staffordshire, c.1795-1810, ht. 215mm. *City Museum & Art Gallery, Stoke-on-Trent, 385.P.1949, 322.P.1949, 386.P.1949, 1648.*

45. Two figures of Winter, on the right earthenware, on the left porcelain impressed on base 'W(***)', c.1790-1810, ht. 190mm. *Geoffrey Godden Collection.*

Several late 18th-early 19th century porcelain figures are known with exactly similar counterparts in earthenware. Some of the porcelain pieces have the impressed mark 'W(***)', which was once thought to represent Enoch Wood; detailed research has not confirmed this and several other theories have been put forward, but no conclusions are yet possible and even a Continental source has not been conclusively ruled out.

in January 1796, and the remaining partners were declared bankrupt in 1797.[12]

The partnership of Lakin & Poole had lasted less than five years; amongst their many fine products is a distinctive range of figures, no doubt a small part of their trade compared to tea and tableware production. Most of these models share common characteristics, in the marbled, square or rectangular base; the figures have plump features with slightly protruding eyes, and their frozen actions portray a realistic lifelessness rather like a Tussaud's waxwork. The modelling is skilled if not inspired and the enamel painted decoration is particularly fine in the depiction of the marble bases. The most well known of their figures is the group entitled 'The Assassination of Marat by Charlotte Corde, of Caen, in Normandy, 1793'. Would that all manufacturers were kind enough to supply such a detailed title and mark their wares so clearly, for there is a large, impressed 'LAKIN & POOLE' on the base. Other marked figures in this group include Rinaldo and Armida, two characters from *Jerusalem Delivered,* an Italian epic poem in twenty books by Torquato Tasso (1544-1595). Armida was a beautiful sorceress with whom the hero Rinaldo 'fell in love and wasted his time in voluptuous pleasure. After his escape from her, Armida followed him, but unable to lure him back, set fire to her palace, rushed into a combat and was slain'. It is left to the reader to decide which part of the story is depicted here. The figures were probably inspired, not by the original poem, but by a popular operetta of the period.

Cephalus and Procris are classical subjects: whilst searching for his errant wife, Cephalus accidentally slew her with a javelin, and when he discovered what he had done he killed himself with the same javelin.

An untitled figure, also in this marked series, is identified as the Trojan boy Ganymede, the cup bearer of Zeus. Ganymede, the epitome of youthful male beauty, was taken up into Olympus and made immortal.

A marked Lakin & Poole figure group, which does not appear to have been modelled by the same hand and for which there is a source, is that of Time Clipping the Wings of Love. James MacArdell (c.1729-1765) produced a mezzotint of this subject after Sir Anthony Van Dyck and it was first produced in Chelsea-Derby porcelain and recorded in the first Chelsea-Derby sale held by Mr Christie in April 1771.[13] It is difficult to be certain whether the print or the Chelsea-Derby figure group stimulated Lakin & Poole to produce this item, but it is usually assumed that earthenware examples automatically followed porcelain prototypes.

These large, important pieces by Lakin & Poole are well known, but it is not known whether or not they engaged in a less ambitious form of figure making

---

12. Blakey, H., 'Thomas Lakin: Staffordshire Potter 1769-1821', *Northern Ceramic Society Journal,* Vol. 5, 1984, pp.79-114.

13. Poole, J., *Plagiarism Personified: European Pottery and Porcelain Figures,* Fitzwilliam Museum, Cambridge, 1986.

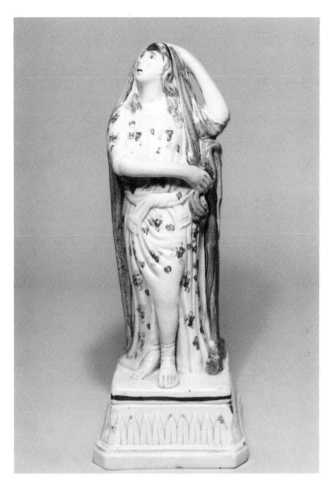

Boy with dog, pearl glazed earthenware with overglaze enamel painted decoration, base impressed 'T. Smith', made by Theophilus Smith, c.1790-1800, ht. 152mm. *Private Collection.*

Hope, pearl glazed earthenware with overglaze enamel painted decoration, impressed 'T. Smith', made by Theophilus Smith, c.1790-1800, ht. 229mm. *City Museum & Art Gallery, Stoke-on-Trent, 15.P.1959.*

Impressed mark 'T. Smith'.

to which they did not feel inclined to apply their mark. It is unlikely that it will ever be known whether any of the mass of smaller, less prestigious figures came from their factory.

Even fewer marked pieces are known from the potter Theophilus Smith, whose impressed 'T Smith' is known on only three pieces. Theophilus Smith seems to have been an ambitious man with access to enough capital to establish a large pottery business. In 1788 he bought an estate in Tunstall where he erected a small town with some forty cottages, shops and an inn, and called it Smithfield. He built his pottery the following year and a family residence called Smithfield Hall for his own occupation, complete with an open air swimming bath. Outwardly he was a successful man, but by 1801 tragedy had struck.[14]

---

14. Wedgwood, H., *Romantic Tales of Staffordshire*, N.D. (c.1860-70).

46. Group of figures, with overglaze enamel painted decoration, made in Staffordshire, c.1800-20, ht. 315mm. *City Museum & Art Gallery, Stoke-on-Trent.*
This group shows the stronger colouring favoured in the 19th century (compare with colour plate 32). The range of subjects includes standard classical models and new contemporary figures such as the reading boy.

Smith had a business agreement with a Liverpool merchant called Peter Wainwright, who formed an attachment with Mrs Smith, and always seemed to call when Theophilus was away from home. By means of an anonymous note Smith lured Wainwright to Tunstall and surprised him by meeting his carriage. As they walked across fields to the house Smith drew a pistol and in the ensuing struggle Wainwright wrested it from his grip, they went on together but Smith drew another pistol, fired at Wainwright and missed. After searching Smith, Wainwright, feeling nervous but fairly safe, continued to the house. Smith, on the pretext of having accidentally left his greatcoat behind, rushed back to fetch it only to produce a third pistol with which he shot the unfortunate Wainwright through the body. The wound did not prevent a fairly violent struggle in which the ever resourceful Smith produced yet another weapon, a knife, with which he endeavoured to cut Wainwright's throat. He was unsuccessful, as Wainwright's cravat and silk scarf deflected the cut, but he did sustain several severe cuts to the jaw. Wainwright survived. At this point Theophilus Smith decided that discretion was the better part of valour and left the scene. He went into hiding in London where he peacefully surrendered to arrest in July 1801.

He was returned to Stafford Gaol and while awaiting trial in January 1802, he received visitors: his children and their governess were allowed into the cell. After their departure his wife went in to see him, whereupon Smith drew two pistols. In the confines of the cell he shot at his wife, but a shoulder wound was the worst he could inflict. He turned the weapon on himself, took his only true aim and died instantly.

His factory was sold and the new owner changed its name to Greenfield in an attempt to erase the memory of the sad end of Theophilus Smith. All that is left to tell the tale is a figure of Hope, a figure of Charity, a boy with his dog and a candlestick.

One of the most well-known potters of the late eighteenth and early nineteenth centuries was Enoch Wood. The figures attributed to his manufacture are many and varied but there are very few marked examples of his work and many of the attributions cannot be substantiated. After leaving his cousin Ralph, in 1789 Enoch took over a whole block of land in a prime position in Burslem. James Caldwell, who joined him as a partner, was a lawyer in Newcastle under Lyme and when he acted as secretary to the General Chamber to the Committee of Potters, may have become acquainted with Enoch.

The two young men had money to invest and the business acumen to achieve success. It is unlikely that their factory complex was completed in one phase, for a development in 1798, several years after their partnership began, was to give the site its name. An engine installed at the works to pump water had pipes laid to a pillar at the gateway of the factory and the town of Burslem was invited to use water free of charge. The estate became known as Fountain Place. Enoch lived within the factory complex and views of the estate, which

'EAST FRONT OF THE MANUFACTORY OF ENOCH WOOD & SONS, BURSLEM',
from Ward's *History of the Borough of Stoke-upon-Trent,* 1843, at the front gate was the
fresh water supply which gave the site its name of Fountain Place.

were published in 1843,[15] show what a splendid site it was. Enoch Wood and
James Caldwell became prominent business men, involved in everything from
raising a loyal Volunteer force to help repel any French invasion, enforcing
local licensing laws, petitioning against the lowering of duty on imported
Oriental porcelains, to acquiring fire engines for the town. In his venerable old
age Enoch became known as The Father of the Potteries.

As the young Wood and Caldwell developed in different directions the
partnership became strained. On 17 July 1818, Enoch noted in his
almanack:[16] 'I therefore have determined to have my accounts adjusted with
Mr C in my lifetime & not leave my successors in difficulties with a man whose
abilities can make black white'. Obviously there had been difficulties for some
time, for the date in the almanack — 17 July 1818 — was the actual date of
the partnership dissolution. The announcement in the *Staffordshire Advertiser* on
1 August stated that the company was to continue as E. Wood & Sons and it
continued to trade under this title until Enoch's death in 1840 at the age of
eighty-two.

The early wares of Enoch Wood made in partnership with Ralph have been
discussed in Chapter 2. It can only be assumed that Enoch continued to make
similar wares in his new partnership with Caldwell, as well as responding to
changes in fashion and increasing the range of his production. The marks used

15. Ward, J., *History of the Borough of Stoke-upon-Trent,* Lewis, 1843, reprinted Webberley, 1984.

16. Enoch Wood's Almanack 1818, in the Department of Medieval & Later Antiquities, The
British Museum.

'WEST VIEW OF THE HOUSE & MANUFACTORY OF ENOCH WOOD ESQ.', from Ward's *History of the Borough of Stoke-upon-Trent,* 1843.

by Enoch are somewhat confusing; the impressed 'E. WOOD' is recorded, which reflects none of the official trading styles of his companies and whilst these pieces have traditionally been ascribed to the late eighteenth century some of them have affinities with excavated pieces which date to the late 1820s, suggesting that the mark may have been used indiscriminately throughout much of Wood's production period. However, pieces marked 'WOOD & CALDWELL' may be assumed to date from their partnership period, 1789-1818.

Wood & Caldwell's partnership occurred during the period when the Grand Tour had become the acceptable conclusion to a young man's education and it often established a collecting zeal which lasted a lifetime. One such young man was Charles Townley, who spent much of his life in Rome and the south of Italy building up a remarkable collection of sculpture. A portrait by Zoffany in 1781 shows Townley sitting in his library with some of his collection.

It was works such as these which offered the sculptor his source material. Plaster makers were in great demand to supply cheaper copies for the home market, not only for display in great houses, but for the lesser arts to copy in their turn. John Cheere was a leading lead and plaster statue supplier and a number of his plasters occur in ceramic form, one of the largest being the 20in. high standing figure of Demosthenes, signed by Cheere and supplied by him to Burton Constable in 1762.

Several ceramic examples of Demosthenes are known, including the one impressed 'E. WOOD' in the Glaisher Collection of the Fitzwilliam Museum, Cambridge (C.900-1928). Demosthenes was a great Athenian orator, sixty of

Portrait of Charles Townley by Zoffany, 1781. This composition shows Townley with many of his favourite 'antique' sculptures and reflects the great interest in classical works of art and the sources which were used by plaster makers and potters. *Townley Hall Museum & Art Gallery, Burnley.*

Demosthenes, pearl glazed earthenware with overglaze enamel painted decoration, reverse impressed 'E. WOOD', late 18th-early 19th century, ht. 482mm. *Glaisher Collection, 900, Courtesy of Syndics, Fitzwilliam Museum, Cambridge.*

whose orations have survived, making him a popular subject for classical scholars. The relief on the pedestal depicts the Greek god Hermes in his role as Eloquence, an allusion to the virtuosity of Demosthenes as an orator. The figure is also referred to as Eloquence, or St. Paul preaching at Athens. Perhaps the potter omitted to inscribe the piece with a title so that it would be suitable for a wide range of customers who could imagine the subject to be either classical or biblical.

It is difficult to be certain that Wood got his model from Cheere's plaster, as other specialist makers also supplied the same subject. A plaster cast of Demosthenses was supplied to Josiah Wedgwood by Hoskins & Grant as a model for a black basalt bust. Charles Harris, a lesser known plaster maker of The Strand, London, also included in his sale catalogue a 20in. high model of Demosthenes at £2.2s. A catalogue of Charles Harris's productions may be found in the Victoria & Albert Museum library (box I.37.Y), which contains many subjects known to have been made by the Staffordshire potters.

Prudence and Fortitude, pearl glazed earthenware with overglaze enamel painted decoration, both impressed 'E. WOOD', ht. 533mm. *Sotheby's New York.*
Prudence is also known impressed 'WEDGWOOD'; it is likely that both potters used the same plaster statuette as a source. See p.169.

Unfortunately, none of Harris's original plasters are known to have survived and thus it is impossible to attribute sources to his workshop with any great confidence. However, it is interesting to note that also included in his catalogue are figures of Prudence and Fortitude which are also known marked 'E. Wood'.

The monument to William Shakespeare designed by William Kent and executed by Peter Scheemakers in 1740, was also an inspiration to those who could produce reduced size reproductions. A bronzed plaster signed 'P. Scheemakers F.1740', was probably made from the terracotta working model for the monument and produced in quantity by John Cheere. The terracotta was once known but now appears to be lost. Other London sculptors making small scale replicas included Peter Vanina. An earthenware example, unfortunately incomplete, was recovered during the demolition of St. Paul's Church in Burslem, when a hidden cache of pottery made by Enoch Wood & Sons was revealed in the foundation of a buttress. It has 'PV' moulded into the

Initials 'PV' moulded into the reverse of Shakespeare found at St. Paul's Church, Burslem. They probably stand for the plaster maker Peter Vanina, whose original model appears to have been used by Enoch Wood.

Figure of Shakespeare excavated on the site of St. Paul's Church, Burslem, 1974, pearl glazed earthenware with overglaze enamel painted decoration, made by Enoch Wood, c.1825-8, the reverse with the initials 'PV' moulded into the body, ht. 410mm. *City Museum & Art Gallery, Stoke-on-Trent.*
The figure is based on Peter Scheemaker's design of 1740 for the monument in Westminster Abbey.

back of the pedestal signifying, I believe, its origin from a plaster supplied by Peter Vanina. One normally dates these pieces to the early Wood or Wood & Caldwell period, but as everything else in the cache appears to have been current production when it was deposited in 1828, perhaps this is evidence of a much longer period of production than was hitherto suspected.

One point of interest is how similar to the bronzed plasters are the bronze glazed earthenwares of Enoch Wood. A ceramic collector might be forgiven for wondering why such a subdued decorative finish was chosen, but I think that direct comparison with plasters which have been bronzed gives us the answer. Set high up on a library shelf, on a bracket or standing in a niche, the casual observer would scarcely be able to distinguish between a true bronze cast or a plaster or ceramic version. Several versions of a large group in the City Museum & Art Gallery, Stoke-on-Trent, traditionally known as Bacchus and Ariadne but which should more correctly be referred to as Priapus and a Maenad, illustrate the range of finishes available to the consumer. A dark brown, glazed example has the appearance of bronze, a lighter colour brown could be identified with popular terracotta casts, whilst enamelled versions offered a colourful alternative to the purely classical reproduction.

Terracottas appear to be the source of yet other Enoch Wood subjects. The

Virgin and Child, pearl glazed earthenware with overglaze enamel painted decoration, made late 18th-early 19th century, ht. 337mm. *City Museum & Art Gallery, Stoke-on-Trent, 648.*

Triton candlestick and bust of Nelson, bronze glazed earthenware, both impressed 'WOOD & CALDWELL', c.1790-1818, ht. 215mm. *Private Collection.*

St. George and the Dragon, pearl glazed earthenware with overglaze enamel and silver lustre painted decoration, impressed 'WOOD & CALDWELL', incised 'Burslem', c.1810-15, ht. 245mm. *Wisbech & Fenland Museum, 1900.26.*

Britannia, pearl glazed earthenware with overglaze enamel and silver lustre painted decoration, impressed 'WOOD & CALDWELL', incised 'Burslem', c.1810-15, ht. 241mm. *City Museum & Art Gallery, Stoke-on-Trent.*

Impressed mark 'WOOD & CALDWELL'.

Virgin and Child by Lucas Faye d'Herbe[17] seems to have been the direct source of an enamel painted earthenware example impressed 'Wood & Caldwell'. The Virgin is seated on a rock and holds the Christ child in a tender and realistic embrace. Other versions of the subject are known in which the Virgin is seated upon a stool, I know of no marked examples of this particular model.

Possibly the most common figure from the partnership of Wood & Caldwell is that of Britannia, of which some particularly striking examples have silver lustre accoutrements. Silver lustre is also used to striking effect on a Wood & Caldwell group marked 'St. George and the Dragon', a particularly lively

---

17. Tait H. 'An unknown Bozzetto of Lucas Faye d'Herbe' *Burlington Magazine,* June 1962, pp.257-65. The terracotta is in the British Museum, acc. no. 1957, 11-1,1.

Pair of lions, pearl glazed earthenware with overglaze enamel painted decoration, base impressed 'WOOD & CALDWELL', c.1810-15, ht. 137mm. *City Museum & Art Gallery, Stoke-on-Trent, 287 & 290.P.1949.*

Boy reading, creamware with overglaze enamel painted decoration, impressed 'WOOD & CALDWELL', c.1810-15, ht. 178mm. *Temple Newsam House, Leeds, 28/37/41.*

This figure is unusual as it has not received the standard pearlware glaze and testifies to the continued use of creamware well into the 19th century. This model can also be found in silver lustre.

James Quinn as Falstaff, pearl glazed earthenware with overglaze enamel painted decoration, impressed on the base 'WOOD & CALDWELL', c.1800-15, ht. 230mm. *Wisbech & Fenland Museum, 1900.19.*

Bust of the Duke of Wellington, pearlware with overglaze enamel painted decoration, impressed 'WOOD & CALDWELL', c.1815, ht. 559mm. *City Museum & Art Gallery, Stoke-on-Trent.*

model with an unusually detailed base. Other figure subjects include popular lion models, and theatrical pieces, all identified from marked examples.

The most commonly found portrait bust from Wood & Caldwell is that of Alexander I of Russia, a neat mantelshelf piece. Rather larger is the 22in. high portrait bust of the Duke of Wellington. This is in the City Museum & Art Gallery, Stoke-on-Trent and is probably that described by Frank Falkener in his book, *The Wood Family of Burslem,* as 'decorated in natural tints; some of the enamel colours have suffered from the fact that this bust was buried with the 'foundations of Burslem Market and was dug up recently when alterations were being made'. The piece is after the marble by Nollekens which is signed and dated 1813. A smaller example may be seen in the Wisbech & Fenland Museum.

Many of the small, square based figures with iron red lines around the base are attributed to Enoch Wood and often date to the early nineteenth century, but I know of no evidence to sustain these suppositions and whilst I am unwilling to say categorically that they were not made by him, I reserve the right to suspend judgement whilst the other figure makers of the period are taken into consideration.

Other subjects which can be attributed to Wood & Caldwell are known from documentary evidence from a London retailer's ledger, which contains entries

Peace or Innocence, pearl glazed earthenware with overglaze enamel painted decoration, impressed on reverse 'WEDGWOOD', c.1790-7, ht. 750mm. *Private Collection.*
This is the largest Staffordshire figure known to the author.

Purity, pearl glazed earthenware with overglaze enamel painted decoration, impressed on reverse 'WEDGWOOD', c.1790-7, ht. 736mm. *Private Collection.*

Impressed mark 'WEDGWOOD', also known as 'WEDGWOOD.' with a stop at the end of the word. A large figure of Prudence in the Atlanta Historical Society Collection is inscribed 'By' and impressed 'WEDGWOOD'.

for goods supplied by Wood & Caldwell in 1810 and 1814-16.[18] Unfortunately, knowing the subject is only half-way to identifying the figure. Figures supplied in 1810 included Justice and Peace, Sportsman and Archer, Stag and Hind, and Pointer and Spaniel. Between 1814 and 1816 figures supplied include Neptune and Venus, Faith, Hope and Charity, Tailor and Mate, and Diana. All these subjects are known in a variety of models; the

18. Information supplied by Ann Eatwell, Victoria & Albert Museum, see appendix 1.

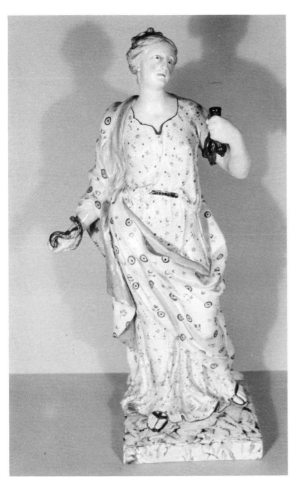

Prudence, pearl glazed earthenware with overglaze enamel painted decoration, impressed on reverse 'WEDGWOOD', c.1790-7, ht. 540mm. *Private Collection.*
This figure is also known impressed 'E. WOOD', it is likely that both manufacturers used the same plaster statuette as a source, see p.162.

Charity, pearl glazed earthenware with enamel painted decoration, impressed with title on front and on reverse with 'WEDGWOOD.', c.1790-7, ht. 190mm. *City Museum & Art Gallery, Stoke-on-Trent, 1641.*

difficulty lies in deciding which are the Wood & Caldwell versions and which are by other potters.

After the dissolution of the partnership in 1818 Enoch Wood carried on in business, trading as Wood & Sons. He continued to manufacture figures and changed his style as fashion dictated, producing subjects with bocage detailing and commemorative pieces in the late 1820s. This later period of Wood's manufacture is discussed in Chapters 5 and 6.

Only one other potter's mark is known on large monumental ceramic pieces in the form of the impressed name 'WEDGWOOD'. It has been suggested that these were also the work of Enoch Wood made to order for the customers of Josiah Wedgwood. There is no evidence in the extensive Wedgwood archives that Josiah or his successors ever made standard earthenware figures. There is also no evidence that they ordered figures to be made on their behalf to be sold through their outlets. I suggest that the mark refers to another Wedgwood entirely and that the figures are the work of Ralph Wedgwood. Ralph was the eldest son of Thomas Wedgwood, cousin and partner of Josiah Wedgwood in

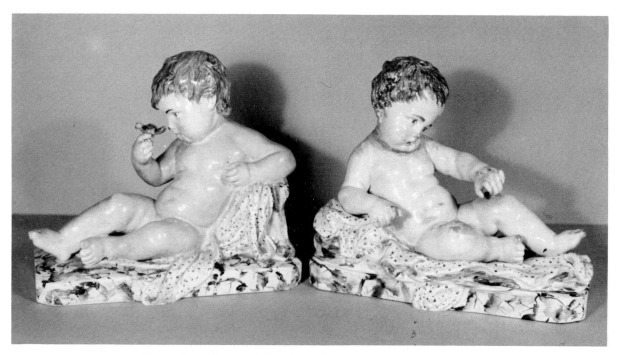

Pair of cupids, pearl glazed earthenware with overglaze enamel painted decoration, impressed on reverse 'WEDGWOOD.', c.1790-7, ht. 1.232mm. *Private Collection.*

Girl with lamb in box, pearl glazed earthenware with overglaze enamel painted decoration, impressed on reverse 'WEDGWOOD', ht. 191mm. *Private Collection.*

Group of figures, pearl glazed earthenware with enamel painted decoration, all impressed 'WEDGWOOD', c.1790-7, ht. of hurdy-gurdy player 232mm. *Sotheby's New York.*

his Burslem factory which made useful earthenwares. Thomas died in 1788, whilst he was in the process of setting up his own pottery business, his younger son Samuel was to be master potter, but on his death in 1790 Ralph reluctantly took on the responsibility.[19]

For seven years Ralph Wedgwood worked in Burslem at the Hill Pottery and lived in the adjoining house; he made the usual wares of the period including creamware, jasper and black basalt and there is no obvious reason why figures should not have been part of his repertoire. Ralph was a brilliant man, an extraordinary inventor, but not possessed of a practical nature. By 1793 his factory appeared to be thriving and a London warehouse had been established where stock was insured for £900, but as trade entered a period of depression in the mid-1790s Ralph became one of the early casualties and in 1797 his bankruptcy occurred. In 1798-9 he entered into a short lived partnership with Messrs Tomlinson & Forster of the Knottingly Pottery, near Ferrybridge in Yorkshire, which was effectively terminated at the end of 1800.

---

19. des Fontaines, J.K., 'Ralph Wedgwood of Burslem, Ferrybridge and London 1766-1837', *Northern Ceramic Society Newsletter*, No.49, March 1983; Blakey H., 'Ralph Wedgwood: Decline and Bankruptcy in Staffordshire and Arrival in Yorkshire', *Northern Ceramic Society Newsletter*, No.53, December 1983.

Whilst there is little doubt that the standard factory mark at Burslem was Wedgwood & Co., it is not clear whether the word 'WEDGWOOD' was used alone although certain authorities believe that it was. Ralph had no reason not to use his own name and it was also used alone and with Wedgwood & Co. at Ferrybridge for some years after he left. The figures that are known with the impressed mark 'WEDGWOOD' appear to be of a type consistent with a 1790s date, and there are no obviously nineteenth century pieces. All the evidence points to a single short lived firm entitled to mark their wares 'WEDGWOOD' and Ralph is the obvious candidate.

Many of the figures marked 'WEDGWOOD' are large monumental pieces typical of the subjects available in plaster form from London. A range of smaller figures includes both enamel and underglaze painted decoration.

The largest producer of earthenware figures outside Staffordshire in the late eighteenth century appears to be the Leeds Pottery in Yorkshire. The factory in Jack Lane, Leeds, was built in 1770 on land owned by Richard Humble and in 1771 the newly constructed factory was insured at a value of £1,000 with Richard Humble in partnership with John and Joshua Green. The earliest products were deep cream coloured earthenwares, but as technology evolved the iron staining was removed from the body and glaze mixture producing a lighter cream which proved more popular.

Production of pearlware came later to Leeds; by about 1776 William Hartley was included in the partnership and in 1781 Humble retired, leaving Hartley Green & Co. in occupation. It is mainly from the 1780-1800 period that I believe the Leeds Pottery figures were produced. John Green had sold up and left the company by 1800 when he was declared bankrupt, but William Hartley was able to run the pottery with great success for a number of years until his death in 1813; from this time it began to decline and by 1820 the firm was bankrupt. Successive attempts to inject life into the company failed, and it struggled to survive until its final closure in 1880. It was probably at this time that J.W. & G.W. Senior obtained the blocks or moulds from the Leeds Pottery and from the 1890s until 1957 they continued to produce the traditional Leeds wares including a range of figures. The reproductions were marketed by W.W. Slee of Leeds and are discussed in Chapter 7.

The original figures follow popular subjects, but much of the modelling is of a distinctive kind and the mould forms are different from those generally used in Staffordshire. The largest known marked monumental piece is that of Isaac Newton, probably taken from a reduced size plaster and the same source as that used by Ralph Wood to produce a similar figure. The Ralph Wood example is slightly better quality in the details of modelling and the handsome marbled base.

Several marked copies of Andromache are recorded, depicting the plump classical lady holding a floral garland and leaning on a large urn. This model is not recorded by any other factory although other versions of Andromache are known.

Isaac Newton, pearl glazed earthenware with overglaze enamel painted decoration, impressed 'LEEDS POTTERY', c.1790-1800, ht. 267mm. *Temple Newsam House, Leeds, 16.199/47.* For a similar figure by Ralph Wood see p.140.

Andromache, pearl glazed earthenware with overglaze enamel painted decoration, base impressed 'LEEDS POTTERY', c.1790-1810, ht. 320mm. *Temple Newsam House, Leeds, 16.196/47.*

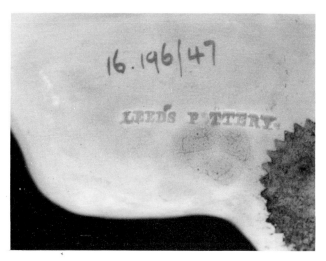

'LEEDS POTTERY', impressed.

Venus, pearl glazed earthenware with overglaze painted decoration, impressed 'LEEDS POTTERY', c.1790-1810, ht. 195mm. *Temple Newsam House, Leeds, 16.194/47.*

Venus and Neptune, pearl glazed earthenware, base impressed 'LEEDS POTTERY', c.1790-1810, ht. 195mm. *Temple Newsam House, Leeds, 16.306 & 304/47.*

Typical open base of a Leeds Pottery figure, where the square base is an integral part of the mould. *Temple Newsam House, Leeds, 16.194/47.*

The figures with distinctive modelling are of fairly small size, 6-10in. high and on square bases. The faces of the figures all exhibit the same sort of pinched features and most have a vague expression which makes them all look like figures of children. The method of construction is by moulds which include the square base as an integral part of the figure, so that when examined from

Autumn from a set of Seasons and a boy with a dog, pearl glazed earthenware, impressed 'LEEDS POTTERY', c.1790-1810, ht. 162mm. *Temple Newsam House, Leeds, 16.302 & 205/47.*

Minerva and Mars, pearl glazed earthenware with overglaze enamel painted decoration and gilding, base impressed 'LEEDS POTTERY', c.1790-1810, ht. 267mm. *Temple Newsam House, Leeds, 16.198 & 200/47.*

Set of Seasons, pearl glazed earthenware with overglaze enamel painted decoration, all except Autumn impressed 'LEEDS POTTERY', c.1790-1810, ht. 158mm. *Temple Newsam House, Leeds, 16.193, 202, 203, 208/47.*

Girl with hurdy-gurdy and boy with tambourine, pearl glazed earthenware, base impressed 'LEEDS POTTERY', c.1790-1810, ht. 190mm. *Temple Newsam House, Leeds, 16. 312, 305/47.*

Falconer, pearl glazed earthenware, base impressed 'LEEDS POTTERY', c.1790-1810, ht. 190mm. *Temple Newsam House, Leeds, 14.20/48.*

Reverse of Falconer showing details of applied leaf and flowers on the tree stump.

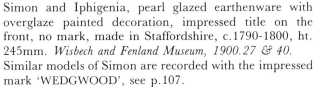

Simon and Iphigenia, pearl glazed earthenware with overglaze painted decoration, impressed title on the front, no mark, made in Staffordshire, c.1790-1800, ht. 245mm. *Wisbech and Fenland Museum, 1900.27 & 40.* Similar models of Simon are recorded with the impressed mark 'WEDGWOOD', see p.107.

Europa and the Bull, pearl glazed earthenware with overglaze painted decoration, made in Staffordshire, c.1800-10, ht. 270mm. *Private Collection.*

beneath a square based figure is hollow. In Staffordshire the figure is usually, but not exclusively, moulded separately from the square base and placed on to it in a separate process, thus the hollow figure cannot be seen into from beneath.

The subjects chosen by the Leeds potters follow the popular demand for classical and allegorical images. Venus and Neptune, Minerva and Mars, represented the classical deities and there were also the familiar seasons and elements. Many of the subjects were produced in plain china or pearl glaze as well as the brightly enamelled versions — a case of penny plain and twopence coloured — to cater for all pockets.

Despite the emphasis placed here on marked examples, the great majority of enamelled earthenware figures are unmarked and unattributable, but they are none the worse for that. It may never be possible to identify the makers of most figures and labelling them for the sake of it should be avoided. Many are of excellent quality, fascinating subjects, and are works of art in their own right with surface decoration that can be subtle, showy, representational or completely abstract. From the monumental to the miniature there is something in the range to suit every taste, which of course is what the potters were striving for, and today's collectors reap the benefits.

Ophelia, pearl glazed earthenware with overglaze enamel painted decoration, made in Staffordshire, c.1780-1800, length 254mm. *Julian Critchley Collection.*

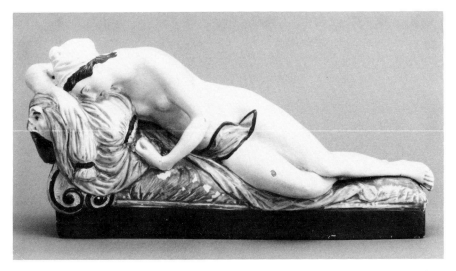

Lucretia, pearl glazed earthenware with overglaze enamel painted decoration, made in Staffordshire, c.1780-1800, length 280mm. *Sotheby's London.*
Lucretia (a suicidal heroine), was made in black basalt as a pair with Cleopatra by James Neale (see *Neale Pottery and Porcelain,* Barrie & Jenkins, 1987, pls. 88 & 89).

5. Enamel painted figures : the second phase

The fashion for square based enamel painted figures persisted well into the nineteenth century. The traditional models of neo-classical inspiration continued to be produced but many were updated to give a more contemporary look. Figures that had been produced in the eighteenth century on bases moulded like grassy mounds were adapted to be set upon square bases; others were remodelled, possibly by new companies which used the established trade quite literally as a model.

The neo-classical deities remained popular and there were many depictions of myth and legend; Neptune and Venus, Bacchus, Diana, Juno and Jupiter can all be found in the figures typical of the early nineteenth century. A new range of classical ladies with urns on pedestals is variously identified as Andromache, Antonia or Charlotte, all weeping heroines pining over the ashes of a loved one. Peace and Justice abounded in the nineteenth century, at least in the ceramic sense, and the old Christian virtues Faith, Hope and Charity remained intact.

Old theatrical favourites such as Falstaff continued to be made and a new range of contemporary stars was added to the potters' output. Actors, clowns and entertainers were the subject of books, theatre posters, popular prints and reproductions, all of which created not only a market but offered sources to the potter. The great Shakespearian characters had a steady sale, but for special gala events the potters had to create commemorative pieces which would capture a short lived but lucrative market.

Biblical subjects changed in emphasis, parables such as the Lost Piece and the Lost Sheep were joined by New Testament tales, and figures of the Virgin and Child through to the Crucifixion offered illustrations of Christ's life. Many of these were made for the followers of Nonconformist religion and in the Potteries this meant the various branches of Methodism, Wesleyan, New Connexion or Primitive; other pieces were destined for a European Roman Catholic market with the titles suitably translated.

The most interesting new subjects of the nineteenth century lay in the depiction of contemporary people. Whilst many of the subjects may romanticise the conditions of life, nevertheless they exhibit an interest in humanity not seen since the naïve creamware figures of the mid-eighteenth century. Sailors leaving and returning to their lasses, women at the water pump, children at play and adults at sport, all can be seen fashioned in clay.

Animal subjects became less important to the earthenware potter, a phenomenon possibly explained by a corresponding increase in porcelain animals made by the growing number of china toy makers. Within the earthenware trade lions remained the most popular of animals, a number appear in pairs, where each animal stands with one paw on a ball; the model is based on the famous stone lions of Florence, which were reproduced in many forms during the late eighteenth and early nineteenth centuries. Another popular animal was adapted as a piece of tableware, in the form of cows cut to use as milk jugs which seem to have saturated the market. Perhaps the bone

Diana, earthenware with overglaze enamel painted decoration, made in Staffordshire, c.1810-20, ht. 280mm. *City Museum & Art Gallery, Stoke-on-Trent, 3119.*

Hercules, earthenware with overglaze enamel painted decoration, made in Staffordshire, c.1810-20, ht. 445mm. *City Museum & Art Gallery, Stoke-on-Trent, 313.*

This model is based on an antique sculpture known as the Farnese Hercules, to distinguish it from other Hercules and because the first record of its existence was in 1556 in the Palazzo Farnese in Rome. Many copies were made of the original and from the early years of the 19th century it was common to affix 'brazen foliage' to render the figure suitable for viewing by ladies. This piece may be taken from a John Cheere plaster, the 'brazen foliage' has a peculiarly English look as the leaves are of acorn and oak; other versions are known.

Juno and the Peacock, earthenware with overglaze enamel painted decoration, title 'Juno' impressed on the reverse, made in Staffordshire, c.1800-20, ht. 216mm. *City Museum & Art Gallery, Stoke-on-Trent, 388.P.1949.*

Figure of a classical woman weeping at a funerary urn, symbolising grief, earthenware with overglaze enamel painted decoration, c.1810-20, ht. 235mm. *City Museum & Art Gallery, Stoke-on-Trent, 3114.*

Figure of Shakespeare, earthenware with overglaze enamel painted decoration, made in Staffordshire, c.1810-20, ht. 387mm. *City Museum & Art Gallery, Stoke-on-Trent, 3134.*
The pair to Milton, both figures also appear in Derby porcelain.

Figure of a classical woman putting a torch to instruments of war, symbolising peace, earthenware with overglaze painted decoration, c.1810-20, ht. 210mm. *City Museum & Art Gallery, Stoke-on-Trent, 1413.*

Figure of the actor John Liston in the role of Paul Pry, earthenware with overglaze enamel painted decoration, made in Staffordshire, c.1826-30, ht. 149mm. *City Museum & Art Gallery, Stoke-on-Trent, 371.P.1949.*

This subject was one of eight of Liston's celebrated characters published as a coloured lithograph in 1826; other examples of Liston figures are recorded in earthenware and in bone china. See Chapter 6.

Virgin Mary, earthenware with overglaze enamel painted decoration, made in Staffordshire, c.1810-20, ht. 185mm. *City Museum & Art Gallery, Stoke-on-Trent, 12.P.1931.*

Girl pumping water, also known as the 'Cow with the iron tail', earthenware with overglaze enamel painted decoration, made in Staffordshire, c.1815-30, ht. 149mm. *City Museum & Art Gallery, Stoke-on-Trent, 375.P.1949.*

Lion, earthenware with overglaze enamel painted decoration, made in Staffordshire, c.1810-20, ht. 241mm. *City Museum & Art Gallery, Stoke-on-Trent, 1389.*

Boy and girl reading, earthenware with overglaze painted decoration, made in Staffordshire, c.1820-30, ht. 152mm. *City Museum & Art Gallery, Stoke-on-Trent, 381 & 382.P.1949.*
Similar subjects exist with underglaze painted decoration, but they do not appear to come from the same moulds.

Pearlware cow cream jugs with overglaze enamel painted decoration, made in England early-mid 19th century, ht. 143mm. *City Museum and Art Gallery, Stoke-on-Trent. 254.P.1963, 321.P.1963, 82.P.1963.*

china dogs and cats catered for the animal lovers at the top end of the market, with underglaze painted earthenwares at the lower end, leaving a very small window of opportunity for the enamel figure makers who turned their hand to more popular subjects.

The techniques of enamel painting did not change from the eighteenth to the nineteenth century, yet the finished product often looks very different. The enamel painted figure of the eighteenth century was usually a top of the range piece; the colours are elegant, often of pastel shade and are carefully applied with floral sprigs on the skirt or breeches in tasteful shades of pink and turquoise. Whilst this style did not cease on 1 January 1800, within a few years a new range of more vibrant colours became popular and eventually dominated production. Bright reds, blues, oranges and greens were often over generously applied and whilst some figures of exceptional quality were produced, elements of refinement were occasionally sacrificed in favour of jolly, cheerful, popular pieces for a wider market.

It is very difficult to identify the makers of the majority of figures, as by 1820 it is likely that between twenty and thirty manufacturers were involved in the trade, at least half of which specialised in 'toy making'. Between 1822 and 1830 local trade directories listed the following specialist figure makers:

Booth Richard, Marsh Street, Shelton	(1828, 1830)
Brammer Thomas, Daisy Bank, Lane End	(1830)
Brown Henry, High Street, Lane End	(1828/9)
Copestick Daniel, Lane Delph	(1830)
Edge Daniel, Waterloo Road, Burslem	(1830)
Ellis James, Pall Mall, Shelton	(1830)
Grocott Samuel, Tunstall	(1822, 1828/9)
Hall Samuel, New Hall Street, Hanley	(1822, 1830)
Heath John, Sitch Lane, Burslem	(1822)
Holland Thomas, Church Street, Burslem	(1828/9, 1830)
Hood George, Tunstall	(1822)
Jones Hannah, George Street, Hanley	(1822, 1830)
Lawton Daniel, Chapel Lane, Burslem	(1828/9, 1830)
Lees Thomas, Sneyd Green	(1822)
Mayer Samuel, Piccadilly, Shelton	(1830)
Mills Henry, Hope Street, Shelton	(1830)
Parr Richard jun., Church Street, Burslem	(1828/9)
Pattison James, High Street, Lane End	(1822, 1828/9, 1830)
Ridgway James, Hill Street, Hanley	(1822)
Salt Ralph, Marsh Street, Shelton	(1828/9, 1830)
Sherratt Obadiah, Hot Lane, Cobridge	(1822, 1828/9, 1830)
Stretton Samuel, Lane Delph	(1828/9)
Tunnicliffe Michael, Tunstall	(1828/9, 1830)
Walton John, Navigation Road, Burslem	(1822)
Wood Ephraim, Nile Street, Burslem	(1822)
Wood Ephraim, Wood's Bank, Burslem	(1828/9)

This list does not take into account those manufacturers of general earthenware who also made figures, such as Enoch Wood, John and Richard Riley and Jacob Marsh. Less than a tenth of these figure makers left any evidence of their production, either in marked examples or in factory records, which leads inevitably towards an over emphasis on those makers whose work can be identified.

The evidence for attributing a wider range of figures to Enoch Wood comes not from a wealth of marked specimens — for there are relatively few — nor from documents, but from the caches of fragments which were left by him to be discovered by posterity. The burial of a time capsule containing material for the use of future generations was a very popular pastime with Enoch. It was an extension of his antiquarian activities, for he was leaving for historians of the future what he would have liked to have found from the past. Using evidence from these caches some currently anonymous models can be tentatively identified.

Possibly the most famous site of recovery is that of St. Paul's Church, Burslem. A large quantity of pottery, typical of wares made for the American market — dark blue printed pieces, yellow glazed wares and peasant enamels

Figure of Joseph Grimaldi, earthenware with overglaze enamel painted decoration, together with an undecorated fragment from the site of St. Paul's Church, Burslem, made by Enoch Wood, c.1828, ht. 146mm. *City Museum & Art Gallery, Stoke-on-Trent, 494.P.1987.*
Made to commemorate Grimaldi's farewell performances in 1828; porcelain versions were made at the Derby factory.

Figure of the actor John Liston as Lubin Log in *Love, Law and Physic,* earthenware with overglaze enamel painted decoration, impressed 'WOOD' & 'K', made by Enoch Wood, c.1826-30, ht. 184mm. *City Museum & Art Gallery, Stoke-on-Trent, 380.P.1949.*
The subject was one of eight of Liston's celebrated characters published as a coloured lithograph in 1826. Fragments found at the site of St. Paul's Church, Burslem, exactly match this figure.

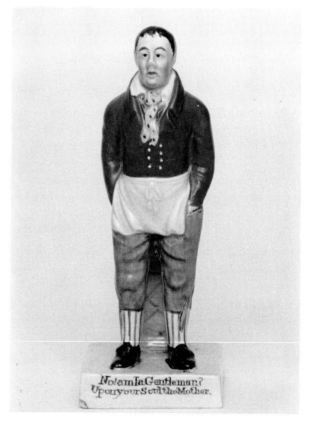

The actor John Liston as Sam Swipes in *Exchange No Robbery,* earthenware with overglaze enamel painted decoration, base impressed '20', c.1826-30, ht. 159mm. *City Museum & Art Gallery, Stoke-on-Trent, 373.P.1949.*
Possibly made by Enoch Wood in a series of John Liston figures, after the celebrated characters published as a coloured lithograph in 1826.

— was exposed within a sealed chamber in the buttress foundations and many of these carried one of the Wood factory marks. No other marked wares were found and there were no inconsistencies within the group, confirming that the whole cache was the product of a single factory. The finds were the property of the demolition contractor, who removed complete items and gave the damaged pieces to the City Museum & Art Gallery, Stoke-on-Trent. The foundations for St. Paul's were laid in 1828 and it seems that Enoch, whilst wanting to leave wares for posterity, was acute enough to leave mostly seconds and wasters.

The only extensive report of these wares was published in the American *Antiques Magazine* in July 1977, when Pamela Kingsbury gave a very detailed discussion of the blue printed wares. The introductory paragraph mentioned only two figures, the figure of Shakespeare signed 'PV', referred to earlier, and 'a very curious pearlware statue of what appears to be an American Indian in European dress'. When I saw a complete example of this figure it was quite obviously a portrait of Joseph Grimaldi and a complete example has been added to the City Museum's collection to complement the excavated material.

Joseph Grimaldi was the original Joey clown. His arduous tumbling and falling act gradually took its toll and in 1821 his health began to fail. In 1828 he performed two farewell benefits: it was in the same year that the pearlware figures were deposited in St. Paul's, which strongly suggests that these were made to be sold in commemoration of his final performances. Two sizes are known in earthenware, but only the larger can be directly related to the Enoch Wood site. Another model was made in porcelain by the Derby factory, presumably for Grimaldi's wealthier fans.

Although no figures other than Shakespeare and Grimaldi have been mentioned in past publications, others were found. A well-known figure of the actor John Liston came from the foundations, which depicts him as Lubin Log in *Love, Law & Physic,* which he played in 1812 and 1823. The subject was one of eight of John Liston's celebrated characters, published as a coloured lithograph in 1826.

The base of a large figure, which is probably that of Diana with a dog at her feet, has no body and therefore it is more difficult to find an exact match. There were some small, fragmentary pieces; one tiny figure usually identified as a Turk had been a popular model with Continental and English porcelain manufacturers for many years. The small earthenware example from Wood's factory has its own parallel in Derby porcelain. A small reclining deer and cradle figure were also present. A figure of a peacock with his tail fanned out has been found in an extant version, the undecorated find is in great contrast to the showy, completed specimen.

One of the most interesting pieces is a figure of a classical figure at an altar; the body of the fragment is vitrified and appears to be biscuit porcelain. It is known that Enoch Wood made porcelain so perhaps this is not just an over-fired, isolated instance, but evidence that he also pursued a porcelain figure trade.

Left: porcelain figure fragment from the site of St. Paul's Church, Burslem, made by Enoch Wood, deposited in 1828; right: classical figure of a woman making a sacrifice, earthenware with overglaze enamel painted decoration, made in Staffordshire, c.1820-30, ht. 197mm. *City Museum & Art Gallery, Stoke-on-Trent, 600.*

In 1938 a number of figure fragments were found beneath the pavement on the south side of Burslem Old Town Hall. Because some of the figures appeared to have coloured glazes (this was in fact a misunderstanding of the results of the misfired colour), they were immediately attributed to Ralph Wood. The accompanying figures with bocage and enamelled decoration were ignored because they pointed to a much later date than Ralph Wood's period. In fact several of the fragments have exact counterpoints in marked examples from Enoch's factory and some are identical to pieces found at St. Paul's, Burslem; this I believe is just cause for supposing that the pieces are from the nearby factory of Enoch Wood.

The model of the actor James Quinn in his role as Falstaff is well known and many of these figures can be found with the impressed mark 'WOOD & CALDWELL'. The identical fragment from the site seems to indicate that the figure retained its popularity well into the nineteenth century, as the Town Hall fragments can be dated to the late 1820s.

Another piece which matches a marked 'WOOD & CALDWELL' example is the Toby jug of the sailor. The marked example can be found in the Victoria & Albert Museum and whilst I do not wish to include Tobies in this volume it serves as a useful confirmation of my attribution.

47. Two mowers, left with coloured glaze decoration, right with overglaze enamel painting, made in Staffordshire, c.1780-1800 and c.1810-20, ht. 203mm. *City Museum & Art Gallery, Stoke-on-Trent, 3015, 825.P.1949.*

48. Two hunters, with overglaze enamel painted decoration, made in Staffordshire, left c.1810-20, right c.1790-1800, ht. 225mm. *City Museum & Art Gallery, Stoke-on-Trent, 3102, and Private Collection.*

These figures show that popular models were adapted to fit new decorative styles and were kept in production over long periods; note particularly the strong colours of the later figures and the delicate shades of the earlier examples.

49. The Lost Piece and Peace setting fire to the instruments of war, with overglaze enamel painted decoration, left, c.1810-20, right, c.1790-1800, ht. 222mm. *City Museum & Art Gallery, Stoke-on-Trent, 602, 1413.*

The actor James Quinn as Falstaff, pearlware undecorated, excavated beneath the pavement outside Burslem Old Town Hall, c.1820-30, ht. 223mm. *City Museum & Art Gallery, Stoke-on-Trent.*
This figure which was first made by Enoch Wood during his earlier partnership with James Caldwell (c.1790-1818), is probably based on a Derby porcelain original taken from a mezzotint by James McArdell (1729-1765).

Figures of St. Sebastian. Left: earthenware with overglaze enamel painted decoration; right: pearlware undecorated, excavated beneath the pavement outside Burslem Old Town Hall, both impressed on the front 'S. SEBASTI O;M.' and the reverse 'Nº 11', the enamel painted piece also with impressed 'E. WOOD' on reverse, made by Enoch Wood, c.1825-30, ht. 255mm. *Private Collection and City Museum & Art Gallery, Stoke-on-Trent.*
This figure was also produced in the 20th century by William Kent of Burslem, see page 286.

A St. Sebastian figure from the site matches an enamelled version in a private collection, both have the impressed model number '11'; the complete example is also impressed 'E. WOOD' on the back of the base. The same model was still in production in the twentieth century, when it formed part of the standard output of the William Kent company of Burslem. Perhaps Enoch Wood's blocks or moulds were acquired when his factories were sold after his death?

Thus at least three fragments from the Town Hall site match marked Wood examples. A large number can be directly matched with fragments from St. Paul's — with the same small animals, small Turks, and a cradle figure — all good, hard evidence for the Town Hall site being an Enoch Wood cache.

Left: Figure of Billy Waters, earthenware with overglaze enamel painted decoration, made by Enoch Wood, c.1821-30, ht. 210mm. *City Museum & Art Gallery, Stoke-on-Trent, 495.P.1987.*
Fragments which exactly match this figure were excavated beneath the pavement outside Burslem Old Town Hall. Billy Waters died in 1823, just as an operatic extravaganza featuring him as a character was enjoying a great success in London.

Right: Group of figures all depicting Billy Waters, earthenware with overglaze enamel painted decoration, on the extreme right is the model produced by Enoch Wood, all made in Staffordshire, c.1821-30, ht. 210mm. *Royal Pavilion Art Gallery & Museum, Brighton, HW 884, 882, 881, 883.*

Among the Town Hall pieces are some interesting models which help to confirm the late 1820s date. Billy Waters was a coloured beggar with a peg-leg, who earned his living playing a fiddle in London's West End. He had a small pension to compensate for the loss of his leg due to an injury sustained when he served in His Majesty's forces, but he had to beg to earn enough to support his wife and two children. With his eccentric feathered hat and peculiar antics he became very popular with his audiences. He was elected King of the Beggars and became a well-known London character. In 1821 Pierce Egan wrote his famous book *Tom & Jerry* subtitled 'Life in London or the day and night scenes of Jerry Hawthorne Esq. and his elegant friend Corinthian Tom in their rambles and sprees through the Metropolis'. The story was of two fictitious Regency bucks in London and featured well-known characters of the day including Billy Waters. The illustrations for the book were by George Cruikshank and Billy features in one drawing of a tavern scene.

The book was reproduced as an operatic extravaganza in three acts by W.T. Moncrief, which opened at the Adelphi Theatre on 26 November 1821, and was an immediate success, having a run of 300 nights and was only stopped because the actors were exhausted, the audience were 'as mad for it as ever'. Billy Waters died in poverty in St. Giles's workhouse in 1823, at the same time as the successful show in which he featured as a character came to the end of its first run. It is a tribute to his popularity that a great many models were made of Billy Waters and he remained in production for many years.

Another character from *Tom & Jerry* was 'a coloured good time girl', by the name of African Sal and she was paired with Dusty Bob. In the London production she was played by Mr Saunders to William Walburn's Dusty Bob.

50. Farmyard group, with overglaze enamel painted decoration, made in Staffordshire, early 19th century, ht. 240mm. *City Museum & Art Gallery, Stoke-on-Trent, 562.P.1984.*

51. Dandies, with overglaze enamel painted decoration, made in Staffordshire, c.1815-25, ht. 210mm. *City Museum & Art Gallery, Stoke-on-Trent, 379.P.1949.*

Figure of African Sal, earthenware with overglaze enamel painted decoration, made by Enoch Wood, c.1821-30, ht. 96mm. *Royal Pavilion Art Gallery & Museum, Brighton, HW891.*
Fragments which exactly match this figure were excavated beneath the pavement outside Burslem Old Town Hall.

Excavated figure of African Sal (all that remains of her partner, Dusty Bob, is the base), pearlware undecorated, ht. 96mm. *City Museum & Art Gallery, Stoke-on-Trent.*

Print of Mr Saunders and William Walburn as African Sal and Dusty Bob in Pierce Egan's *Tom & Jerry*, first performed in 1821. (I am grateful to Delia Napier for drawing this print to my attention.) *Theatre Museum, London.*

Venus and Bacchus, earthenware with overglaze enamel painted decoration, made by Enoch Wood, c.1820-30, ht. 152mm. *Private Collection and City Museum & Art Gallery, Stoke-on-Trent, 3164.*

Venus and Bacchus, excavated from beneath the pavement outside Burslem Old Town Hall, pearlware undecorated, made by Enoch Wood, c.1820-30, ht. 152mm. *City Museum & Art Gallery, Stoke-on-Trent.*

African Sal appears in fairly complete form in the Wood cache, but all that remains of Dusty Bob is his base. A glorious technicolour version of Sal can be found in the Willett Collection and a Derby porcelain version is also known, but no extant examples of Dusty Bob have been recorded.

A pair of neat figures of Bacchus and Venus have been identified from fragments from the Town Hall site and models of Neptune and Elijah were also found. All of these exist as extant pieces and for the first time one can assign them to a manufacturer with some degree of confidence.

The eighteenth century figures of Old Age were updated by Enoch Wood and fragments were found which help to identify his work. A range of female figures with baskets, sheaves of corn and flowers may represent the Seasons or be part of traditional bucolic subjects. A pair of a boy and girl with baskets of fruit has the unusual addition of wings which makes them rather distinctive. There are many other small fragments still awaiting titles and identification; those that were not too fragmentary can be found illustrated in this volume. It is interesting to note that, whilst there are no marked examples from the site, a number of pieces have impressed letters and/or numerals, for a complete list of these see Appendix 2.

52. Gardener, possibly representing Earth from a set of elements, with overglaze enamel painted decoration, made in Staffordshire, c.1810-20, ht. 224mm. *City Museum & Art Gallery, Stoke-on-Trent, 3107.*

53. Group of lions, with overglaze enamel painted decoration, made in Staffordshire, c.1800-20, ht. 235mm. *City Museum and Art Gallery, Stoke-on-Trent.*

The lion with his raised paw on a ball is based on the antique marble lions which stand at the entrance of the Loggia dei Lanzi in Florence. These lions were well known as small scale reproductions in stone, marble, bronze and plaster. The lion was also a popular symbol of British nationalism during the 19th century.

54. The bare knuckle fighters Cribb and Molyneux, with overglaze enamel painted decoration, made in Staffordshire, c.1812-15, ht. 203mm. *Private Collection; photograph by Gavin Ashworth, New York.*

Tom Cribb was one of England's greatest fighters; Tom Molyneux was a young American champion who challenged Cribb to a championship fight. The fight took place on 18 December, 1810. Cribb won when Molyneux fell exhausted and unable to continue in the 30th round. A return fight was held in September, 1811 and Cribb was victorious again. The figures are probably based on a commemorative print which was published by George Smeeton, 17 December, 1812, to commemorate their second fight.

Pair of figures of Old Age. Left: excavated from beneath the pavement outside Burslem Old Town Hall, pearlware undecorated; right: earthenware with overglaze enamel painted decoration, both impressed '18' on base, made by Enoch Wood, c.1820-30, ht. 127mm. *Royal Pavilion Art Gallery & Museum, Brighton, 320010 and City Museum & Art Gallery, Stoke-on-Trent.*

Venus, earthenware with overglaze enamel painted decoration, titled on the front, made by Enoch Wood, c.1820-30, ht. 152mm. *Julian Critchley Collection.*

Pair of figures of Old Age, earthenware with overglaze enamel painted decoration, both impressed '18' on the base, made by Enoch Wood, c.1820-30, ht. 127mm. *Royal Pavilion Art Gallery & Museum, Brighton, 320010, 320011.*

The most unusual pieces are the religious figures, with biblical subjects represented as well as clerics and saints. These are not commonly found in Britain and perhaps enjoyed a greater success overseas. Whereas small specialist manufacturers may have found it difficult to pursue foreign trade, the large factories making tablewares relied on it for commercial success and had established methods of export.

Two figures of Neptune. Left: excavated from beneath the pavement outside Burslem Old Town Hall; right: earthenware with enamel painted decoration, made by Enoch Wood, c.1820-30, ht. 242mm. *Private Collection and City Museum & Art Gallery, Stoke-on-Trent.*

Neptune, earthenware with overglaze enamel painted decoration, made by Enoch Wood, c.1820-30, ht. 242mm. *Private Collection.*

Group of biblical subjects, pearlware undecorated, excavated from beneath the pavement outside Burslem Old Town Hall. From the left: the Pieta impressed on the front 'N.S.DA. PIEDADE', reverse with 'Nº.6', the Virgin and Child impressed on the reverse 'Nº.28', Christ or a disciple impressed on the reverse 'Nº.20' and Elijah and the Ravens, all made by Enoch Wood, c.1820-30, ht. 250mm. *City Museum & Art Gallery, Stoke-on-Trent.*

Virgin and Child, earthenware with overglaze enamel painted decoration and some gilding now worn, titled on the base 'N.S. DOBOM DESPACHO', the head is pierced possibly for fixing a metal halo, made by Enoch Wood, c.1820-30, ht. 200mm. *Royal Pavilion Art Gallery & Museum, Brighton, HW 752.*
This piece is identical to fragments found in excavations beneath the pavement outside Burslem Old Town Hall and appears to have been made for the Continental Roman Catholic market.

55. Group of porcelain figures, with overglaze painted decoration, early 19th century, ht. 237mm. *Geoffrey Godden Collection.*

The Virgin Mary with impressed numeral '40' on the reverse. The shepherd and shepherdess group with impressed numeral '88' on the reverse. The group entitled 'contest' with impressed numeral '133' on the reverse. These figures all have counterparts in Staffordshire earthenware, suggesting that one manufacturer, as yet unidentified, made both porcelain and earthenware figures.

56. Two shepherd and shepherdess groups, left in porcelain, right in earthenware, made in Staffordshire, c.1800-20, ht. 273mm. *Geoffrey Godden Collection; City Museum & Art Gallery, Stoke-on-Trent, 3149.*

Group of religious subjects, pearlware
undecorated, excavated from beneath the
pavement outside Burslem Old Town Hall.
From the left: two clerical figures both impressed
on the reverse '24', St. Sebastian impressed on
the front 'S. SEBASTI O:M' and on the reverse
'N⁰.11', St. Barbara impressed on the front 'S.
Barbar.V.M.' and on the reverse 'N⁰.3',
c.1825-30, ht. 256mm. *City Museum & Art
Gallery, Stoke-on-Trent.*

Figure of Elijah and the Ravens, earthenware
with overglaze enamel painted decoration,
possibly made by Enoch Wood, c.1810-30, ht.
242mm. *Private Collection.*
This model appears to be identical to fragments
excavated from beneath the pavement outside
Burslem Old Town Hall, except for details of the
base which may have been adapted to fit on top
of a square base.

Apollo, earthenware with overglaze painted decoration, impressed 'FELL', c.1817-20. *Courtesy Geoffrey Godden.*

Bust of Shakespeare, pearlware undecorated, impressed on reverse 'Bott & Co', c.1807-10, ht. 413mm. *Southport Museum, 198.*

Many of the other figures from the Town Hall site have bocage (a model of a tree-like structure) to the rear, and whilst they obviously date to the same late 1820s period as the rest of the fragments, they are discussed with other bocage figures in Chapter 6.

Other than Enoch Wood, very few makers of early nineteenth century figures can be identified. A portrait bust of William Shakespeare impressed 'Bott & Co' is the only figurative example known from this Longton firm. The firm of Bott and Bond is noted from 1807 until the dissolution of partnership in 1810. Mr Bond continued taking other partners after Mr Bott died in 1811. Their products are said to include earthenware painted busts, figures, painted vases and lustre ware; two silver lustre decorated bulb pots are the only other known pieces.

A marked 'FELL' enamel painted figure of Apollo is a very rare example of that factory's work and dates to the 1817-20 period. We are more familiar with the high temperature underglaze painted pieces and coloured glazes from this factory and they are discussed elsewhere in this book. The Apollo is rather heavily modelled and is similar in certain respects to an example from a set attributed to Lakin & Poole 1791-6, possibly the model was inspired by the

57. Group of spill vases, with overglaze enamel painted decoration, made in Staffordshire, c.1810-20, ht. 263mm. *Private Collection; City Museum & Art Gallery, Stoke-on-Trent 309.P.1949, 303.P.1949.* Spill vases were often incorporated into figure groups in the 1810-20 period. They were made in many types of pottery and were usually set upon mantels above an open fire and filled with spills made from slivers of wood or twisted paper. The spills were used to transmit flame to a candle or pipe before the match was developed.

58. Tam O'Shanter and Souter Johnny, with overglaze enamel painted decoration, made in Staffordshire, c.1820-30, ht. 135mm. *City Museum & Art Gallery, Stoke-on-Trent, 3174, 3127.*
The subjects are taken from a poem by Robert Burns and many popular engravings existed which could have served as inspiration for these models.

same design source or, less likely, Fell based his example on the earlier Staffordshire piece.

Marked examples are, of course, the best source of reliable information. Documentary evidence is useful in establishing a list of figure makers but does not identify their wares, even when the subjects of their manufacture are known it is not usually possible to identify individual specimens by title only. A London retailer's ledger referred to in Chapter 4[1] recorded the following:

W.S. Bailey & Co.	supplied
	2 setts china female persian
1815 Wm. Moseley	supplied
	4doz Boys & girls with dog & lamb
	6/-
	" Shepherds &
	shepherdess 6/-
	" Gardener &
	Mate 6/-
1819 Wm. Moseley	1 set of ornaments set no 415
	11/6
1810-20 John & Richard Riley	1 set of ornaments 3 in set 415 11/6
1821 Ann Peover	set of ornaments No. 3 £1 for 5
1823 T. & Benj. Godwin	supplied
	small sheep with bush
	squirrels
	Strawberry Gatherers
	Pair Close Gardener & Mate
	Shepherd & Mate
	Gardener & Mate
	small fruit boy
	large fruit boys

Of W.S. Bailey no trace can be found; it is possible that he was a member of the Bailey family of Longton, which in the early nineteenth century specialised in decorating ceramics, but as the reference specifically refers to sets of china figures, his work need not detain us here.

The second reference is to William Moseley, who is first recorded in business with John Moseley as an Egyptian black manufacturer in *Holden's Triennial Directory*, 1809-1811. By 1818 William was working alone and was noted as an earthenware and Egyptian black maker at the Black Works, Burslem.[2] On 6 November 1819, the *Staffordshire Advertiser* gave notice that William Moseley was retiring from business and that his works were to be let; in May of 1820 an auction of his potters' utensils was advertised. Some of his figures must have

---

1. Information supplied by Ann Eatwell, Victoria & Albert Museum, *see* Appendix 1.

2. *Staffordshire General and Commercial Directory*, W. Parson and T. Bradshaw, 1818.

been very small: at one shilling and sixpence a dozen possibly they were the cheaper, underglaze painted, rather than enamelled pieces, but the set of ornaments no. 415 at eleven shillings and sixpence were obviously of the best quality and as there is no record of Moseley making china, the pieces must have been of quite elaborate earthenware or Egyptian black.

It is interesting to note that in the year of Moseley's retirement and sale of utensils, John and Richard Riley supplied set no. 415 for the same price; perhaps they had bought some of the moulds in the auction. John and Richard Riley began in business about 1796, at the Hole House works in Nile Street, Burslem. In 1811 the brothers bought the Hill House estate from the Wedgwood family, formerly tenanted by John Heath from 1802, and prior to that by the Ralph Woods. The Rileys had to rebuild the tumbledown premises and the date of 1814 can be seen over the entrance to the works, which is still in operation today. Both the brothers died in 1828 without sons to succeed them, and the business went on to the market. The *Staffordshire Advertiser,* 2 April 1831, gave notice of the auction of the premises and stock, the Property of the late Messrs J. and R. Riley, which included 'chimney ornaments'. So far only one large portrait bust in porcelain has been identified as the work of the Riley brothers, in the form of a large model of Princess Charlotte; two examples have been recorded with the overglaze enamel painted inscription 'J. & R. Riley 1819'.[3] Ann Peover, the fourth name on the list, is again associated only with bone china production and is therefore not relevant to this discussion.

Thomas and Benjamin Godwin were in partnership by about 1809-11, at their factory in Navigation Road, Burslem. They continued to work together until Benjamin's death in 1833, when Thomas continued the business alone. The Godwins have never been regarded as figure makers, but it seems that in 1823 they did supply several models to our London retailer. This time there are no prices to give any guidance. It would not be difficult to find examples of these subjects with enamel painted decoration, but it would be difficult to attribute them to the Godwins on subject alone.

What can be learned from these tantalising entries is that many manufacturers were involved in figure making, besides the specialists listed in trade directories, and that any definitive attribution of an unmarked specimen is both dangerous and foolish. Perhaps we should accommodate a more restrained approach from which we may nominate a likely source, but acknowledge the possibility that one may never know for sure.

As well as manuscript sources, figures themselves occasionally have interesting details, including inscriptions and dates which help to classify the mass of unmarked material. Many of the examples have a name incised into the base, whereas others have painted details. So few of these can be traced to

---

3. Pomfret, R., 'John & Richard Riley China & Earthenware Manufacturers', *Journal of Ceramic History,* Vol. 13, City Museum & Art Gallery, Stoke-on-Trent, 1988.

Inkstand, earthenware with overglaze enamel painted decoration, inscribed 'John Forster made this at Hanley Agust the 29 1820', ht. 145mm. *Glaisher Collection, 981, Courtesy of Syndics, Fitzwilliam Museum, Cambridge.*
Inkstands of this form are also known in bone china impressed Spode.

Bust of Neptune, inscribed on the reverse with the date '1826', ht. 346mm. *Private Collection.*

Figure of a lion, pearlware undecorated, inscribed on the base 'B.Plant Lane End', c.1818-25, ht. 248mm. *Salford Museum.*

Figure of a vestal virgin carrying her lamp and jug of oil, earthenware with overglaze enamel painted decoration, made in Staffordshire, c.1810-20, ht. 205mm. *Wisbech & Fenland Museum, 1900.23.*

Juno and Jupiter, earthenware with overglaze enamel painted decoration, made in Staffordshire, c.1810-20, ht. 155mm. *Wisbech & Fenland Museum, 1900. 28 & 29.*

A tiger mauling a man in uniform, earthenware with overglaze painted decoration, made in Staffordshire, early 19th century, ht. 241mm. *Royal Pavilion Art Gallery & Museum, Brighton, HW 1155.*

This figure depicts the death of Captain Munroe, who was savaged by a tiger in 1793.

a known factory owner that they are usually considered to be the work of an individual operative engaged in the making of figures. Workers in the 'clay end' of the factory would have had the opportunity to write in the wet clay figure before firing, and decorators could more easily add their inscription at the painting stage. This practice is not unknown in the Potteries and many families in North Staffordshire have a treasured heirloom with a grandmother's or father's name on the base. (My own grandmother was allowed to inscribe her name 'Lucretia Elkin' in yellow enamel on the back of a stoneware plate which she decorated; the special occasion on which this was allowed is not known but is always assumed to be the date on which her last trainee piece was completed.) Many pieces would have been inscribed by workers and passed through the kiln by sympathetic colleagues, who could expect a free pint in the local pub for turning a blind eye. However the pieces came into being, they are the most tantalising objects, from which crumbs of information can be gleaned but rarely the complete story.

Reginald Haggar illustrates a fine portrait bust of the Empress Josephine, painted in enamel colours and incised on the back 'Thomas Gruitt 1809'.[4] As I have never seen the piece it is impossible for me to comment on the accuracy or legibility of the transcription, however, Mr Haggar was the most reliable of ceramic historians. The local trade directories do not record this as the name of a pottery, nor does Gruitt, or variations of this name, occur in local genealogical indexes. Was it made elsewhere or is the inscription totally misread?

A large figure of a lion is known in several versions, with plain pearl glaze, with enamel painting and silver lustre detailing, inscribed with initials or in full 'Benjamin Plant, Lane End'. Despite extensive research no manufacturer of this name is recorded, but a Benjamin Plant is listed as a pottery worker in 1818 and specifically as a potter's presser in 1822. It is likely that the marked examples are the work of this man, who may have worked for any of the Lane End earthenware manufacturers.[5]

An interesting inkstand in the Glaisher Collection at the Fitzwilliam Museum, Cambridge, is modelled in the form of a boy astride a dolphin; the base is inscribed 'John Forster Made this at Hanley Agust [sic] the 29 1820'. Several similar inkstands survive and date to 1820; whether they are the work of John Forster is impossible to tell, but John Forster is not known as a manufacturer in his own right and must have been employed at a factory in Hanley when this was produced.

A fine portrait bust of Neptune is widely regarded as a late eighteenth to early nineteenth century piece, but the only example with any clue as to the production period has a large cursive inscription '1826', a much later date than one would normally associate with this figure.

4. Haggar, R.G., *Staffordshire Chimney Ornaments*, Phoenix, 1955, pl.36.

5. Hampson, R., 'Longton Potters 1750-1865', *Journal of Ceramic History*, Vol. 14, City Museum & Art Gallery, Stoke-on-Trent, 1991.

Leopard, earthenware with overglaze painted decoration, made in Staffordshire, early
19th century, ht. 140mm. *Wisbech & Fenland Museum, 1901.78.*

Two red earthenware figures decorated with silver lustre, made in Staffordshire, early
19th century, ht. 168mm. *City Museum & Art Gallery, Stoke-on-Trent 1646, 52.P.1952.*
Figures similar to the boy are known, with overglaze enamel painted decoration
impressed 'WOOD & CALDWELL', see p.166.

Pair of deer, earthenware with enamel painted decoration, made in Staffordshire, c.1815-30, ht. 184mm. *Private Collection.*

Figure of a man in Turkish costume, earthenware with overglaze enamel painted decoration, early 19th century, ht. 152mm. *Private Collection.*

Group of figures, earthenware with overglaze painted decoration, made in Staffordshire, early 19th century, ht. 127mm. *Sotheby's London.*

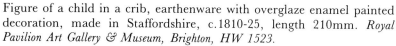

Figure of a child in a crib, earthenware with overglaze enamel painted decoration, made in Staffordshire, c.1810-25, length 210mm. *Royal Pavilion Art Gallery & Museum, Brighton, HW 1523.*

The child in a crib was a popular figure for many years; traditionally the first were said to be representative of the dead child of Admiral Rodney, but this has not been substantiated. Cradles were found amongst the fragments deposited by Enoch Wood at St. Paul's Church, Burslem, in 1828.

Elephant and Castle watch stand, earthenware with overglaze enamel painted decoration, made in Staffordshire, early 19th century, ht. 202mm. *Private Collection.*

The castle has a pottery clock face on one side and a hole on the other to view the time by the pocket watch, which may be placed inside the turret.

Pair of figures of musicians, earthenware with overglaze enamel painted decoration, c.1820-30, ht. 148mm. *City Museum & Art Gallery, Stoke-on-Trent, 281, 282.P.1949.*

A similar pair of figures has been reported with the impressed mark of Dudson, but the report has not yet been verified. These figures are based on porcelain models produced at Derby.

Figure of George IV, earthenware with overglaze enamel painted decoration, made in Staffordshire, c.1820-30, ht. 165mm. *Royal Pavilion Art Gallery & Museum, Brighton, HW68.*

Figure of a watch seller, earthenware with overglaze enamel painted decoration, made in Staffordshire, c.1820-30, ht. 155mm. *Royal Pavilion Art Gallery & Museum, Brighton, HW678.*

The common feature of the inscribed pieces is that they all indicate that the production of figures is often much later than one would have thought. The lesson here must be not to classify wares into too narrow a date band and that we should expect popular subjects to be made over a long period of time. Any manufacturer worth his salt will continue to use established models as long as they are popular, to avoid the cost of acquiring new blocks and moulds. It is still normal practice within the pottery industry to continue the production of old favourites, whilst introducing one or two new lines to test the market; the vast majority of new lines are discontinued, but occasionally one turns into a winner which the manufacturer hopes will stay in production for many years.

Figure group of golfers, earthenware with overglaze enamel painted decoration, made in Staffordshire, c.1830-40, ht. 197mm. *Royal Pavilion Art Gallery & Museum, Brighton, 320021.*
This subject is taken from a mezzotint by Valentine Green after F. Abbot, c.1790, depicting a member of the Blackheath Golf Club, the golfer in military uniform was William Innes, his caddy was a Greenwich Pensioner.

We all know those subjects and models which occur over and over again and must have been beloved by both customer and maker, for different reasons. We also all meet the unusual model, the rare and now unique piece which must not have appealed to the customer and must have been a commercial failure. It is ironic that these rare pieces now are often thought to be more desirable than the common ones.

The majority of the figures produced were not marked in any way and it may never be possible to identify their makers. Nevertheless we can enjoy the visual and tactile qualities which speak volumes to the true devotee of earthenware figures, a situation in which familiarity does not breed contempt but contentment.

6. Bocage and table base figures

Bocage Figures

Earthenware bocage figures were introduced during the nineteenth century. The term 'bocage' is derived from a French word meaning woodland and refers to the spreading, leafy tree that supports the main figure or figures. The tree form was used extensively in the eighteenth century by Continental and British porcelain makers and whilst it appeared to be an extravagant, ornamental touch, it was also functional. The composition of early porcelains, especially English ones, was very experimental: the material inclined to warping and melting, thus the tree behind the figure allowed some degree of movement during the critical firing process, but offered suitable support to prevent collapse. The manufacturer of earthenware had a much more stable material to work with and no bocage was needed, but it was added in the early years of the nineteenth century for purely cosmetic reasons.

Group of man and woman with birds in hand and overlooked by birds in a tree, pearl glazed earthenware with overglaze enamel painted decoration, made in Staffordshire, c.1815-25, ht. 267mm. *Royal Pavilion Art Gallery and Museum, Brighton, HW1326.*
This is a splendid example of an exaggerated bocage towering above the figures.

Reverse of group, showing how leaves are also applied to the back of a bocage; usually the flowers are omitted.

The Sailor's Return, pearl glazed earthenware with overglaze enamel painted decoration, made in Staffordshire, c.1815-25, ht. 232mm. *Royal Pavilion Art Gallery & Museum, Brighton, HW 306.*

Large figure of a stag, pearl glazed earthenware with overglaze enamel painted decoration, made in Staffordshire, c.1815-25, ht. 330mm. *Private Collection.* The unusual bocage has individual sprays of two oak leaves with acorns at the edge.

'SHOWMAN', pearl glazed earthenware with overglaze enamel painted decoration, made in Staffordshire, c.1815-25, ht. 159mm. *Royal Pavilion Art Gallery & Museum, Brighton, HW 1229.*

Group of religious subjects, from left to right: 'CHRIST TEACHETH NICODEMUS', 'ST PETER' and Abraham about to sacrifice Isaac, all have different bases and bocages, pearl glazed earthenware with enamel painted decoration, made in Staffordshire, c.1820-30, ht. 343mm. *Sotheby's London.*

Many of the earthenware bocage groups are quite naïvely made and rarely achieve the elegance one might associate with the finest Enoch Wood or Neale figures, yet their peculiar, rustic charm and their bright, cheerful colours often compensate for their lack of refinement.

These pieces must have been quite costly to produce, as the bases are often elaborately moulded and have separate floral details. The figures themselves are made from complex, multi-part moulds and the bocage is an intricate, decorative detail requiring the individual application of foliage sprays and flower heads. The whole assembly must have taken quite some time to put together and therefore have been relatively expensive.

The bocages themselves are of infinite variety and whilst there may be a few styles common to many manufacturers, it is possible that there are some distinctive leaf models which are peculiar to individual makers. One may tentatively identify unmarked examples by comparing with details of positively attributed pieces, but it is not possible in the present state of knowledge to

Tithe-Pig group, pearl glazed earthenware with overglaze enamel painted decoration, made in Staffordshire, c.1815-25, ht. 168mm. *City Museum & Art Gallery, Stoke-on-Trent, 305.P.1949.*

Tithe-pig groups are common in both earthenware and porcelain. There exist slightly different models based on a printed source which includes an explanatory poem.

Faith, pearl glazed earthenware with overglaze enamel painted decoration, the cross in purple lustre, made in Staffordshire, c.1815-25, ht. 203mm. *Julian Critchley Collection.*

identify every figure maker. It would be useful to have a classification that can be built on in the future, therefore I propose to discuss the work of the known manufacturers and then to group unidentified wares according to their bocage and other similar moulded details. If future excavation or research should unearth the maker of a particular type of figure we should then have a ready assembled group of work for reference, but one word of caution: please make sure your bocage is original, because replacements and restorations may be based on the leaf pattern of a different manufacturer and thus cannot be relied upon as a means of identification.

Even with a completely original figure caution is necessary in attributing any unmarked figure. It is known that factories, models and moulds changed hands, that some modellers were independent tradesmen who could sell their work to one or more customers, and it is probable that workers moved from factory to factory, possibly taking ideas, patterns and skills with them. Taking all these factors into consideration one might require several points of evidence before attributing a figure to a particular maker.

Stylistically it would seem that the bocage was introduced to earthenware figures about 1810-20; it is difficult to pin-point the date more accurately as there are no subjects which offer a close date, nor are there any marked pieces from an early short-lived company. By 1822 twelve specialist figure makers were recorded in local trade directories; by 1834 the number had risen to twenty-four and by 1841 to thirty-nine. In all sixty-four specialist toy makers are recorded during this time (some of whom may have produced china toys) and other general manufacturers are known to have included figures in their productions. Of these many factories less than ten left any evidence of their work and in recent years the commercial pressure to find a maker's name for a figure has led to the majority of unmarked examples being attributed to three or four of the known makers. Statistically it must be unlikely that four factories could have made so many surviving pieces whilst the work of the other sixty has disappeared.

The subjects used by the manufacturers illustrate the great wealth of material available in the nineteenth century. The classical subjects lingered on and we find that popular models of Diana are given bocage additions. Rustic and rural subjects continued to be popular with a particular passion for sheep, shepherds and shepherdesses. Gardeners, sportsmen, archers and rustic amusements, were all updated and produced with less finesse, but more liveliness, than previous models. New subjects included theatrical and circus groups; travelling menageries are depicted with monkeys riding dogs, and bears dancing to hurdy-gurdy music. Along with the amusing anecdotal pieces are groups with political and satirical significance, such as the New Marriage Act of 1823, and the Tithe-Pig group, depicting the Farmer's Wife offering her tenth child to the vicar along with their tithe or tenth of all their goods for the year. Religious subjects increased in number, in the eighteenth century the Old Testament and the parables were popular but with the rise of popular Nonconformist religions there was a resultant demand for more direct depictions of biblical events. Alongside the figures of Elijah and the Widow of Zarephath are found new models, including the Holy Family's flight to and return from Egypt, there are parables and episodes from the Old Testament, together with the appropriate text and models of the saints.

There was also a steady increase in the number of porcelain subjects available, for not only were factories such as Rockingham and Derby producing good quality wares for the top end of the market, but small Staffordshire outlets were making a range to satisfy the middle market demands. There never seems to have been a point at which English porcelain figure production matched that of earthenware in quantity, but as porcelain became more affordable more figure makers seem to have entered this market. The onset of the Victorian era saw a distinct change in demand and, as flatback portrait figures began to dominate the market, the manufacturers reverted once more to the simplest, cheapest, streamlined forms, with many of the porcelain makers moving to the use of Parian, which allowed intricate slipcast pieces to be produced for those of a more discerning nature.

One of the names most commonly associated with bocage figures is that of John Walton. It has been suggested that some of his work may date from as early as 1790, but no evidence can be found to substantiate this claim. Local trade directories of the potteries have been searched and his name does not occur in 1800, 1802, 1805 or 1809, but some time after this date he became established as a colour maker and earthenware figure maker and was listed as such in 1818.[1] The 1818 *Directory* is a particularly comprehensive document, but only three specialist figure makers are listed, all in the same area of the Potteries:

Longport, Burslem, Cobridge, Hot Lane &c.

Heath John, earthenware (toys), manufacturer, Sitch

Hobson Ephraim, black Egyptian and earthenware toy manufacturer, Cobridge.

Walton John, colour maker and earthenware figure manufacturer, near New Road

Both John Heath and Ephraim Hobson were in business for about ten to twelve years, yet nothing is known of their work; there must be figures which came from their factories but lack of evidence prevents identification. It is fortunate that John Walton left a body of marked wares which can be used for reference. John Walton was in business from about 1810-35, his last trade directory entry was in the *National Commercial Directory,* published by J. Pigot & Co., 1835, where he is listed under:

Earthenware Manufacturer

Walton Jno. Navigation rw, Burslem

Toy and Ornamental china Manufacturers

Walton John, Waterloo rd, Burslem.

Another Walton recorded as a figure maker was Joshua Walton, who was first listed as a modeller and an earthenware figure maker in *Pigot's Directory* of 1830.[2] Joshua Walton continued in business until his last entry in 1841 when he is recorded as making Toy and Ornamental China (fine).[3] I do not think that this member of the Walton family can be responsible for many of the bocage figures for I believe the majority pre-date his period in business.

John Walton was christened at St. John's Church, Burslem, on 20 February 1780 and married Ermine Whitmore at Newcastle under Lyme on 27 October 1800. It is not known what his trade was at this time; perhaps he was being trained in the pottery industry as a businessman rather than a practical potter, for by 1818 he had two separate works, a colour makers in Pleasant Street, and an earthenware manufactory at the Hadderage, both in Burslem, and his house was nearby in New Street. By 1822 Walton had rationalised his interests

1. *Commercial Directory 1818-20,* J. Pigot & R.W. Dean.

2. *National Commercial Directory,* Pigot & Co., 1830.

3. *Royal National and Commercial Directory and Topography of the Counties of. . . Staffordshire,* Pigot & Co., 1841.

59. Group of figures with bocage, with overglaze enamel painted decoration, made in Staffordshire, c.1815-25, ht. 222mm. *Private Collection; City Museum & Art Gallery, Stoke-on-Trent.*
This group shows a typical range of bocage figures and illustrates the wide variety of bocage types that were produced.

A selection of figure fragments from a site in Tunstall; some of the pieces are similar to extant figures but none appear to be identical. A number of figure makers worked in Tunstall, including George Hood, Samuel Grocott, and Michael Tunnicliffe. It has not yet been possible to attribute these pieces to any particular toymaker. *City Museum & Art Gallery, Stoke-on-Trent.*

Some of these pieces are similar to Walton examples. George Hood was John Walton's son-in-law and eventual successor at the Navigation Road site and is a prime contender for the role of maker, however, more than this circumstantial evidence will be required to attribute these pieces with any confidence.

and occupied only one business premises in Navigation Road, Burslem, where he was recorded as a 'toy figure and Egyptian black manufacturer'.[4]

The Navigation Road premises continued to be used as an Egyptian Black and Toy manufactory and in about 1835 an additional Toy and Ornamental China Works was established in Waterloo Road, Burslem.[5] This was a short-lived venture, for by 1841 Walton is no longer recorded at this address and a new name enters the directories, that of Abraham Wood. Perhaps Wood continued to make figures in the Walton tradition, but unfortunately there is no evidence to help draw any conclusions.

John and Ermine Walton had a number of children. Their second daughter, Susannah, was christened on 10 January 1808 and on the 6 February 1830 she married George Hood, of Brownhills near Burslem, a toy and figure maker of Tunstall, whose fortune became interwoven with that of the Walton family. A

---

4. *Newcastle and Pottery General and Commercial Directory 1822-23,* T. Allbut.
5. *National Commercial Directory,* J. Pigot, 1835.

number of figure fragments have been recovered from a site in Tunstall which bear great similarity to those marked 'WALTON'; direct comparison shows some differences but it is possible that they are the work of John Walton's son-in-law. The site cannot be positively associated with any particular Tunstall potter with our present state of knowledge and we do know that other 'toy-makers' were at work in Tunstall, however, George Hood must be a strong, if unconfirmed candidate.

Sometime in the 1830s John Walton's Navigation Road works passed to George Hood, who by 1839 had run into financial difficulties probably due to his Tunstall potting activities. From a succession of notices in the local newspaper, the *Staffordshire Advertiser,* the decline of Hood's business can be observed.

In the *Staffordshire Advertiser* of 15 June 1839 there was a notice of an earthenware manufactory to be auctioned in Navigation Road, Burslem, for many years occupied by John Walton and subsequently by George Hood. The description of the works shows it to be a typical, small figure factory with only one biscuit and one gloss oven. A notice the following month advertised the 'utensils &c.' of the Navigation Road works late in the occupation of George Hood and promised further details later. The additional details never appeared and it seems that Hood managed to stay in occupation of the works for some time longer. He had, however, to face bankruptcy proceedings and he let his factory in Tunstall to John Hancock. Between 1840 and 1844 there were various sale notices for his new house, new manufactory with 5 hovels and 6 kilns &c. The whole estate was placed on the market in 1844; the sale by auction was advertised on 18 March when the lots included: 'Extensive earthenware manufactory at Brownhills formerly occupied by George Hood & now by the executors of John Hancock'. Whilst his Tunstall business was wound up Hood continued to occupy the Navigation Road works, which was not only small but apparently in need of repair, for in January 1841 the *Staffordshire Advertiser* reported that the 'floor of the biscuit warehouse of George Hood's in Navigation Road gave way onto 20 persons working below, 3 girls were seriously hurt and 8-10 tons of ware were lost'. In 1843 Hood was sued for £6,000 by a Mr Bourne who claimed that he had advanced money to set up Hood's business. The court examined the books kept by Hood's clerk, his brother-in-law John Ellison Walton, and found in favour of Hood. In January 1848 the *Staffordshire Advertiser* announced the death of George Hood potter, Burslem, aged sixty-eight. It is not stated, but one can infer that the wretched state of his business and the vagaries of the potters' trade must have taken their toll on his health. An interesting account of Mr G.H.'s toy manufactory is given by Charles Shaw,[6] which is generally thought to be that of George Hood (a section is quoted in the Introduction to this volume). The Navigation

---

6. Shaw, C., *When I was a Child,* originally printed 1903 by Methuen, reprinted by Caliban, 1977.

60. Musicians, with overglaze enamel painted decoration, made in Staffordshire, c.1815-25, ht. 272mm. *City Museum & Art Gallery, Stoke-on-Trent, 313.P.1949.*
This is one of the more ambitious figures with a large bocage spray linking two musical groups placed on a rectangular base.

61 Elijah and the Widow of Zarephath, with overglaze enamel painted decoration, impressed on scroll on reverse 'WALTON', made by John Walton, Burslem, c.1810-20, ht. 273mm. *City Museum & Art Gallery, Stoke-on-Trent, 3079, 3080.*

62. Bare knuckle fighters Spring and Langan, impressed on a scroll at each end with the appropriate name and on the reverse with 'WALTON', made by John Walton, Burslem, c.1824-5, ht. 178mm. *Private Collection; photograph by Gavin Ashworth, New York.*
Tom Spring of England and Jack Langan of Ireland fought twice in 1824. Spring won both matches, each of which lasted over 75 rounds; he never fought again. The group is probably based on a coloured aquatint after a picture by Clement, depicting the first fight at Worcester Racecourse on 7 January, 1824.

Diana, pearl glazed earthenware with overglaze enamel painting, impressed 'WALTON' on a scroll, c.1815-25, ht. 300mm. *Private Collection.*

Royal Coat of Arms, pearl glazed earthenware with enamel painted decoration, impressed 'WALTON' on a scroll, c.1820-30, ht. 147mm. *Private Collection.*
Possibly made for the accession to the throne of George IV in 1820, or William IV in 1830.

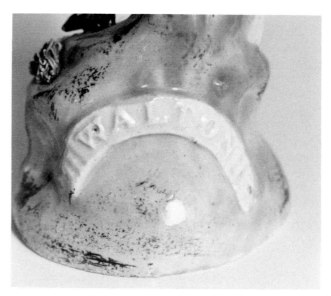

Walton mark impressed on scroll.

Walton mark in relief on scroll.

Road works appears to have passed to Bowers & Lloyd by 1846 and to Joseph Harding by 1850. These names follow the disappearance of Hood from the records, but bearing in mind the age and the structure of the premises they may have been demolished and the new names belong to a new and different factory.

It is possible that the bocage on Walton marked figures will help identify unmarked examples. Detailed moulded bases may also be compared but even tentative attributions should be based on *identical* matching features; *almost* the same means that the features are different and therefore invalid.

Detail of bocage on a marked Walton figure.
This is the most common bocage found on marked Walton figures, the applied florets are occasionally different but the leaves are usually in this form.

Detail of bocage on reverse of marked Walton figure.

Detail of bocage on a marked Walton figure.

This is a more unusual bocage found on a few marked Walton figures.

Detail of bocage on reverse of marked Walton figure.

Figure of a hunter, pearl glazed earthenware with overglaze enamel painted decoration, impressed 'WALTON' on a scroll, c.1815-25, ht. 165mm. *Julian Critchley Collection.*

Figures of this type are occasionally seen in groups, with models of hunters and dogs, on separate bases to be arranged to taste.

Pair of figures birdnesting, pearl glazed earthenware with overglaze enamel painted decoration, 'WALTON' in relief on scroll, c.1815-25, ht. 135mm. *Private Collection.*

63. Pair of gardeners and a lady archer, with overglaze enamel painted decoration, impressed 'SALT' on the reverse in the body of the gardeners, and 'SALT' in a scroll on the archer, made by Ralph Salt, Shelton, c.1820-30, ht. 170mm. *City Museum & Art Gallery, Stoke-on-Trent, 1404, 1398, 559.*

64. Guitar player, with overglaze enamel painted decoration, impressed on reverse 'I DALE BURSLEM', made by John Dale, Burslem, c.1825. *City Museum & Art Gallery, Stoke-on-Trent.*

65. Two figures depicting Abraham offering up his son Isaac, with overglaze enamel painted decoration, made in Staffordshire, c.1825-30, ht. 315mm. *City Museum & Art Gallery, Stoke-on-Trent, 153.P.1965, 601.*
The figure on the left depicts the scene where God sends an angel to stop Abraham sacrificing Isaac. A plaque to one side is impressed with verse 12 from Genesis, Chapter 22 'HE SAID LAY NOT THINE AND [sic] UPON THE LAD NEITHER DO THOU ANYTHING UNTO HIM'. The figure on the right is entitled 'ABRAHAM OFFERING HIS SON ISAAC'.

66. Equestrienne, with overglaze enamel painted decoration, made in Staffordshire, c.1825-30, ht. 235mm. *Royal Pavilion Art Gallery & Museums, Brighton, 329276; photograph by Gavin Ashworth, New York.*

Figure of a girl holding a bird, possibly representing Air from a set of elements, pearl glazed earthenware with overglaze enamel painted decoration, impressed 'WALTON' on a scroll, c.1815-25, ht. 178mm. *Private Collection.*

Girl with tambourine, pearl glazed earthenware with overglaze enamel painted decoration, impressed 'WALTON' on a scroll, ht. 152mm. *Royal Pavilion Art Gallery & Museum, Brighton, HW 885.*

Small spill vase, depicting a dog with a man asleep under a tree, pearl glazed earthenware with overglaze enamel painted decoration 'WALTON' on a scroll, c.1815-25, ht. 105mm. *Private Collection.*

Gardener and his companion, pearl glazed earthenware with overglaze painted decoration, impressed 'WALTON' on a scroll, c.1815-25, ht. 132mm. *Private Collection.*
A similar figure is also shown with a different base.

Gardener, pearl glazed earthenware with overglaze enamel painted decoration, 'WALTON' in relief on a scroll, c.1815-25, ht. 140mm. *Saffron Walden Museum, 1900.67.60.*

Shepherd and gardener, pearl glazed earthenware with overglaze enamel painted decoration, both with 'WALTON' on a scroll, c.1815-25, ht. 143mm. *Private Collection.*

Shepherd, pearl glazed earthenware with overglaze enamel painted decoration, impressed 'WALTON' on a scroll, ht. 153mm. *Saffron Walden Museum, 1900.67.50.*

Woman and child, pearl glazed earthenware with overglaze enamel painted decoration, impressed 'WALTON' on a scroll, c.1815-25. *Royal Pavilion Art Gallery & Museum, Brighton, HW 1305.*

'TENDERNESS', pearl glazed earthenware with overglaze enamel painted decoration, impressed 'WALTON' on a scroll, c.1815-25, ht. 206mm. *Royal Pavilion Art Gallery & Museum, Brighton, HW1617.*

'REMUS & ROMULUS', pearl glazed earthenware with overglaze enamel painted decoration, unmarked, made in Staffordshire, c.1815-25, ht. 240mm. *Wisbech & Fenland Museum, 1901.62.*

The bocage is similiar to the marked Walton Songsters, but there is no other detail to confirm a Walton attribution.

Gardeners, pearl glazed earthenware with overglaze enamel painted decoration, unmarked, made in Staffordshire, c.1815-25, ht. 191mm. *Royal Pavilion Art Gallery & Museum, Brighton, HW 1354.*

The bocage is similiar to the marked Walton Songsters, but there is no other detail to confirm a Walton attribution.

'SONGSTERS', pearl glazed earthenware with overglaze enamel painted decoration, impressed 'WALTON' on scroll, c.1815-25, ht. 216mm. *Saffron Walden Museum, 1900.67.96.*

67. Group of figures with table bases, with overglaze enamel painted decoration, made in Staffordshire, c.1825-35, ht. 290mm. *City Museum & Art Gallery, Stoke-on-Trent.*
This shows a typical range of table base figures with a variety of different table details.

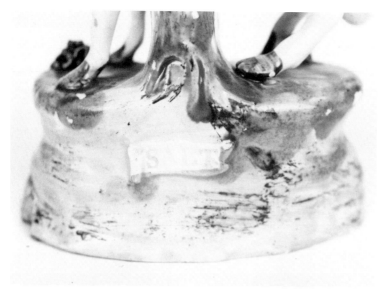

Salt mark impressed on scroll.

Salt mark impressed on reverse of figure.

The number of marked Walton figures indicates that a wide range of subjects was produced during his twenty-five years or so as a manufacturer and it is not impossible that they subsequently continued to be made by George Hood. The figure of Diana on a mound on top of a square base shows the traditional figure model adapted to the new style, but it seems that most of the marked Walton pieces are of figures that are either new subjects or contemporary models based on old themes. There are two distinctive bocages known on marked pieces and a great variety of moulded base forms. Many factories appear to have made similar subjects at this time and every detail should be scrutinised before attributing unmarked pieces to Walton.

One of Walton's most notable contemporaries was Ralph Salt, who also marked some of his figures enabling a body of reference material to be built up. Ralph Salt was born in 1782; nothing is known of his early life except that he was already a partner in a decorating company before March 1816. On the 13 March 1816 the *Staffordshire Advertiser* records the dissolution of partnership between Ralph Salt, Joseph Gould and Charles Massey, 'lusterers of China & Earthenware Hanley'. It seems that Ralph Salt and Charles Massey continued the work in New Street, Hanley, as 'Lusterers painters & gilders of earthenware', but there were still problems in the partnership. Within two months Ralph left the business to be carried on by William and Charles Massey and moved around the corner to set up on his own account.

In the *Newcastle & Pottery General and Commercial Directory* for 1822-3, published by T. Allbut, the alphabetical list of occupants of Shelton includes: 'Salt Ralph, lusterer, enameller & figure maker, Miles bank'. By 1829 Ralph Salt had moved to Marsh Street in Shelton where he worked until he gave up business in 1841. He is variously listed during that time as an 'Earthenware Manufacturer Toy only', 'China & Earthenware Toy Manufacturer...figures & porcelain tablets' and as a Fine 'Toy & Ornamental china Manufacturer'. During his twenty or more years in business we see that he specialised in figures, in both porcelain and earthenware and that he also made porcelain tablets. The latter would

Detail of bocage on front of marked Salt figure.

Detail of bocage on reverse of marked Salt figure.

'FIRE', from a set of the elements, pearl glazed earthenware with overglaze enamel painted decoration, impressed 'SALT' on a scroll, c.1820-30, ht. 165mm. *Saffron Walden Museum, 1900.67.111.*
See a similar subject impressed 'I DALE BURSLEM', p.243.

'GARDNERS', pearl glazed earthenware with overglaze enamel painted decoration, impressed 'SALT' on reverse, c.1820-30, ht. 153mm. *Private Collection.*

probably have been for painted decoration and producing flat sheets of porcelain for this purpose was a difficult art to master.

It has been said that when Ralph Salt gave up trading he was succeeded by his son Charles. No evidence of this can be found, in fact the *Staffordshire Advertiser,* of April 1841, advertises for auction several copyhold premises in Shelton, including:

68. Polito's Menagerie, with overglaze enamel painted decoration, made in Staffordshire, c.1825-35, ht. 336mm. *Private Collection; photograph by Gavin Ashworth, New York.* Mr. S. Polito purchased the Exeter Change Menagerie of London in about 1810, but for some years prior to this had toured a menagerie around England. Although Polito died in 1814, the touring show continued in his name for many years. It is said that the end finally came when the menagerie and the ship transporting it were lost crossing the Irish Sea on the way to tour Ireland in 1836.

69. Wombwell's Menagerie, with overglaze enamel painted decoration, made in Staffordshire, c.1825-35, ht. 372mm. *Private Collection; photograph by Gavin Ashworth, New York.* George Wombwell's Menagerie began its peregrinations throughout Britain in about 1807. By the time of his death in 1850, there were three travelling menageries belonging to various branches of the family who continued in business; the last finally closed in 1884.

70. Wombwell's Menagerie, with overglaze enamel painted decoration, made in Staffordshire, c.1825-35, ht. 211mm. *Art Gallery & Museum, Newcastle under Lyme, Staffordshire.* This is a very small menagerie figure; the variety of sizes and models suggests that more than one potter produced these subjects. The capital investment required to acquire all the models and moulds would have been very high and it is unlikely that one potter would wish to commit such a high proportion of his resources to producing many versions of a subject.

'ARCHAR', pearl glazed earthenware with overglaze painted decoration, impressed 'SALT' on scroll, c.1820-30, ht. 165mm. *Private Collection*

Pair of bone china figures of John Liston in character parts, decorated with gilding on enamel painted bases, impressed 'SALT' on a scroll, c.1826-30, ht. 159mm. *Royal Pavilion Art Gallery & Museum, Brighton, HW928,929.* Taken from lithographs of John Liston published in 1826.

Impressed 'SALT' on a scroll on reverse of these porcelain figures.

'...a house fronting Marsh st. with separate yard and garden behind held by Mr Ralph Salt, another house adjoining occupied by him as an ornamental china figure warehouse with yard and garden, and one other house beyond with yard and garden held by Mr John Salt. The premises range in a row one or two removes from the Black Horse public House, have a communication backwards to & from the street by a private entry, over an area of 695 sq. yds and are supplied with water by taps...'

Ralph Salt was almost sixty when he stopped work and his retirement was brief; his death was noted in the *Staffordshire Advertiser* of 28 November 1846.

Salt figures have many similarities with the Walton wares but close examination shows that on the whole they are less sophisticated. The misspelling of titles is not uncommon and we find 'ARCHAR', 'SHEPHERDISS' and 'GARDNERS' impressed on the fronts of bases. Some rare examples of his porcelain toys are known, but the overall impression is of a range of colourful naïve models.

Two sheep, pearl glazed earthenware with overglaze enamel painted decoration, on the left impressed 'SALT' on a scroll, on the right impressed 'HALL' on a tablet, c.1820-30, ht. 110mm. *Private Collection.*

Ram, pearl glazed earthenware with overglaze enamel painted decoration, impressed 'HALL' on tablet, c.1820-30, ht. 115mm. *Jonathan Horne.*
The bocage is made up of single broad leaves with simple florets.

Reverse of ram showing back of bocage with single, overlapping, broad leaves and impressed mark 'HALL' on tablet.

Sheep, pearl glazed earthenware with overglaze enamel painted decoration, impressed 'HALL' on tablet, c.1820-30, ht. 110mm. *Christie's.*

Samuel Hall was a neighbour of Ralph Salt and whilst many authorities have credited the marked Hall figures to the Burslem and Tunstall factories of John and Ralph Hall, I see no reason to suggest that they were not made by Samuel Hall. As I have said in the Introduction, figure making was a humble part of the potting trade and there is no evidence to suggest that the large scale manufactories of J. & R. Hall, which specialised in blue printed wares for the American market, ever produced any figures. However, the documentary evidence records Samuel Hall as a potter and specialist figure maker from 1818 to the 1850s, producing this class of ware for about forty years. These figures will therefore be discussed as the work of Samuel Hall, who was born in 1784 and is first recorded in 1818[7] in the alphabetical lists of occupants of Shelton as 'potter, New Hall street'. The term potter was usually confined to employees in this particular directory, the term manufacturer indicated a factory owner. From 1822[8] Samuel is listed as an earthenware toy maker, as

7. *Commercial Directory 1818-20,* J. Pigot & R.W. Dean.

8. *Newcastle and Pottery General and Commercial Directory 1822-23, T. Allbut.*

Reverse of Dandy with 'HALL' impressed directly into the body.

Figure of a Dandy, pearl glazed earthenware with overglaze enamel painted decoration, impressed 'HALL' on reverse, c.1820-30, ht. 170mm. *Saffron Walden Museum, 1900.66.31.*

'WIDOW', the widow of Zarephath, pearl glazed earthenware with overglaze enamel painted decoration, impressed 'HALL', c.1820-30, ht. 89mm. *Newcastle under Lyme Museum, 68.P.1943.*

Deer, pearl glazed earthenware with overglaze enamel painted decoration, impressed 'TITTENSOR' on the reverse, c.1820-25, ht. 77mm. *City Art Gallery & Museum, Stoke-on-Trent, 422.P.1990.*

Reverse of deer showing detail of bocage and impressed mark.

Boy reading, pearl glazed earthenware with overglaze enamel painted decoration, impressed on reverse 'TITTENSOR', c.1815-25, ht. 171mm. *Private Collection.*

a china and earthenware toy maker in 1834[9] and finally in 1841 as a china toy manufacturer.[10] The various trade directories are not consistent with their classifications, but it seems likely that Samuel Hall followed the pattern of moving from the cheaper earthenwares to porcelain, and possibly to Parian as

9. *History, Gazetteer and Directory of Staffordshire,* W. White, 1834.

10. *Royal National and Commercial Directory and Topography of the Counties of Staffordshire,* Pigot & Co., 1841.

Impressed mark 'I DALE BURSLEM'.

Girl playing mandolin, pearl glazed earthenware with overglaze enamel painted decoration, impressed on reverse 'I DALE BURSLEM', c.1825, ht. 121mm. *Private Collection.*

this alternative material became increasingly popular in the mid-nineteenth century.

Marked Hall figures are not common; sheep are the most numerous, and other subjects, apart from the two figures illustrated here, include a model of St. Peter which was sold at Sotheby's in 1973.

The history of the Tittensor family has been discussed in Chapter 3 but it is necessary to remind ourselves that potters did not always produce only one

Detail of bocage on front of marked Dale figure.

Detail of bocage on reverse of marked Dale figure.

'WATER', from a set of the Elements, pearl glazed earthenware with overglaze enamel painted decoration, impressed on the reverse 'I.DALE BURSLEM', c.1825, ht. 176mm. *Southport Museum, 133.*

'FIRE', from a set of the Elements, pearl glazed earthenware with overglaze enamel painted decoration, impressed on the reverse 'I.DALE BURSLEM', c.1825, ht. 165mm. *Atlanta Historical Society.*
See a similar subject impressed 'SALT', p.235.

class of figure, but made a variety of types as fashion and the pocket dictated. The Tittensor high temperature decorated figures would have been fairly cheap compared with the enamel painted pieces, but marked examples of both kinds are known and it is interesting to note that several models occur in both decorative finishes. Perhaps a closer study of his work may help to identify unmarked examples.

Of other marked figures that are recorded, many have shadowy origins. John Dale is a potter of whom little is known; the name is not uncommon in the Potteries and the known facts may refer to one or more men of the same name. John and William Dale were involved in various pottery partnerships with George and Samuel Poulson and with Stevenson and Godwin during the early years of the nineteenth century. A son, John, was born to John and Hannah Dale and christened on 8 May 1791. In 1818 the trade directories recorded in the alphabetical section: 'Dale John, China &c. manufacturer, — house Stoke'. Subsequently a marriage was recorded in the *Potteries Mercury:* 'John Dale engraver & toy manufacturer was married at Astbury to Sarah Walker 14th February 1825'. There is no evidence to connect these two John Dales, but at least it is known that figures were produced by a maker of that name around 1825.

Detail of front of bocage of marked Edge & Grocott figure.

Boy birdnesting, pearl glazed earthenware, undecorated, impressed 'EDGE & GROCOTT' on a tablet on reverse, c.1825, ht. 152mm. *Private Collection, courtesy Jonathan Horne.*

Detail of reverse of bocage of marked Edge & Grocott figure.

Detail of moulded base of marked Edge & Grocott figure.

Mark of 'EDGE & GROCOTT' on a tablet on reverse of figure.

Boy with a basket of flowers, pearl glazed earthenware, undecorated, impressed 'EDGE & GROCOTT' on a tablet on reverse, c.1825, ht. 135mm. *Christie's.*
(This figure was kindly brought to my attention by Jonathan Horne.)

There are, in fact, very few marked Dale pieces: a set of the Elements is in the Victoria & Albert Museum and 'Fire' from this series is in the Atlanta Historical Society; a figure of Mercury passed through the London salerooms in 1973 and a damaged figure of Aesculapius through another London saleroom in 1987; a small figure of a girl playing a mandolin is in the Geoffrey Godden reference collection and a portrait bust of John Wesley is known in a private collection.

There are even fewer marked examples of Edge and Grocott pieces: two of their figures are often described in the existing literature, but the whereabouts of only one of them is known. There is no documentary evidence concerning a partnership between these two potters and along with previous authors I can only speculate on the possibility that it was a short-lived venture, possibly involving Samuel Grocott of Tunstall, who is recorded in business from 1822 to 1828 and Timothy or Daniel Edge, who had potworks in Burslem. Woolliscroft Rhead was the first to mention a marked figure of a boy birdnesting and the undecorated, china glaze figure is known in a private collection. The second recorded figure was 'a boy partly draped, holding a basket of flowers, standing on an irregular base, tree background: rather strongly coloured', it is listed in the catalogue of an exhibition held in Dublin in 1911 and its present whereabouts are unknown. A third figure, not previously recorded, recently went through a London saleroom and appears to be an undecorated china glaze example of the boy with a basket of flowers.

Oak leaf bocage, excavated from Burslem Old Town Hall site, Enoch Wood, c.1825-30, the use of oak leaf and acorn is an unusual feature and may be a means of identifying unmarked Enoch Wood figures. *City Museum & Art Gallery, Stoke-on-Trent.*

Small leaf bocage, excavated from Burslem Old Town Hall site, Enoch Wood, c.1825-30, the veins of the leaves are quite deeply scored and the stalks are quite prominent, the reverse is made up of single, overlapping leaves. *City Museum & Art Gallery, Stoke-on-Trent.*

Standard bocage, excavated from Burslem Old Town Hall site, Enoch Wood, c.1825-30, the front has overlapping large single leaves with florets arranged in twos (this latter is not a moulded pair and so the florets could occur singly), the reverse also has overlapping large single leaves. *City Museum & Art Gallery, Stoke-on-Trent.*

Palm frond bocage, excavated from Burslem Old Town Hall site, Enoch Wood, c.1825-30, the front and reverse both made up of sprays of palm-like fronds. *City Museum & Art Gallery, Stoke-on-Trent.*

The most well-known figure maker, who produced unmarked and therefore previously unrecognised bocage groups, is Enoch Wood. His history is detailed in Chapter 5 and it is only necessary here to refer once more to excavated examples of his work, which offer some evidence of his bocage figure productions. In 1938 figures and fragments were found beneath the pavement on the south side of Burslem Old Town Hall; the attribution of these to Enoch Wood has been dealt with in Chapter 5 and needs no further explanation. The group retrieved from Burslem Old Town Hall was a range of figures, some fairly complete, others quite fragmentary, including a number of theatrical subjects which dated the cache to about 1828. There were a number of bocage forms — some of them are quite distinctive — which should be an aid to identifying unmarked specimens. Four bocage forms were found, one of the most original being the acorn and oak leaf, found without any figure attached and a long search has resulted in only one similar complete piece coming to light, that of 'JESUS PRAYING'. Jesus appears to be in the garden of

A group of bocage figures excavated from Burslem Old Town Hall site, Enoch Wood, c.1825-30, ht. 130mm. *City Museum & Art Gallery, Stoke-on-Trent.*

A group of bocage figures excavated from Burslem Old Town Hall site, Enoch Wood, c.1825-30, ht. 150mm. *City Museum & Art Gallery, Stoke-on-Trent.*

Faith, Hope and Charity, earthenware with overglaze enamel painted decoration from a set all impressed '19', Charity matches an excavated piece from Burslem Old Town Hall site, attributed to Enoch Wood, c.1825-30, ht. 190mm. *City Museum & Art Gallery, Stoke-on-Trent, 1407, 400.P.1949, 1400.*

Two figures of Charity, on the left excavated from Burslem Old Town Hall site, on the right a complete example with overglaze enamel painted decoration, attributed to Enoch Wood, c.1825-30, both impressed '19', ht. 190mm. *City Museum & Art Gallery, Stoke-on-Trent, 1400.*

Andromache and Hygeia, earthenware with overglaze enamel painted decoration, the palm frond bocage matches excavated pieces from Burslem Old Town Hall site, Andromache, impressed '3', Hygeia impressed '10', attributed to Enoch Wood, c.1815-25, ht. 175mm. *Manchester City Art Gallery, 1923.903 & 901.*
This pair of figures is listed as being purchased from Wood & Caldwell in 1810 and 1815, at a cost of two shillings the pair, see Appendix 1.

'JESUS PRAYING', earthenware with overglaze enamel painted decoration, the acorn bocage matches excavated pieces from Burslem Old Town Hall site, attributed to Enoch Wood, c.1820-30, ht. 190mm. *Private Collection.*

Gethsemene, praying that the cup be taken from his lips, a cherub at his right shoulder bears the bitter draught. (I was first attracted to this piece because of the magnificent halo and only later noted the significance of the bocage.) The second is also a distinctive bocage from the site, it has small leaves with deeply scored leaf veins and prominent stalks, the reverse has single overlapping leaves. Third is a fairly standard form of bocage and can be seen in the tender group of a cow and calf, which matches in every detail that found on the Old Town Hall site. The fourth is a more novel bocage and looks like a palm or fern frond and a number of decorated and undecorated pieces were found. Only one find has been made to match this last bocage exactly, but there must be others. In Manchester City Art Gallery is a pair of Andromache and Hygeia with the palm frond bocage; this unusual combination of subjects is known to have been sold by Wood & Caldwell between 1810 and 1816 and is recorded in a retail pottery dealer's ledger.[11]

---

11. Information supplied by Ann Eatwell, Victoria & Albert Museum, see Appendix 1.

Cow and calf, earthenware with overglaze enamel painted decoration, the standard bocage matches fragments found on Burslem Old Town Hall site, attributed to Enoch Wood, c.1820-30, ht. 127mm. *Private Collection.*

Goat, earthenware with overglaze enamel painted decoration, matching fragments found at Burslem Old Town Hall site, attributed to Enoch Wood, c.1820-30, ht. 100mm. *Private Collection.*

Bocage excavated on the site of the Dudson pottery, Hope Street, Hanley, c.1815-25, ht. 60mm. *Dudson Bros. Ltd.* The leaf form appears to be made of single overlapping leaves, with overglaze enamel painting in a distinctive yellow and green; the florets with red and blue enamels.

Cherub, earthenware with overglaze enamel painted decoration, base impressed '3', the figure matches fragments from the Burslem Old Town Hall site and the bocage is the single large leaf variety found on the site, attributed to Enoch Wood, c.1820-30, ht. 102mm. *Private Collection.*

Diana, earthenware with overglaze enamel painted decoration, base impressed '6' or '9', the base is similar to that from Burslem Old Town Hall site and the bocage is the single large leaf variety found on the site, tentatively attributed to Enoch Wood, c.1820-30, ht. 293mm. *Julian Critchley Collection.*

Bocage figures from the site include several animal models, of a goat and kid, reclining deer in various sizes and the inevitable sheep; there are shepherds and shepherdesses, boys and girls with baskets and cherubs with flowers. It seems quite likely that Enoch Wood was a major figure producer throughout his lifetime, perhaps reflecting his interest in sculpture and modelling which, in later years, he confined to life-size portraits of himself and his son. The Wood factories were finally closed in 1840 on the death of Enoch Wood.

Excavated evidence may also lead to the identification of another maker of bocage figures. The Dudson family became established as potters about 1800,

Deer, pearl glazed earthenware with overglaze enamel painted decoration, made in Staffordshire, c.1815-30, ht. 184mm. *Private Collection.*
This model has a large leaf bocage with the fruit moulded in with the foliage.

Reverse of large leaf bocage with individual, overlapping sprays.

the Hope Street Works in Hanley was begun in about 1809 and is still standing today. Thomas Dudson who first ran the factory was joined by his two sons, the eldest of whom, James, succeeded to the business in 1845. Although the factory has remained in family hands there is unfortunately no complete archive. From a variety of primary sources a history of the family and its products has been compiled[12] but no documentary references have been found relating to figure production in the 1815-25 period. This 'toy' end of the trade must have been a small part of the overall output of the factory. The bocage excavated within the boundaries of the site is of distinctive form and colour but as yet no complete figures have been identified.

The majority of bocage groups consist of those specimens which are unmarked. They contain some very distinctive foliage forms, and we await either the elusive and unlikely marked piece to surface, or for future excavation to reveal the identity of the makers. Some of the anonymous pieces are amongst the finest examples of this class of figure. The large leaf form is a particular personal favourite and the pine cone leaf form has such delightful figure groups that one instinctively feels that a first class figure maker must be responsible. As well as bocage, we can look at the base details, to reveal some

12. Dudson, A.E., *Dudson — A Family of Potters since 1800,* Dudson Publications, 1985.

Man with lost sheep, pearl glazed earthenware with overglaze enamel painted decoration, c.1815-30, ht. 206mm. *Private Collection.*
The large leaf sprays are applied edge to edge to make an unusual bocage.

Mother and child, pearl glazed earthenware with overglaze enamel painted decoration, made in Staffordshire, c.1815-25, ht. 223mm. *Royal Pavilion Art Gallery & Museum, Brighton, HW 1531.*
The bocage is of the pine cone type, the base is moulded with overlapping leaves.

Arbour group sometimes found entitled 'Perswasion', pearlware with overglaze enamel painted decoration, made in Staffordshire, c.1815-25, ht. 223mm. *Royal Pavilion Art Gallery & Museum, Brighton, HW 777.*

Detail of pine cone bocage.

The bocage is of the pine cone type, the base has moulded and applied details in red and blue enamel against the white body of the 'patriotic' group.

Figure titled 'SCRIPTURES PRESERVED JEREMIAH CH 34', pearl glazed earthenware with overglaze enamel painted decoration, made in Staffordshire, c.1815-25, ht. 279mm. *City Museum & Art Gallery, Stoke on Trent, 618.* The moulded details on bases of figures of this type are often enamelled red and blue against the white body, hence my classification of the 'patriotic' group.

'Patriotic' group bocage, the front with a five fingered leaf spray and single large floret.

'Patriotic' group bocage, the reverse with a five fingered leaf spray with single, overlapping leaf at junction with branch.

Figure titled 'CHRIST TEACHETH NICODEMUS JOHN 3 CH3', pearl glazed earthenware with overglaze enamel painted decoration, made in Staffordshire, c.1815-25, ht. 297mm. *City Museum & Art Gallery, Stoke-on-Trent, 13.P.1931.*

'SCRIPTURES. PRESERVED. JEREMIAH CH.34.' pearl glazed earthenware with overglaze enamel painted decoration, c.1815-25, ht. 254mm. *Royal Pavilion Art Gallery & Museum, Brighton, HW 750.*
The heavily modelled bocage with integral fruit, the base with applied leaf sprays.

Detail of bocage.

Detail of reverse of bocage.

Flight into Egypt, pearl glazed earthenare with overglaze enamel painted decoration, made in Staffordshire, c.1815-25, ht. 191mm. *Royal Pavilion Art Gallery & Museum, Brighton, HW 758.* The bocage on this figure has distinctive curly leaves.

Abraham sacrificing Isaac, inscribed 'HE SAID LAY NOT THINE AND UPON THE LAD NEITHER DO THOU ANY THING UNTO HIM', pearl glazed earthenware with overglaze enamel painted decoration, c.1815-25, ht. 184mm. *Royal Pavilion Art Gallery & Museum, Brighton, HW738.* The bocage is of the curly leaf type.

Detail of front of curly leaf bocage.

Reverse of curly leaf bocage.

Tithe-pig group, pearl glazed earthenware with overglazed enamel painted decoration, c.1820-30, ht. 191mm. *Private Collection.*

distinctive moulded features which we assume must come from the same hands and include bases with S and C-scrolls where the white body is enhanced with red and blue enamels, leading to my less than academic title of the 'patriotic' group.

There will be many other sub-groups which arise out of classifying bocage figures in this way, but at least they will be based on something tangible and form a foundation on which future research can stand. Systematic classification is a slow process and has only just begun. It has taken scientists centuries to classify the natural world and amendments still continue. Pottery figures are less amenable to taxonomy, but that is no excuse for not beginning.

Dandies, pearl glazed earthenware with overglaze enamel painted decoration, made in Staffordshire, c.1815-25, ht. 210mm. *Royal Pavilion Art Gallery & Museum, Brighton, HW1649.*
The bocage is of anthemion type.

Detail of anthemion bocage with flattened fruit moulding.

Detail of flower and fruit bocage, front.

Shepherdess, pearl glazed earthenware with overglaze enamel painted decoration, made in Staffordshire, c.1815-25, ht. 171mm. *Royal Pavilion Art Gallery & Museum, Brighton, HW 1312.*
The bocage is of flower and fruit type.

Detail of flower and fruit bocage, reverse. It is unusual for the bocage to have florets on the reverse.

Detail of multi-leaf bocage with alternate red and blue florets.

Cow attacked by a snake, pearl glazed earthenware with overglaze enamel painted decoration, made in Staffordshire, c.1815-25, ht. 155mm. *Royal Pavilion Art Gallery & Museum, Brighton, HW 1343.*

Detail of multi-leaf bocage, reverse.

Group depicting a 'Dame School', pearl glazed earthenware with overglaze enamel painted decoration, the back with applied grape and vine to signify an outdoor arbour, made in Staffordshire, c.1825, ht. 155mm. *Royal Pavilion Art Gallery & Museum, Brighton, HW1350.*

A lack of historical methodology in the past has led to an over-simplification of the problems in identifying earthenware figures, with the result that certain names have become associated with wares without any evidence whatsoever. This is not only academically unsound, but restricts our understanding of the pieces and so limits our enjoyment. One particular group of wares, the table base group, has suffered more than any other from the rash desire to find a maker at all costs.

259

Group entitled 'THE.NEW.MARRIAGE.ACT' and 'JOHN. FRILL. AND. ANN. BOKE. AGED. 21. THAT. IS. RIGHT.SAYS.THE.PARSON. AMEN.SAYS.THE.CLERK.', pearl glazed earthenware with overglaze enamel painted decoration, made in Staffordshire, c.1825, ht. 159mm. *Royal Pavilion Art Gallery & Museum, Brighton, HW824.*
The group refers to the Act of 18 July 1823, repealing Hardwick's Marriage Act of 1753; in view of the number of clandestine marriages the 1823 Act declared that marriages performed without the benefit of banns or licence were to be valid, but that the clergyman who officiated would be guilty of a felony.

Group of card players, the figure on the right probably depicting Dr. Syntax, pearl glazed earthenware with overglaze enamel painted decoration, made in Staffordshire, c.1825, ht. 152mm. *Royal Pavilion Art Gallery & Museum, Brighton, HW1475.*
Dr. Syntax played cards in *Dr. Syntax in Search of a Wife;* the illustration by Thomas Rowlandson shows Dr. Syntax at a large indoor games table and is therefore not the direct source for the subject.

There is a variety of figure groups, which are depicted within an interior setting, rather like 18th century arbour groups. These pieces have individual figures which might be found within bocage or table base groups.

Neptune and Venus, pearl glazed earthenware with overglaze enamel painted decoration, made in Staffordshire, c.1830, ht. 245mm. *City Museum & Art Gallery, Stoke-on-Trent, 298 & 292.P.1949.*

Table Base Groups

Table base groups are exactly what they sound like: figures or groups mounted on a base that resembles a table. This is the least emotive phrase which can be applied to these pieces and should generally be accepted as a classification in which there are subdivisions based upon the differences in style of base and other details.

Table base groups are invariably of pearl glazed earthenware and are decorated with enamel painted colours. They are of multi-mould construction and occasionally incorporate the stylised trees known as bocage. The figure groups themselves often include two or more figures, castellated buildings, bocage, applied floral sprays and an inscription, all placed on to a table base; they must have been expensive to produce and thus top of the range models for earthenware manufacturers. Through studying the similarities of detail between table base and bocage figures it may be possible to group certain pieces together and tentatively identify them as the production of individual factories as yet unknown. The pieces described here have been grouped according to their base form and other similar moulded features.

The models chosen by the potters to be depicted in this way include a number of subjects which can be fairly accurately dated. These include 'The Red Barn Murder', 1827-8, portraits of King William IV and Queen Adelaide, who succeeded to the British throne in 1830, and 'Teetotal' (a word which only came into the English language in 1834). These dates indicate that table base groups may have been introduced around 1825 and continued in popularity for ten years or more. Many of the subjects covered were continuations of the themes established in the previous century. Classical subjects such as Neptune and Venus were produced in quite large numbers but were updated to give Venus a stylish 1820s hairstyle. Characters and tales from mythology and biblical subjects also remained popular; the front of the table base offered a suitable tablet for titles and inscriptions. The move towards producing more topical subjects such as the Royal family, famous murderers and popular actresses, show table base groups to be transitional between the early nineteenth century fanciful pieces and the Victorian portrait figures.

There are no recorded marked examples of table base figures, nor is there any documentary or archaeological evidence to support their attribution to any particular manufacturer.

The name of Obadiah Sherratt is often given as the source of all table base groups and has crept stealthily into ceramic mythology during the last thirty years until almost any ornate base is attributed to his manufacture. It is often said that Obadiah Sherratt is a traditional attribution for table base groups and yet it appears that the earliest date this was suggested was 1955. In his *Staffordshire Chimney Ornaments,* Reginald Haggar wrote:

> 'Obadiah Sherratt is generally considered to have made the ''Bull-baiting'' groups...Various versions of the ''Bull-baiting'' group have been recorded...Two very distinctive types which may perhaps be associated

Frog mug, pearl glazed earthenware with overglaze enamel painted decoration, the inside with moulded frog, the base impressed 'O. SHERRATT', c.1825-30, ht. 110mm. *City Museum & Art Gallery, Stoke-on-Trent, 714.P.1987.*

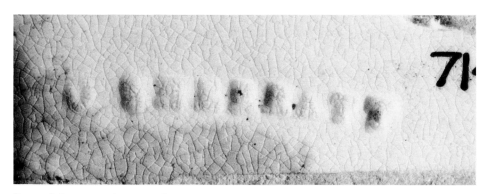

Base of frog mug impressed 'O. SHERRATT'.

with Obadiah Sherratt are mounted upon a specially-shaped six-legged table base...This particular form of stand occurs with a wide variety of models, mostly of a crude type, some moralistic, some religious, which may have been the work of one potter, who, I suggest, was Obadiah Sherratt.[13]

Reginald Haggar's subsequent researches and study of the Staffordshire pottery industry became a model of historical methodology and he often regretted that his 'suggestions' became fact without the benefit of any supporting evidence.

---

13. Haggar, R.G., *Staffordshire Chimney Ornaments,* Phoenix, 1955, p.92.

I tried to trace the source of the 'traditional' opinion which associated the name of Sherratt with bull-baiting, but could not get any further back than 1920, when in *The Earthenware Collector* G. Woolliscroft Rhead wrote:

'Obadiah Sherratt was a maker of figures in Burslem about 1822, and produced among other groups one of Bull-baiting — a man holding staff, with both arms upraised, a dog attacking, another tossed on the top of the bull. A number of these groups are extant, the earliest being attributed to Ralph Wood.'[14]

In 1929 Herbert Read published his *Staffordshire Pottery Figures* and referred to:

'The excellent bull-baiting groups, of which two are illustrated here (Plates 62 and 63), are attributed to Obadiah Sherratt, who had a pottery in Burslem about 1822 and died about 1855. Mr. Woolliscroft Rhead states. . .that he also made some of the perfunctory but amusing figures of famous personages, such as are illustrated in Plates 69 and 70.'[15]

Plates 69 and 70 are flatback figures of Wellington and Prince Albert, from the Balston Collection. The two bull-baiting groups illustrated were both flat based, one has a tethered bull attacked by one dog and is fairly crudely painted in enamel colours, with the stepped rectangular base in one colour with a contrasting line, and the other has a man and one dog with the bull on a rectangular base, decorated in enamel colours to resemble marble, but not a table base in sight. There seems to be no hard evidence to suggest that Obadiah Sherratt has any more claim to the production of table based groups than Michael Tunnicliffe, Maria Maskery, or any of the other twenty-five or so figure makers of the 1830s.

Little is known of the history of Obadiah Sherratt, as there is no trace of his birth in local parish registers, but it is known that he was married to Ann Davenport in 1797 and that they had several children before Ann died in 1810. Obadiah's second marriage to a widow, Martha Austin, took place within two months of Ann's burial. There were at least four children, including a son named Hamlet who died in infancy and a later son also called Hamlet who was christened in 1814. Nothing is known of the early potting career of Sherratt, as the very comprehensive trade directory of 1818[16] does not record his name; the conclusion must be that at that time he worked in some capacity for another person. Sometime between 1818 and 1822-3 Obadiah set up in business for himself. There are two trade directories for 1822-3;[17] Pigot's makes no mention of Obadiah Sherratt, but Allbut's, which is much more

---

14. Rhead, G.W., *The Earthenware Collector,* Herbert Jenkins, 1920, p.295.

15. Read, H., *Staffordshire Pottery Figures,* Duckworth, 1929, p.20.

16. *Commercial Directory 1818-20,* J. Pigot & R.W. Dean.

17. *London & Provincial New Commercial Directory 1822-23.* Pigot & Co; *Newcastle and Pottery General and Commercial Directory 1822-23,* T. Allbut.

Bull-baiting group, pearl glazed earthenware with overglaze enamel painted and purple lustre decoration, made in Staffordshire, c.1830, ht. 222mm. *Royal Pavilion Art Gallery & Museum, Brighton, HW1021.*

The two flat based bull-baiting groups are similar to the type illustrated by Herbert Read in 1929 and captioned 'Perhaps made by Obadiah Sherratt'. From this tentative suggestion a chain can be followed which next leads to 'Obadiah Sherratt probably made bull-baiting groups on table bases as well' to 'Obadiah Sherratt definitely made all table base groups' finally 'Let's call anything with a florid base Obadiah Sherratt'.

Bull-baiting group, pearl glazed earthenware with overglaze painted decoration, made in Staffordshire, c.1830, ht. 310mm. *Sotheby's London.*

Bull-baiting group, entitled 'BULL. BEATING' and 'NOW CAPTAIN LAD', pearl glazed earthenware with overglaze painted decoration, made in Staffordshire, c.1830, ht. 247mm. *City Art Gallery & Museum, Stoke-on-Trent, 3178.*
This example has a flat-footed table base, the feet have no decorative detail.

There is no evidence of any kind to suggest what type of figure Obadiah Sherratt made, and as he was only one of many specialist makers at that time it is likely that table base groups were made by more than one factory.

Bull-baiting group, pearl glazed earthenware with overglaze enamel painted decoration, made in Staffordshire, c.1830, ht. 187mm. *Stoke-on-Trent, 59.P.1936.*
This example has a ridged foot table base.

Detail of ridged foot table base.

Detail of front of ridged foot table base, pearl glazed earthenware with enamel painted decoration, with characteristic impressed title within elliptical panel above relief moulded swags.

Table bases have a variety of details which can be used to classify them, on the form of table and foot, bocage (where it exists) and moulded figures on the table bases. One feature is common to many of the groups and consists of small sprays of flowers applied to the base. These appear to be very similar in many cases and may indicate a common manufacturer using a range of similar sprig moulds, or the slight differences could indicate that several manufacturers are involved. Without further evidence it is not possible to give a definitive judgement. The table base groups have been subdivided here by obvious differences of base and bocage.

Group entitled 'ALE-BENCH', pearl glazed earthenware with overglaze enamel painted decoration, made in Staffordshire, c.1830, ht. 241mm. *Royal Pavilion Art Gallery & Museum, Brighton, HW1476.*
This example is on a ridged foot table base and has a version of a turreted building and a distinctive bocage.

Reverse of 'ALE-BENCH' with view of turreted background.

Detail of front of single leaf bocage with four petalled floret on ridged foot table base group titled 'GRECIAN & DAUGHTER'.

'GRECIAN & DAUGHTER', pearl glazed earthenware with overglaze enamel painted decoration, made in Staffordshire, c.1830, ht. 260mm. *Royal Pavilion Art Gallery & Museum, Brighton, HW 598.*
The figure with ridged foot table base and single leaf bocage with four petalled floret.

Detail of reverse of single leaf bocage on ridged foot table base group titled 'ALE-BENCH'.

Figure group titled 'W. CORDER & M. MARTEN', pearl glazed earthenware with overglaze painted decoration, made in Staffordshire, c.1828, ht. 196mm. *Royal Pavilion Art Gallery & Museum, Brighton, HW608.*
This figure group with ridged foot table base, was made to commemorate the murder at the Red Barn, Polstead, near Bury St. Edmunds, Suffolk. In 1827 Maria Marten was shot, stabbed and strangled, then buried beneath the floor of the Red Barn. William Corder was arrested, tried and found guilty of her murder and in 1828 was publicly hanged at Bury.

Detail of front of triple leaf spray bocage with three florets.

Detail of reverse of triple leaf spray bocage.

Figure entitled 'THE READING MAID', pearl glazed earthenware with overglaze enamel painted decoration, made in Staffordshire, c.1825-30, ht. 305mm. *Royal Pavilion Art Gallery & Museum, Brighton, HW1532.*

This example on a pearl beaded foot, with triple leaf spray bocage with three florets. The subject of the reading maid appears to have been popular with a number of manufacturers and made over a number of years, see pp. 110 and 183.

Detail of pearl beaded foot, the title often appears in an elliptical panel on the front of the base.

Figure group entitled 'COURT SHIP' pearl glazed earthenware with overglaze enamel painted decoration, made in Staffordshire, c.1825-30, ht. 190mm. *Royal Pavilion Art Gallery & Museum, Brighton, HW1634.*

This example is not on a table base but has the triple leaf spray bocage with three florets found on some pearl beaded foot table bases.

comprehensive, lists for Burslem, 'Sherratt Obadiah, toy and figure maker, Hot Lane'. This discrepancy may lie in the degree of detail included in the directories or may indicate that Sherratt's business was either too new or too small for Pigot's consideration. It is not unreasonable to suggest that Sherratt was established in business in a small way by about 1820. Some ten years later he had removed to premises in nearby Waterloo Road, which by 1846 was listed in the occupancy of Hamlet Sherratt, figure manufacturer.[18] By 1859 the premises were advertised for sale; the description suggests a manufactory on a small scale, consistent with all other evidence relating to the manufacture of figures. The *Staffordshire Advertiser* of May 1859 gives notice of an auction including 'Dwelling house...and extensive frontage to the road, No 13 occupied by owner Hamlet Sherratt and a compact & convenient China Toy Mfy an oven and enamelling kiln with usual workshops & showrooms'.

Obviously Obadiah Sherratt made something. Woolliscroft Rhead wrote also that he produced a number of cow cream jugs and tells us of 'a joke long current in the Potteries to the effect that Sherratt formed the teats of his cows and Wellington's nose from the same mould!'[19] (this could lead to two figures which could be identified). The only positively attributable piece of Sherratt's manufacture is a frog mug, two of which impressed 'O. SHERRATT' are known and are the only pieces which can be assigned to him with any degree of confidence or accuracy.

The table base groups appear on a variety of moulded feet, but many other moulded features seem to link the models together, suggesting that very few and possibly only one or two makers are responsible. Considering the complexity and massive scale of some of the pieces it is most surprising to find no indication of maker. However, the vogue for anonymity seems to have swept through the figure making fraternity from the 1830s onwards, for the amazing numbers of Victorian portrait figures have even less distinguishing features on which to begin a serious classification.

The number of table base groups is quite small compared to bocage figures, and there are many subjects which are seen over and over again. Polito's and Wombwell's menageries are particularly numerous in museum and private collections, if not exactly freely available at the average antiques fair. Some of the menageries appear to have come from the same hand, with a range of component moulded figures assembled in various combinations to give variety, but others are quite different from the standard model, and one wonders if it would pay one maker to have several Politos or Wombwells in stock or whether more than one factory is involved. In the light of current knowledge it is not possible to answer this question.

The comparison of moulded features may enable one or two self-contained groups of table base figures to be assembled, but the cross-referencing of these

18. *Williams' Commercial Directory for Stafford and the Potteries*, J. Williams, 1846.
19. Rhead, op.cit., p.297.

Christening group, pearl glazed earthenware with overglaze painted decoration, made in Staffordshire, c.1830, ht. 203mm. *Royal Pavilion Art Gallery and Museum, Brighton, HW210.*

This example with pearl beaded foot and a version of the turreted building, the bocage is of a swirling leaf form which links this group to another form of table base, see p.271.

Detail of front of swirling leaf bocage with single multi-petalled florets.

Detail of reverse of swirling leaf bocage.

Figure group depicting Jesus in the Garden of Gethsemene titled 'O MY.FATHER.LET.THIS.CUP. PASS.FROM.ME.', pearl glazed earthenware with overglaze enamel painted decoration, made in Staffordshire, c.1830, ht. 311mm. *Royal Pavilion Art Gallery & Museum, Brighton, HW765.*
This example on grotesque footed base with the swirling leaf bocage seen on pearl beaded foot groups.

Figure group depicting Abraham about to sacrifice his son Isaac, titled 'ABRAHAM STOP' and with appropriate text from Genesis Ch.22, pearl glazed earthenware with overglaze enamel painted decoration, made in Staffordshire, c.1830, ht. 304mm. *Royal Pavilion Art Gallery & Museum, Brighton, HW739.*
This example on grotesque footed table base with a standard five fingered leaf spray bocage.

Detail of grotesque footed table base, larger figure groups may have an additional centre foot.

'POLITOS' menagerie, pearl glazed earthenware with overglaze enamel painted decoration, made in Staffordshire, c.1830, ht. 307mm. *Royal Pavilion Art Gallery & Museum, Brighton, HW1220.*
This example has a grotesque footed table base.

Detail of grotesque footed table base with additional centre foot.

One of the world's first zoos was the Royal Menagerie, which was established in the Tower of London, when three leopards were given to King Henry III. Visitors were admitted to view the ever-growing collection of animals and there were popular demands for wider access to 'Living curiosities of the known world'. The Exeter Change in London was host to one of the most famous menageries and one of its earliest proprietors, a Mr Pidcock, also toured animals around the country from the 1780s. The Exeter Change menagerie was in the hands of Mr S. Polito from at least 1810, and for some years before this time he had toured a menagerie throughout England. Polito died in April 1814, but a touring show continued in his name for many years; a number of circus authorities have written that the end finally came when the menagerie and the ship transporting it were lost crossing the Irish Sea on the way to tour Ireland in 1836.

'POLITOS' menagerie, pearl glazed earthenware with overglaze enamel painted decoration, made in Staffordshire, c.1830, ht. 324mm. *Sotheby's London.*
This example has a grotesque footed table base.

details is not an easy task. Features worth noting are details of legs of base, bocage, moulded backgrounds such as the turrets that are commonly found, moulded figures and floral sprays. It is very difficult to make these comparisons from photographs or from memory of pieces in many collections. Unfortunately, no large collection of table base groups is known to me and therefore the simple classification undertaken here may require further refinement in the future.

One source of additional information lies buried deep, for quite literally, the City of Stoke-on-Trent is built on the accumulated ceramic waste of generations. It is almost impossible to put a spade into the earth without finding pottery fragments. Inevitably the great majority of waste is tableware, the major product of the industry. Few figure fragments are found, but of those that have been recovered, not a single piece from a table base group has been noted. It can only be hoped that one day a hole in the ground will reveal all.

'WOMBWELL' menagerie, pearl glazed earthenware with overglaze enamel painted decoration, made in Staffordshire, c.1830, ht. 280mm. *Royal Pavilion Art Gallery & Museum, Brighton, HW1219.*
The base is broken, but appears to be the grotesque footed type.

Mr Wombwell's travelling menagerie began its peregrinations throughout Britain c.1807 and by the time of his death in 1850 there were three travelling menageries belonging to the family, the last appearing to continue until 1884.

Figure groups depicting these menageries usually include a number of showmen and women, together with musicians, in front of a door which leads to the animals, above this is the painted advertising canvas with the name of the menagerie and a legend which usually reads 'ROYAL. MENAGERIE. OF. THE. WONDERFULL. BURDS. AND. BEASTS. FROM. MOST. PARTS. OF. THE. WORLD. LIONS. &c.'

Figure group titled 'SAMUEL.ANOINTED.DAVED. SAMUEL.CH.16', pearl glazed earthenware with overglaze enamel painted decoration, made in Staffordshire, c.1830, ht. 241mm. *City Museum & Art Gallery, Stoke-on-Trent, 608.*
This example is on a variation of the grotesque footed table base, the table top is stepped and the modelling of the figures is unlike that of the standard grotesque footed pieces.

Figure group titled 'PETTER.RISING.THE.LAME. MAN.ACTS.CH.3', pearl glazed earthenware with overglaze enamel painted decoration, made in Staffordshire, c.1830, ht. 261mm. *Royal Pavilion Art Gallery & Museum, Brighton, HW786.*
This example is on a variation of the grotesque footed table base, the table top is stepped and the modelling is unlike that of the standard grotesque footed pieces.

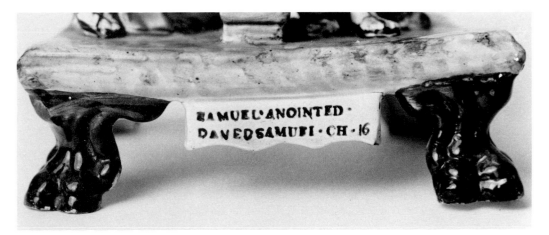

Detail of variation of grotesque footed base, the foot has less moulding and does not stretch right across the stand but stops either side of a title plaque.

7. The Real Thing

Many collectors, and even museum curators, worry about whether they have the real thing in their possession or whether they have been deceived. It is most unnerving to have doubt cast upon one's treasures, not only if the piece has cost a lot of money to acquire, but also if the piece has claimed a special place in one's affections. The loss of face associated with owning a non-genuine piece is as acute as the loss of finance. Figures are not normally bought merely for their superficial attractiveness: whilst the true lovers of earthenware figures will never buy a piece they do not like, they do not buy only a pretty piece, they buy a piece of history. Whether they are conscious of the fact or not, collectors buy a piece of the past which speaks to them. It may say 'Don't I have a sensual, silky eighteenth century glaze?' or 'Am I not a good example of how much better craftsmanship was in the past?' or 'Here I am 200 years old and no one else in this antique fair has recognised me'. Whatever your piece says to you, if you find you have been deceived and the piece was made yesterday, then its prettiness is as nothing. The associated values of quality, craftsmanship and age are amongst the intangible, yet vital aspects which make a figure desirable or disreputable.

In order to learn more about fakes, reproductions and forgeries I thought it would be a good idea to have a rogues gallery at the City Museum & Art Gallery, Stoke-on-Trent, but I found it almost impossible to assemble. No one admits to selling such pieces and therefore it is difficult to buy them, except at genuine prices. I hoped that collectors might show me some of their 'wrong' pieces, but I never met any collectors who had any they wished to publicise. The only place one can openly talk about fakes is in museums, where curators can always blame someone else for their acquisition and therefore avoid loss of face. One other place where one can talk in whispers about fakes is behind the scenes in auction houses, where occasionally a black museum is kept for the purpose of training and comparison. I believe that a museum of fakes and forgeries would be a useful adjunct to the reserve collections at Stoke and hope that one day we can unashamedly say 'Come and see our fakes'.

The terms 'fakes', 'forgeries' and 'reproductions' are emotive and confusing, therefore it would be best to set out my terms of reference before entering the perilous world of identification.

The term 'fake' will be used to cover all those pieces made deliberately to deceive, that is pieces made to imitate earlier figures and intended to be sold as such. Fakes are not common and will not feature widely in this chapter. The term 'reproduction' implies those pieces made in imitation, usually of an earlier figure. Reproductions are not necessarily made to deceive, some even have modern factory marks proclaiming their true origins but others are left anonymous. The manufacturers of anonymous examples sell to wholesalers and some offer the choice of crazed or uncrazed pieces in an attempt to provide a realistic product, declaring that they have no responsibility for their subsequent sale description. The reproduction market is most buoyant in the area of Victorian portrait figures, which lies outside the scope of this volume, but some bocage figures are also made.

Pair of lion and unicorn figures, made by Beswick, Staffordshire, c.1985-7, ht. 145mm. *City Museum & Art Gallery, Stoke-on-Trent, 460.P.1987.*

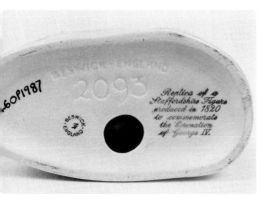

Base of unicorn showing full factory marks (and museum accession number) indicating that the figures are reproductions.

Two figures of lions: left made by Beswick 1985-7; right, impressed 'WALTON' on a scroll, c.1820, ht. 150mm. *City Museum & Art Gallery, Stoke-on-Trent, 460.P.1987, 1408.* The difference in colour is not just the taste of the period, but the technical changes in colours and glazes which offer a wider palette in the 20th century.

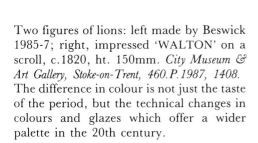

Reverse of two lions: left made by Beswick 1985-7; right, impressed 'WALTON' on a scroll, c.1820, ht. 150mm. *City Museum & Art Gallery, Stoke-on-Trent, 460.P.1987, 1408.* The reverse shows the simple, all-in-one moulding of the bocage on the 20th century example; this is a modern, economical way of reproducing the tree-like structure at the back of the figure.

One of the more difficult areas to assess is that of traditional manufacture, by which is meant that some potteries never stopped making Staffordshire figures in the early nineteenth century style. William Kent of Burslem is the most well known of these traditional makers because of the company catalogues which still exist. Kent's continued until the 1960s and their moulds have been passed on to other potters since then. In a similar way Leeds Pottery figure production was continued from about 1890 to 1957 by the Senior family and marketed by W.W. Slee. I cannot believe that bocage figures were so desirable in the early years of the present century that there was a great deal of money to be made from forging them. Kent's were merely continuing to produce an old-fashioned popular line. How many thousands of Jobson & Nell must have been sold at 80 shillings per dozen for large and 21 shillings for small? How many Jobson & Nell do you see advertised as twentieth century examples? Are these fakes when sold as early editions? They were not made as fakes but have been mis-attributed, either deliberately or through ignorance.

Mis-attribution is the most common form of confusion. Errors of this kind occur not only when reproductions are confused with originals, but also when nineteenth century foreign wares are confused with earlier English pieces. English creamware figures decorated with underglaze oxides were simple and fairly easy to produce, as pottery technology was in its infancy. It may not be surprising to find that Continental earthenware factories went through a similiar evolutionary process in the nineteenth century and that some of their products bear a likeness to those of an earlier period in England. When these enter the English antique market, they have an appearance similar to our own wares and may be accepted as such; an incomplete understanding of Continental earthenwares prevents us from discriminating between some English eighteenth century wares and similar later products.

Fakes are the easiest to deal with. The first figure fakes seem to have occurred in the 1915-25 period, when early creamware figures were at their most collectable and a veritable orchestra of musicians appeared on the market. The fakes were not identical to any known figures but were made to imitate them; in the making the potter used his twentieth century values and produced a twentieth century piece. The identification of the fakes has always been a subjective judgement until thermoluminescence testing confirmed expert opinion. The mid-eighteenth century originals may have been simply made, but they were not crudely made and it was this confusion that confounded the forger. The originals have much more detail in their depiction and are more robust in their demeanour; the fakes have narrow, mean shoulders and limbs with curves rather than joints. The use of names impressed into the reverse and on the bases proved to be the undoing of the faker, for his poor understanding of ceramic history led him to famous potters who would not have been in business at the time the originals were made, for there are pieces marked Wedgwood, Wood, and even Elers. No doubt there are other fakes yet to be recognised and inevitably, when early simple pieces

Two cream coloured earthenware figures with coloured oxide decoration under the glaze: left, made in Staffordshire, mid-18th century; right, impressed on reverse 'WOOD BURSLEM', early 20th century, ht. 124mm. *City Museum & Art Gallery, Stoke-on-Trent, 143.P.1949, 142.P.1949.*

Reverse of two cream coloured earthenware figures.

Fakes of mid-eighteenth century musicians and allied figures, appear to have been made during the 1915-25 period. It is likely that they were made in London in response to the high prices which collectors were prepared to pay for the simple, naïve models. The reproductions are not so detailed as the originals, they do not usually have a coat open over a waistcoat, nor the falls of lace at neck and wrist; the marking of buttons and buttonholes, pockets and pleats is either perfunctory or missing from the copies. (For further illustrations of originals see Chapter 1.)

can command a high price, there exists a great temptation for the unscrupulous to try their hand.

Reproductions, if they are not originally meant to deceive, should be easier to identify. Modern production methods are so unlike those of the early potteries in many ways that a comparison of making methods may help. Almost without exception early Staffordshire earthenware figures were made by the press moulding method, whereas modern copies use the slip casting process. These making methods are more fully explained elsewhere in this volume; only the physical result is of interest in assessing the date of a piece. When figures are press moulded, sheets of clay are pressed into the moulds, which results in figures with walls of varying thickness with a relatively smooth or flat interior. In slip casting a thin layer of clay is deposited evenly inside the moulds and the contours of the interior reflect the external shape of the figure. This is easy to see in the open base figures. When figures are placed on to square plinths it is not possible to see inside and therefore other features must be taken into consideration. One indication of press moulding is that it is

Two figure groups, early 20th century, ht. 127mm. *Colonial Williamsburg, 1963, 200 & 204.* See pages 35 and 36.

Equestrian group, early 20th century, impressed 'FELL' ht. 206mm. *Colonial Williamsburg, 1963, 2228.*
The impressed mark is not from the same die as the early 19th century Fell pieces.

A number of the creamware figures of the 1750-70 period have been reproduced; it is not possible to be confident that they were all made as fakes, for the Burslem School of Art in the Potteries encouraged young students to make copies of earlier wares in order to learn how the craft of pottery making evolved. Some of the copies may have subsequently been sold as original pieces. The problems experienced in trying to reproduce creamware figures are of two kinds, firstly of style and secondly of technique.

If the figures illustrated here are compared with their prototypes illustrated in Chapter 1, it is possible to see which figures were copied and that the modelling is not quite right, as it is more laboured and less natural. The originals have a soft, creamy, lead glaze, stained by iron occurring naturally in the raw materials. The improvements in preparing glazes and bodies meant that by the 20th century any cream colour had to be added to the glaze mix, and often the colour in no way resembles that of 18th century wares but can be a greeny-yellow rather than cream.

usually heavier than slip casting; this is a difficult assessment to make as steps could be taken to ensure the weight is amended, also one has to be very familiar with originals to dismiss an otherwise good figure on the grounds of weight alone. If a piece is crazed one may ask why? Crazing is not necessarily a sign of age, as some of the best pots of the eighteenth century exhibit no crazing at all. Crazing is induced by a fault in the piece which results in the glaze not fitting properly, which can happen during firing if the body and the glaze are incompatible, and thus it can be deliberately produced by making the necessary adjustments to the glaze and body mixes. During firing the body and glaze shrink; if the glaze shrinks faster or more than the body it will not 'fit' and therefore, like a small overcoat worn by a fat man, it splits at the seams. Earthenware which leaves the factory in perfect condition may subsequently become crazed if subjected to poor conditions in which it is cracked or chipped and the body is in some way exposed to the atmosphere; moisture may then

Two small bocage figures: left, shepherdess, impressed 'WALTON' on scroll, c.1970-2; right, cupid impressed 'WALTON' on scroll, c.1815-25, ht. 142mm. *City Museum & Art Gallery, Stoke-on-Trent, 11.P.1972, 1616.*
The late reproduction is much paler in colour and has florets moulded with the bocage rather than applied separately, which one would normally expect in an original. A shepherdess similar to this example, but placed on a square base, was advertised as 'GIRL WITH A LAMB No456' in William Kent's catalogues of 1955 and 1960.

Reverse of two 'WALTON' marked figures; left, c.1970-2; right, c.1815-25, ht. 142mm. *City Museum & Art Gallery, Stoke-on-Trent, 11.P.1972, 1616.*
The late reproduction has no bocage on the reverse and the mark 'WALTON' has no serifs; it is possible that earlier reproductions of Walton figures may have full bocage and period lettering.

The bases of two 'WALTON' marked figures; left, c.1970-2; right, c.1815-25. *City Museum & Art Gallery, Stoke-on-Trent, 11.P.1972, 1616.*
The reproduction on the left exhibits all the signs of slip casting, a technique popularly used for figure making in the 20th century. The interior reflects the contours of the exterior, as an even coating of clay has built up on the inside of the mould. The original example on the right exhibits all the signs of press moulding, the most popular 18th-19th century method of making earthenware figures, where the clay is pressed into the mould and smoothed so that the interior is relatively even and does not reflect the contours of the exterior.

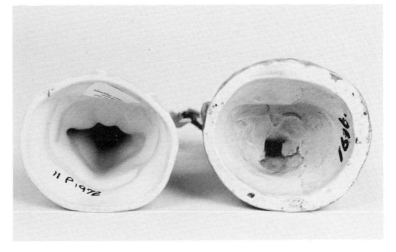

Figure group titled 'TENDERNESS', impressed 'WALTON' on a scroll on the reverse, early 20th century, ht. 506mm. *Temple Newsam House, Leeds 28/21/41.*

This example is of very white earthenware, quite untypical of the bluish pearl glaze of the original: the lettering of the title and of the potter's name is sanserif, the original would have had serifs; the subject 'Tenderness' in exactly the same size occurs as no. 506 in William Kent's catalogues of 1955 and 1960. For original see page 232.

be absorbed by the body, causing it to expand, thus stressing the glaze which cannot expand, and so crazing results. Deliberately induced crazing exhibits a different pattern from that which occurs accidentally. Therefore study your own pieces to become familiar with crazing on original models.

Decoration should also be scrutinised, for not only have technological advances been made which assist the pottery manufacturer in making reproductions, but legislation has been passed which prohibits the use of certain materials, and practices. Glazes with free lead can no longer be used, certain colours such as those produced by uranium and cadmium are banned and intermittent coal fired ovens have been superseded by a continuous firing process: these are some of the points which may indicate when a piece was made. Collectors will not always know the technical reasons for differences in glaze, colour or feel, but they should be aware that such differences may exist between right and wrong pieces.

Once a reproduction reaches the market it may be subjected to processes which promote the piece as an early example. There are ways of ageing wares in the same way that furniture can be distressed. One common practice has been to darken the crazing, making it look as if it has been subjected to the dirt and grime of many years, however, the story exists that a good cup of coffee can be made by pouring boiling water over the piece and thus releasing the colouring agent. It is not known at what stage this additional process occurs, but it must make reproductions into fakes. It is not advocated that the boiling water test is tried on any pieces, but just be aware that the means of

Two figures of sheep; left, impressed 'SALT' on a ribbon, c.1820-30; right, c.1970-2, ht. 160mm. *City Museum & Art Gallery, Stoke-on-Trent, 57.P.1962, 6.P.1972.*
The reproduction on the right is very white in the body but very heavily crazed and stained, which is not typical of 19th century pieces.

Reverse of two figures of sheep; left, c.1820-30; right, c.1970-2.

Bases of two sheep.
The reproduction on the left is enclosed, which is typical of modern reproductions; the heavy, stained crazing is more obvious from this angle, the foot ring is dry and exhibits signs of wear as if it has been rubbed over sandpaper, a feature which one would not expect to find on an original piece. The original Salt sheep on the right exhibits the typical features of an early 19th century press moulded figure, with the open base with smooth interior not reflecting the contours of the exterior.

Plate from *Olde Staffordshire Ware, The Story of Old Staffordshire Pottery* by William Kent of Burslem, published c.1955.

The top picture is titled 'Craftsmen at work' in which the workers appear to be releasing parts of figures from the moulds and assembling them. On the shelf in the background is a range of factory products and a large jug for pouring slip into moulds in a continuous stream, to produce a smooth cast. The centre left picture is titled 'A second generation craftsman at Kent's' and depicts a worker releasing parts from a plaster mould; cow cream jugs stand on the shelf behind.

The centre right picture is titled 'Our youngest artist' and depicts a young woman painting what appears to be animal figures. On the shelf behind are what appear to be a shepherdess and the figure of a man on a square base. The bottom picture is titled 'Artists All' and depicts a typical factory painting shop. On the table in the foreground is the figure which is commonly known as 'The Parson & Clerk', but which Kent calls 'Inebriates'; other figures which can be seen include a Dr. Syntax, a sheep, Virgin and Child and a Toby jug.

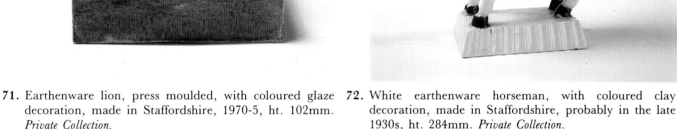

71. Earthenware lion, press moulded, with coloured glaze decoration, made in Staffordshire, 1970-5, ht. 102mm. *Private Collection.*

This piece is based on a Wood & Caldwell lion (see page 166). It was not made as a copy or as a fake 18th century piece but as a contemporary ornamental figure reflecting an interest in the past. Whilst some inexperienced collector might mistake the lion for an 18th century coloured glaze piece this confusion should not arise for this type of glaze decoration is not compatible with a model in the early 19th century style.

72. White earthenware horseman, with coloured clay decoration, made in Staffordshire, probably in the late 1930s, ht. 284mm. *Private Collection.*

This figure is modelled from a white salt glazed stoneware horseman, an example of which can be found in the Victoria & Albert Museum. The piece was probably made for the amusement of the modeller and is similar to a range of rolled clay figures produced by students at Burslem School of Art. The naïvety of the modelling and the simple 18th century subject should not really deceive a collector, for the piece is a very white, clear glazed earthenware of a type associated with more recent pottery production.

73. Two cats, earthenware with underglaze oxide and coloured glaze decoration, Continental, late 19th century, ht. 110mm. *Private Collections.*

The cats are made of a cream coloured earthenware heavily speckled with impurities. They are modelled and decorated in a traditional style, which is superficially similar to 18th century Staffordshire wares. When Staffordshire potters began to refine their wares many Continental factories continued in the traditional manner; their work was not created to copy early Staffordshire wares but is sometimes misattributed. The cat on the left has the impressed mark of the factory of Manuel Cipriano Gomes Mafra founded at Caldas da Rainha, Portugal in 1853, this mark dates from the 1870s. The cat on the right had been sold with an old exhibition label attached giving provenance: on checking the exhibition label it was discovered that it had been removed from a plate that had been exhibited and attached to the cat to give it some authenticity!

Pages from the earliest known of the catalogues produced by William Kent entitled 'Price List William Kent Manufacturer of Earthenware Figures etc. including reproductions of Old Staffordshire Ware', the catalogue is undated but is thought to be from c.1926-35. Some of Kent's wares were marked with a Staffordshire knot and the words 'Olde Staffordshire Ware', but this mark is often abraded so that the late date of the piece is not so obvious. Note the figure of St. Sebastian; for the original see page 190.

deceit are many and devious. One of the most cynical and useless practices observed is that of removing manufacturers' marks. I would willingly buy a piece of Kent's Olde Staffordshire Ware if a marked example could be found, but only damaged pieces exist in which the glaze is abraded where the mark used to be: again the point is reached where a reproduction is turned into a fake.

The traditional manufacturers have made the greatest contribution to our confusion. William Kent began in business in 1878, presumably with a stock of second-hand moulds which included marked Walton figures, which at the time would have been considered old-fashioned rather than antique. If Kent produced his novelty and gift ware from that date, how are we to tell which pieces he made in 1890, 1920 and 1960, or indeed were made in 1980 by Kent's successors? We can use some of the assessments suggested in the section

287

74

75

76

77

74-81. Pages from a catalogue of *Old Staffordshire Pottery* produced by William Kent of Burslem in 1955. William Kent's factory was established in about 1878 and appears to have acquired an assortment of old figure models which they continued to produce until 1962. Since that time some of the models have been leased to other small figure making factories. The figures included marked 'WALTON' pieces and models known with an earlier Enoch Wood mark. The author of the catalogue writes: 'Kents "Old Staffordshire" pottery is not "reproduction" in the strictest sense of the word,

78

79

80

81

because, except for a period during the wartime, the pottery has been produced continuously from the early days. We who appreciate these examples of a period in Staffordshire pottery have to thank members of the Kent family for preserving the manufacture of traditional pottery at the expense of modern development'.

Some of the figures may be found with a Staffordshire Knot mark and the words 'Olde Staffordshire Ware'. The vast majority of pieces are unmarked and occasionally even the marked examples have the details erased.

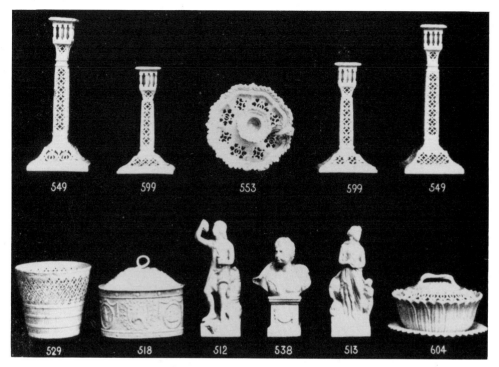

Plate from *Reproductions of Leeds Pottery. . .* published by W.W. Slee of Leeds, October 1913; the pottery was made by J.W. & G.W. Senior from the 1890s to 1957 and many of the old Leeds moulds were used. In this plate are seen 512 Bacchus ht. 7inches price 5shillings; 538 Air ht. 6inches price 4sh.6d; 513 Charity ht. 6½inches price 3sh6d. *Courtesy Leeds Central Library.*

Plate from *Reproductions of Leeds Pottery. . .* published by W.W. Slee of Leeds, October 1913; the pottery was made by J.W & G.W. Senior from the 1890s to 1957 and many of the old Leeds moulds were used. In this plate are seen 593 Shepherd ht. 8inches price 3sh6d; 517 bust of Shakespeare ht. 13inches price 10sh.6d; Horse ht. 16½inches price £1.10sh. *Courtesy Leeds Central Library.*

on reproductions and we can also apply further tests. The main point of making pottery is to make money, manufacturers therefore choose the cheapest way of solving a problem and over the years certain adaptations may have been made by manufacturers to reduce production costs. Certainly later bocage figures do not have leaves attached to the back of the tree-like support, and a cheap form of bright gold is used, which emerges from the kiln with a brassy shine, rather than the more expensive deep golden gilding which requires burnishing after the firing. The range of colours will be confined to those which fire at the same temperature and during the twentieth century the introduction of new sources of colour means that the palette widens. The materials for making pottery have improved over the years and many of the later pieces will have a very white body and clear glaze, except in the case of the Leeds pieces, where a cream coloured earthenware was produced by means of a stained glaze.

It is almost impossible to learn to differentiate between originals and fakes or copies from reading alone. Photographs may help, but what one needs to do is to see and handle a large number of good pieces. Many museums have collections which include figures and if the curator is assured that your visit is for serious study you may be allowed to handle pieces. Even if you are not allowed to handle, visit and look. Find out when the pieces were collected by museums: if they have labels with accession numbers this may offer a clue, as obviously a piece must have been made some time before its acquisition and if that was some time in the nineteenth century then there is more chance of it being original.

Auction houses and good vetted antiques fairs are also places to visit to see and handle fine quality pieces. Reputable dealers may not be too pleased to think that their stock is being used as a teaching collection, but if they understand that you are familiarising yourself with the subject prior to starting a collection, then you are likely to be treated with great courtesy and offered sound advice as a potential long term customer.

It is impossible to be 100% sure about any figure, because there may be fakes in existence which we are using as type specimens, forming a basis for assessing all other pieces. There are some pieces which one feels instinctively are correct: the reliability of one's instinct is in direct proportion to experience. There are other pieces which shout 'I was made yesterday', and again the reliability of this communication is in direct proportion to experience. There is, however, a vast grey middle area in which suspect pieces are 'let off' for lack of evidence, when the verdict 'unproven' offers little comfort, and when no amount of experience gives one a definitive result. If a new model turns up, a new style of decoration appears, or a new subject is discovered, should you condemn it merely because in your limited experience you have never seen its like?

No one can guarantee that you will never meet a fake, even though fakes must be greatly outnumbered by the genuine article; no one can guarantee that

82. Two classical figures, made from a yellow clay with coloured clay and coloured glaze decoration, made in Apt, France, 19th century, ht. 238mm. *City Museum & Art Gallery, Stoke-on-Trent, 125 & 126.P.1933.*

Figures of this type are not widely known outside France and may be misattributed to 18th century Staffordshire because of their naïve modelling and familiar subject matter. However, figures of this colour body were not made in Staffordshire.

83. King and Queen, decorated with underglaze oxides and coloured glazes, 19th century, ht. 173mm. *City Museum & Art Gallery, Stoke-on-Trent, 161 & 169.P.1949.*

Occasionally referred to as King Arthur and Queen Guinevere, these pieces were once thought to be excellent examples of mid-18th century Staffordshire pottery. However, recent examinations of the details of modelling, body, decoration and glaze have led to the conclusion that these are 19th century pieces, origin as yet unknown.

84. Chinese manservant, made from buff coloured clay with coloured glaze decoration, made in China, 19th century, ht. 202mm. *City Museum & Art Gallery, Stoke-on-Trent, 4293.*

Examples of this kind of figure are occasionally found misattributed to Staffordshire; this particular example has an old collection label which reads 'An Astbury figure of a chinaman'.

85. Two musicians, cream coloured earthenware with underglaze oxide decoration, c.1920, ht. 122mm. *City Museum & Art Gallery, Stoke-on-Trent, 139 & 140. P.1949.*

86. These two musicians show the lack of detailed modelling of the fakes. Compare these two with black and white illustrations in Chapter 1 and Chapter 7.

87. Girl with an apron of flowers, white earthenware with overglaze enamel painting and gilding, made in Staffordshire, 1972, ht. 202mm. *City Museum & Art Gallery, Stoke-on-Trent, 5.P.1972.*

This example is based on an early model but the decoration is thoroughly modern. The enamel colours are pale and patchy; the black outline around the bodice is poorly painted and would not be found on an original. Gilding is not normally found on 18th and early 19th century figures; in the rare exceptions the gilding is usually worn but where it still remains is a deep rich gold; the reproduction has modern liquid gold which has a harsh glittery finish.

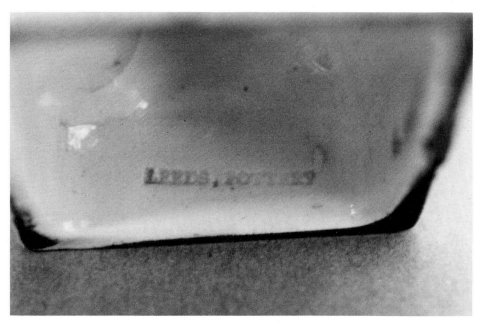

Impressed mark 'LEEDS.POTTERY', found on the work of J.W. & G.W. Senior 1890s-1957. Note the stop between the words LEEDS and POTTERY.

Sheep and lamb, impressed 'LEEDS.POTTERY', made by the Senior family 1890s-early 1900s (see page from the Slee catalogue) ht. 126mm. *Temple Newsam House, Leeds.* This example is of a hard body and very bright enamel painted decoration.

Bacchus & Venus, creamware, undecorated, impressed 'LEEDS.POTTERY', made by
the Senior family, 1890s-early 1900s (see page from the Slee catalogue), ht. 185mm.
Temple Newsam House, Leeds, 16.192/47, 16.195/47.
This example is of a hard body with finely crackled glaze.

you will not buy a reproduction in mistake for the real thing. It is up to the
individual to study the subject; if you find a bargain, be suspicious; if a twin
replaces the piece you have just bought, be very suspicious; if a dealer is
reluctant to give a receipt with a description, ask yourself why?

In the end it comes down to you, your taste, your confidence and your
instinct; for some collectors this challenge is avoided by buying only from
reputable dealers with a money back guarantee; for others, the risk, the search,
the challenge, is the motivating force. Whichever kind of collector you are, use
mistakes as learning experiences and through them come to a more thorough
appreciation of the genuine article.

88 and 89.

The death of Munroe, white earthenware with overglaze painted decoration, the base with painted inscription 'Obadiah Sherratt', 20th century, ht. 165mm. *Private Collection.*

This piece purports to be by Obadiah Sherratt, who potted in Burslem from around 1820 to 1845. The group is not a 19th century example but has typical 20th century features, it is of a modern white earthenware rather than pearl glaze, it is slip cast rather than press moulded and the colours are from a bright modern range some of which were not available in the 19th century. Here a modern figure maker has fallen victim to 20th century speculations that Sherratt may have made table base figures and has allowed this unsubstantiated theory to influence his figure reproductions.

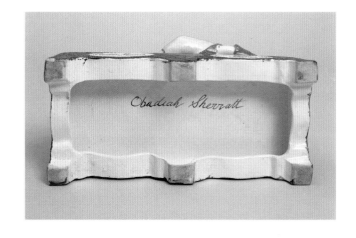

8. Techniques of Figure Making

Many collectors dismiss the technical development of figure making as superfluous information. Others feel that the very word technical infers that the processes involved are beyond the understanding of the average person. I hope to show that this additional facet of information will help to add a new dimension to the enjoyment derived from ceramics.

Methods of making pottery changed in the eighteenth and nineteenth centuries and styles evolved to reflect the changes in taste and fashion. An understanding of making methods will help the collector to place a figure in its historical context as well as giving the added pleasure of enjoying the craftsmanship involved in its production. Perhaps even more important is that an appreciation of techniques may assist in recognising the date of production and distinguishing between original pieces and later copies.

The technology involved in pottery making is relatively simple and easy to understand, as hands are the major tools, assisted by moulds. Terms used to describe pottery processes may be unfamiliar, but they are likely to be simple dialect and much more friendly than modern computer jargon.

Clay Preparation

Staffordshire's native clays vary in colour from a grey/buff to dark red/brown. White clays are rarely found and not in large enough quantities to fulfil the requirements of the local industry. The majority of figures produced in Staffordshire in the period under discussion were made from white clays imported from Devon and Dorset. These clays were transported by sea, river and land and later by canal, to the Potteries where they were prepared for pottery making. There they were mixed with water, sieved and combined with other ingredients, such as ground flint, before being dried to a plastic consistency.

Figures were made from either liquid clay or plastic clay. Liquid clay is known as slip and is formed by mixing a proportion of water with the clay mixture which is stirred either manually or mechnically until an even, cream-like consistency is achieved. Plastic clay must contain no air bubbles, which can expand and burst during the firing cycle, so all the air has to be removed, either manually in a process called wedging in which the clay is kneaded to a homogeneous mass, or mechanically using a pug-mill, which is not unlike a large sausage machine.

After the clay has been prepared for use it is sent to the relevant workshop for the next process.

Hand Modelling

Hand modelling, the most primitive form of clay manipulation, involves taking the moist raw material and by squeezing, rolling and pinching, a figure gradually emerges. This is the method a child might use with any malleable material such as clay or plasticine.

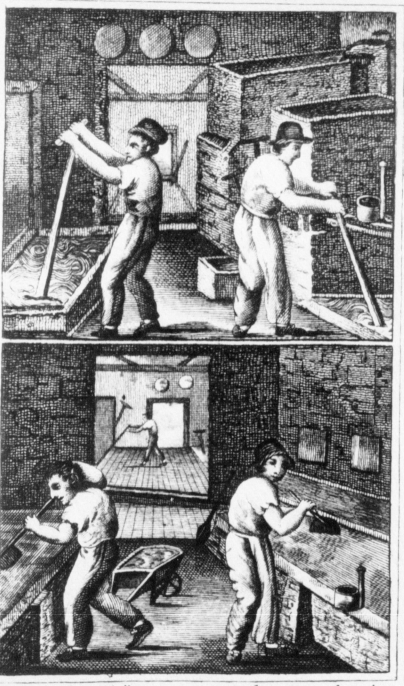

"Blending" or mixing the materials with water, forming a Compound called Slip.

"Boiling the Slip" to evaporate the water, leaving a clay about the consistence of dough.

Top: ' "Blending" or mixing the materials with water, forming a Compound called Slip" '. Bottom: ' "Boiling the Slip" to evaporate the water, leaving a clay about the consistence of dough'. *Enoch Wood's Manufactory 1827.*
These two illustrations show stages of clay preparation; once an homogeneous, plastic consistency is achieved, the clay can either be used for pressing or mixed with water to make slip.

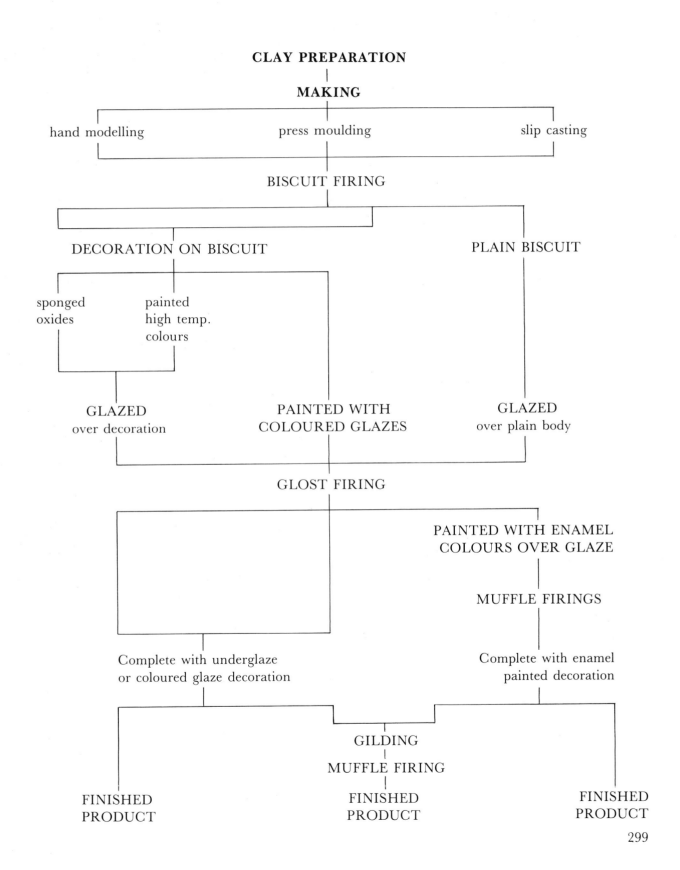

Modelling final details of figure

Hand modelling of figures has been used from the earliest times and is still used by children and sculptors today, many early Staffordshire figures were moulded but had hand modelled details.

Figures of horsemen, earthenware with coloured slips and underglaze oxide decoration, made in Staffordshire, c.1760-80. *Weldon Collection.*
The basic figures are press moulded but the accoutrements are hand modelled.

The Moddler or Sculptor from whose productions are taken casts or moulds for the potter.

'The Moddler or Sculptor from whose productions are taken casts or moulds for the potters', *Enoch Wood's Manufactory 1827*.

Except for a short period in the twentieth century, completely hand modelled figures are exceptionally rare in Staffordshire earthenware and may be confined to a few pew groups (most of which are salt-glazed stoneware). Hand modelled details, however, may be found on moulded figures and include musical instruments, soldiers' accoutrements or horse harness. The technique of hand modelling is not really commercially viable in an industrial context, but small country potters may have continued to produce figures this way.

A hand modelled figure is likely to be one of the following: either a rare mid-eighteenth century example from Staffordshire; a country pottery production of eighteenth-twentieth century date; a foreign earthenware production akin to our country pottery; a twentieth century studio piece in a contemporary style, or a twentieth century piece in imitation of an earlier example. Features of style, decoration and glaze, as well as the production method, may help to resolve the difficult problems of authenticity and these points are covered in other chapters.

Moulding

Moulding is a more complicated method of production than hand modelling but is still fairly simple to understand. The widespread adoption of plaster of Paris moulds is said to have begun about 1740-5 when they were introduced to North Staffordshire by Ralph Daniel and their use was advocated for production of tea and table wares.

Figure of Winter, earthenware decorated with coloured glazes, made in Staffordshire, c.1780-1800, ht. 115mm. *City Museum & Art Gallery, Stoke-on-Trent 162.P.1949.*
This simple model is made from a two-part mould consisting of the front half and back half of the figure.

Pair of musicians, the man with hurdy-gurdy the woman with castanets, man impressed '74', woman impressed '73', earthenware decorated with coloured glazes, made in Staffordshire, c.1780-1800, ht. 160mm. *Wisbech & Fenland Museum, 1900.55 & 59.*
These are complex moulded figures, the basic torso from one two-part mould, with separately moulded parts including arms, head, musical instrument, feet/legs, bases and cloak.

The first stage in the moulding process is to acquire a model which is a full-scale prototype. The majority of models are made of clay, carved and hand built by craftsmen. It has been suggested that during the late eighteenth and early nineteenth centuries fashionable plaster models may have been acquired from specialist makers in London, to provide sources for the model or block makers.

Once a satisfactory clay model is constructed, moulds may be taken using plaster of Paris. The peculiar qualities of plaster and the process of making master and working moulds need not detain us here as more detailed descriptions are available elsewhere for those whose appetites have been whetted.

The completed plaster of Paris mould is a negative of the required figure. Streamlined figures with no appendages could be made from a simple two-part mould reflecting the front and the reverse of the figure. Subjects with extended limbs or extra details such as additional people or animals, would be broken down at the model stage into constituent parts, each part requiring its own mould, and the moulded parts would then be made, dried and later assembled with slip (clay mixed with water to a creamy consistency) before firing. The use of multiple moulds to create a figure or group added considerably to the cost, requiring capital investment in expensive moulds and in extra production expenditure, with additional time needed to assemble the completed item.

Plaster of Paris moulds can be made for use in two different production methods, either press moulding or slip casting.

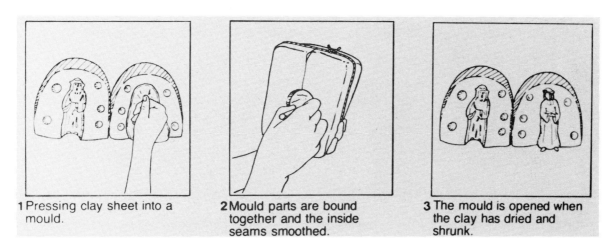

1 Pressing clay sheet into a mould.

2 Mould parts are bound together and the inside seams smoothed.

3 The mould is opened when the clay has dried and shrunk.

Stages in making a simple two-part press moulded figure, where complex figures are made using a number of small moulds to produce the requisite parts before assemblage.

Press moulding

Press moulding involved taking plastic clay and flattening or batting it out into small thin sheets. One of these sheets was pressed firmly into each half of the negative mould, with care taken to fill every crevice. Like many seemingly simple procedures this was an extremely skilled task, as pressure had to be evenly and strongly applied to avoid air pockets, which could mar the surface, rendering a figure imperfect, e.g. a head with an incomplete nose would have to be scrapped, wasting time and money.

When clay had been satisfactorily pressed into both halves of the mould, the edges were moistened with water or slip and the two halves brought together and bound tightly. Some moulds had an open base through which the seams were smoothed and consolidated, a long narrow tool could be inserted into tall thin pieces to complete this process. If necessary a thin roll of clay could be pressed into the joint to give added strength.

The plaster of Paris mould absorbed water from the clay causing it to dry and shrink away from the surface of the mould, and when the clay became firm the piece was released. The mould was then set to dry before it could be used again. The moulded piece was also put to dry until it was leather hard and could be safely handled. At this stage the seam lines were fettled or smoothed away using paring tools and any surface imperfections were removed by towing or sponging, i.e. using tow or coarse hemp or natural sponge to polish the surface.

If the moulded item was complete in itself it was now ready for the first firing. If it was only part of an elaborate assemblage the pieces had to be joined together. This was done using slip as an adhesive medium and the process was known as 'sticking up'. The resulting union was very strong and after a final sponge the piece was ready for firing.

 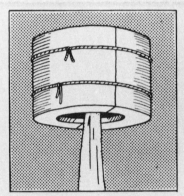 

1 The mould parts are bound together and filled with slip; as the water is absorbed, the level drops and more slip is added

2 When enough water is absorbed to deposit a layer of clay inside, the mould is inverted and the remaining slip is poured out

3 When the pot has dried and shrunk from the mould it is released.

Stages in slip casting; it is likely that the body of the figure will need added moulded limbs, etc.

Slip casting

The use of liquid clay in making earthenware figures was not common until the twentieth century. It is a more costly method of production and thus was reserved for those wares which could command a sufficient price to cover the extra costs in making. The additional expense came from the fact that a large quantity of water was needed to produce slip, which, when poured into the mould, saturated the plaster of Paris. This absorption, together with natural evaporation, left a thin skin of clay on the interior walls of the mould. When the skin reached the desired thickness the moulds were inverted and the excess slip poured out. It took some time before the figure was firm enough to be

A Potters Oven when firing or baking, the ware being therein placed in Safeguards, or Saggers.

'A Potters Oven when firing or baking the ware being therein placed in Safeguards or saggers'. *Enoch Wood's Manufactory 1827.*
The ovens in which the wares are fired are protected by an outer wall, which rises into a chimney, which helps to create the right draught to assist in the firing process, this bottle-like construction around the oven is known as a hovel.

released from the mould and even more time for the mould to thoroughly dry before it could be used again. The recurring saturation wore the surface of the moulds smooth and they had to be replaced more frequently than press moulds. The need for drying meant that a room had to be set aside and heated for this purpose and that extra moulds had to be made to ensure continuous production. During the present century a chemical additive ensures the breakdown of clay in the minimum amount of water and so the process has become the major forming method for hollow wares. Figures made by the slip casting method may also be made in multi-part moulds and assembled in a similar way to press moulded examples.

Biscuit firing

When the figure was thoroughly dried it was fired for the first time, which involved a number of processes. First of all the piece was placed in a saggar, a clay box which protected the ware during the firing process. The figures were then bedded on sand or flint inside the saggars which were then carried into the oven and stacked one on top of the other in tall 'bungs' inside the circular firing chamber. The experienced oven man, knowing the peculiarities of each oven, had every saggar stacked in the hottest or coolest place according to its contents; rings of moist clay between each saggar compressed to form an effective seal and the top of each bung was capped with a flat saggar known as a hiller. The entrance to the oven was sealed with bricks and a sand mortar, and firing then began.

During the period under discussion, firing took place in a construction now known as a bottle oven. The firing chamber was a domed shape with a number of hearths known as fire mouths distributed around its circumference. It is not possible to be specific as to the size of these ovens as they varied enormously according to their purpose. What was suitable for the first or biscuit firing, when a large capacity was required, was certainly unsuitable for small select firings of enamel painted pieces. The distinctive bottle shape so often associated with the Potteries landscape was constructed to protect the oven, it also served as a shelter for the fireman and occasionally provided storage space for his equipment, it produced the required draught for the fires and funnelled the smoke and flames away above roof height.

Heat was introduced into the oven through a number of fire mouths which were fuelled with coal and then lit. The man in charge of the firing was the fireman and he was responsible for building an even heat throughout the oven until the optimum temperature was reached. He did this by controlling the air flow through the oven and by fuelling the fire mouths at the appropriate times. He checked by taking trial pieces from inside the oven using long rods inserted through small trial holes in the wall. When the required temperature had been reached it had to be held for a specified time called the soaking period. In firing biscuit earthenware the required temperature was likely to be 1100-1150 degrees C. After the soaking period the oven was allowed to burn itself out and was left undisturbed for at least twenty hours, at which point the oven entrance could be opened and ten hours later the fire mouths were cleaned out. A big oven of 20ft. or over would take from 45 to 55 hours to fire consuming 17 to 22 tons of coal. After about two days cooling, the oven can be drawn, that is the saggars carried out and emptied. The completed pots are taken to the biscuit warehouse where they are closely examined. Defective pieces were referred to the worker responsible, who was only paid for perfect pieces, a system known as 'good from oven'. Perfect ware was brushed clean of sand or flint and sanded smooth, if necessary, before being passed to the next stage.

The next stage in figure production depends upon the type of wares required. Some figures were decorated at this point, others were glazed and decoration might follow later.

Underglaze, painting and glazing

Decorating on the biscuit earthenware had its limitations. The gloss firing temperature of about 1000°-1100° centigrade meant that a restricted palette had to be used. The only colours which could withstand that heat were those derived from metal oxides: cobalt for blue, copper for green, manganese for a purplish brown, tin and antimony for yellow; iron was used to add depth to yellow, and brown and could make green; a mixture of iron and cobalt made black.

'Glazing or dipping the ware in a prepared liquid, which produces the glossy surface'.

'Glazing or dipping the ware in a prepared liquid, which produces the glossy surface'.
Enoch Wood's Manufactory 1827.
This glassy material in the glaze mix was lead, which is a cumulative, debilitating poison and many workers suffered from the effects of lead poisoning before legislation required that glazes should be prepared without free lead.

The metal ore was burnt, crushed to a powder and mixed with water before painting on to the biscuit earthenware surface; an alternative decorative effect could be produced by applying the colour with a sponge. After decorating the figure was allowed to dry before it was dipped into the glaze tub where it received a coating of lead glaze to seal the body and the colours. The piece was then sent for gloss firing.

Glazing

The biscuit earthenware figure was glazed by immersion in a tub of liquid glaze mix made from powdered lead oxide suspended in an earthenware slip. During the mid-eighteenth century iron impurities in the body and glaze gave the ware a cream coloured finish which varied with the quality of the ingredients, their preparation and the exact formula used. Most of the figures in the period under discussion have a glaze to which a small amount of cobalt oxide has been added; the blue stain makes the figure appear whiter than creamware. The contemporary name for this product was china glaze, the modern term is pearlware. Pearlware can easily be discerned by close examination of crevices in the modelling where the pools of glaze can be seen to be a translucent blue. Simple, undecorated glazed figures are the most inexpensive of the potters' range.

'Placing the dipped ware ready for its being fired or baked in the Glazing oven'. *Enoch Wood's Manufactory 1827.*
The placer loaded ware into saggars as economically as possible; in the background can be seen the loaded saggars being carried into the oven.

Painting with coloured glazes

An alternative treatment for the biscuit earthenware figures was to paint them with coloured glazes. The base glaze is the bluish pearlware stained with colours derived from metal oxides which can withstand the 1000°-1100° centigrade firing (see above).

Coloured glazed wares were more expensive than china glaze or underglaze painted figures because of the extra time taken in the careful application of colours. In their haste to complete the required number of figures the workers often missed the more difficult corners of a figure, under arms, between fingers and at junctions, there is often bare earthenware body exposed, confirming this type of decoration.

Glost firing

When the figures were coated with glaze they were dried ready for placing in saggars for their second firing. The saggars were brushed and washed with glaze to prevent the absorbent saggar sucking the glaze from the ware. The molten state of the glaze during firing required the pieces to be kept apart during this process. There is a variety of kiln furniture employed to support the wares and designed to leave the smallest possible mark. The saggars full of ware were stacked in bungs inside the oven to the instructions of the experienced oven man, rings of clay between each saggar once more formed an effective seal and the top was sealed with the hiller.

The firing began and each fire mouth was constantly checked for an even burning. Spy holes and trial pieces enabled the fireman to observe the progress of the firing. Once the optimum temperature was reached it was held for the required 'soaking period'. After the oven was cooled sufficiently it was drawn or emptied and the ware sent to the sorting house.

In the sorting house the ware was examined, cleaned and classified into best, seconds and thirds or lump. Wares that were complete were sent to the warehouse for sale. Other pieces were sent for the next process which might be overglaze painting or gilding.

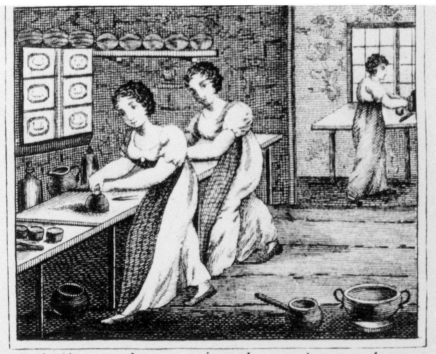

'Grinding and preparing the various colours for the Enamellers or Painters'. *Enoch Wood's Manufactory 1827.*

Painting with enamel colours over the glaze

There were many advantages to painting in overglaze enamel colours, not least the wide range of shades that was available as a consequence of lower firing temperatures which may be employed after glazing is completed.

The colours were produced by making a coloured glass which was ground

'Painting and Gilding China or Earthenware'. *Enoch Wood's Manufactory 1827.*

to a powder for mixing with an oily binding medium, allowing the painter to apply it with a brush (known as a pencil in the pottery industry). The finest and cleanest medium was fat oil, but this could be diluted with additions of Stockholm tar or turpentine. The enamel was applied using a variety of pencils and designs were as simple or complex as the workers' skills allowed. It was possible to produce exquisitely painted pieces as the change of colour during firing was small and easily accommodated by an experienced hand.

Muffle firing

It was true, however, that colours matured at a variety of temperatures and some might have to be fired before others could be applied. Browns, greens and blues could withstand the highest temperatures and they were applied first and fired in the hottest part of the oven. The more delicate colours such as coral, red and flesh colour were applied after the stronger colours had been fired and their saggars were placed in the less hot parts of the oven. Enamel kilns were usually like bottle ovens of a very small size, which made it easier to assemble sufficient quantities of the different, suitable colours to fill them. The interior of enamel kilns differed from the larger biscuit and glost ovens in that flames and smoke were not allowed to enter the firing chamber but the heat was directed through the walls by means of flues. This separation of the fire from the wares gave rise to the alternative name muffle oven. As a rule when placing the oven, the more delicate colours needed to be in the centre of the kiln, surrounded by colours that would sustain the greater heat without detriment. Therefore, if delicate colours such as coral, red and flesh tones had to be fired it was necessary to have a certain quantity of the stronger colours

Top: 'Examining and dressing the ware after its coming from the potter's and glazing ovens'. Bottom: 'Packing China and Earthenware in Crates'. *Enoch Wood's Manufactory 1827.*

such as brown, green or blue to be placed in the hottest parts of the kiln and form a protection for the more delicate ones.

By the time an enamel figure was complete it may have been subjected to the hazard of fire four or five times at temperatures between 800°-1000° centigrade, consequently enamel painted figures were quite costly to produce.

Gilding

Gilding is the most expensive decorative treatment and may be applied to any kind of figure, but it is not found on underglaze painted pieces. The mid to late eighteenth century figures which were enhanced with gilding included the china glazed and the coloured glazed wares. Many of these now show little sign of their former richness, as the technology of gilding was not fully understood by the Staffordshire earthenware potters until long after their porcelain counterparts had developed the skill. The Staffordshire potters seem not to have realised that a flux or glassy binding medium was needed as with enamel colours, in order to fix the gold permanently to the glaze surface. Until this was understood the gold was fixed by dusting ground gold leaf on to a pattern painted in size, this held the gold until a final fire fixed it lightly to the surface of the figure. Much of this size gold has worn away over the years, however, by the end of the century the problem was solved and some very finely gilded pieces serve to show how skilful the potters could be if necessary.

The application of gold made figures considerably more expensive because of the cost of the raw material, the cost of the painting process and the subsequent firing. The most expensive figures of all were the finely enamelled examples with gilding.

After the final decorating process and firing the pieces are sent to the glost warehouse where they can be stored or used to fill orders.

Development of Making Methods

The middle and later years of the eighteenth century are amongst the most exciting in ceramic history, yet we cannot assume that when one new technique was introduced that all makers immediately adopted it. Figures which exhibit primitive making methods are not necessarily early pieces, but are much more likely to be the result of simple production methods and therefore cheap. When new and more expensive ideas were introduced there would still be a market for the old style cheaper product and this should be borne in mind when making methods are used to assist dating. It is much easier to assess the beginning of a new style than its end: for instance it is much easier to state that pearlware was introduced about 1775 than to say when it was no longer used, but this only helps us to decide that a pearlware figure must then post date 1775, not that all pearlware figures were made in 1775.

It is obvious that when one compares an earthenware figure of Whieldon's production with one of James Neale's, that the eighteenth century saw a dramatic development in techniques. The developments were almost certainly introduced to raise the standards of tableware production but were none the less applied to figure manufacture. Improvements in the preparation of raw materials give finer, whiter bodies and glazes. The influence of the porcelain makers on salt glaze manufacturers brought coloured enamel painting to the Staffordshire Potteries. The increasingly successful master potter became more familiar with the finer things of life and his standards were suitably raised. Expansion of the retail trade with London outlets and warehouses and shops in major provincial centres brought the challenge of more sophisticated tastes and demands from the ever increasing ranks of middle class consumers.

It must not be thought that every potter rose to the challenge with equal vigour, for it is in the natural way of things that there are men who strive for improvement and are willing to take risks, there are those who sit back, satisfied with their lot, and there are those who, try as they will, cannot make headway. Thomas Whieldon, Enoch Wood and Ralph Wood each fit one of these categories, the reader should be able to deduce which is which from the pages of this book.

Exterior of a Pottery.

FINIS.

Appendix 1

Documentary evidence relating to figure production is not widely available. This appendix contains transcripts of figures supplied by John Wood, Ralph and Enoch Wood and Enoch Wood and James Caldwell. Anyone wishing to pursue research through these records is advised to consult the original documents.

John Wood

The following records are from a John Wood sales ledger listing goods sold by him between 1783 and 1787. The figures formed a minor part of his business and are all listed below. The ledger is part of the collection of the City Museum & Art Gallery, Stoke-on-Trent.

30 May 1783 to Mr Joseph Tidmarsh (p2)

6 Shepherd &c	3	..
6 Gardener &c	2.	6
6 Sailor &c	2.	6
2 Sets Faith hope &c	3.	-
2 Pipers	..	9
2 Men with lost sheep	1.	6
2 Clowns	..	7
6 Stags & Hinds	4.	6
1 Sheep & Goat	1.	8
1 Lord Chatham	1.	9

6 October 1783 to Mr Tho Dickins (p39)

1 pair dolphin flower pots coloured	2.	-
3 pair Shepherd & Shepherdess	3.	-
3 Ditto Gardener & Wives	2.	6
3 Ditto Sailor & Lasses	2.	6
1 Ditto Neptune & Venus	2.	6
1 Elephant	1.	3
3 pair Stags & Hinds	4.	6
2 Men with lost sheep	1.	6
2 Sheep & Goats	1.	8
2 Clowns		8

31 December 1783 to Mr John Shaw (p57)
2 Doz. Satyr Head drinking Cups & Cream Jugs

30 March to Mr Robt Dickinson (p153)

2 pair Stags & Hinds	3/-	2 pair Sheep & Goats 3/4		6.	4
1 pair Spaniel & pointer dog	1/6	1 Do Fox & Greyhound 1/6		3.	-
1 pair Shepherd & Shepherdess				2.	-

2 pint Jugs Do			" 9
4 Toby Jugs coloured 10/ 2 China Glaze 4/			14 "
12 Sauce Terrines small Royal			10
12 — Ditto fluted tops			" 10
12 Long sets of Boys 6 Short			11 —
6 Do blue painted 7/6 3 Short Do 3/			10 . 6
1 Doz shallow Shells 1 Doz Do 1 Doz Do			4 —
1 Doz deep Do			2 —
28 two Quart Bottles 28 Three Do Do			1 . 4 . 6
Image Toys			
3 Sets faith hope & charity 1/6			4 . 6
2 Van Tromps	1/3		2 . 6
2 pair Spaniel & Pointer	1/6		3 —
4 Game keepers	1/3		5 —
3 pair Sportsman & Lady 1/4			4 —
6 pair Boy & Girl with Baskets 10d			5 "
2 pair Neptune & Venus's 2/6			5 —
5 pair Mower & Haymakers with Rakes for the women } 1/8			8 . 4
5 pair Gardener & Mate 1/			5 . —
3 Dianas & 1 Appollo	1/3		5 —
3 pair Stag & Hind	1/6		4 . 6
2 Sets faith hope & charity China Glaze Gilt } 2/6			5 —
1 pair Sportsman & Lady Do			2 . 4
1 pair Mower & Haymaker Do			2 . 6
1 pair Diana & Appollo Do			3 . 6
1 pair Gardener & Mate Do			2
1 pair Lyon & Panther with Cupids coloured & Gilt }			4 . 6
		13 . 17 . 3	13 . 17 . 3
Bill sent	36 crates Hovers 8/9		

Page 221 from John Wood's sales ledger, with details of figures supplied to Mr. John Edwards 9th December 1785. *City Museum & Art Gallery, Stoke-on-Trent, John Wood MS.*

2 men with lost Sheep	1/6	2 Diana's 2/-	3.	6
2 Appollo's	1/8	4 pairs Gardeners & Wives 3/4	5.	-
4 pair Haymakers	3/-	6 Bagpipers 1/9	4.	9
1 pair Neptune & Venus	2/6	1 George & Dragon 1/9	4.	3
3 Sets faith hope & Charity			4.	6
1 Gunner			1.	

Groups of figures, earthenware decorated with coloured glazes, made in Staffordshire, 1780-1800. *City Museum & Art Gallery, Stoke-on-Trent.*
The subjects can be found in the lists of goods supplied by John Wood and Enoch and Ralph Wood. It is not usually possible to identify the maker of any particular figure from the title alone as there is often a number of versions of each subject.

Group of figures, pearl glazed earthenware with overglaze enamel painted decoration, made in Staffordshire, c.1800-15. *City Museum & Art Gallery, Stoke-on-Trent.*
The subjects can be found in the lists of goods supplied by Wood and Caldwell. It is not usually possible to identify the maker of any particular figure from the title alone as there is often a number of versions of each subject.

25 May 1785 to Mr John Long (p173)
1 Sportsman with gun 1/3
1 Pair Haymaker 10d   Do Gardener & Wife 1/-
1 Do Boy & Girl 5d   Do Stag & Hind 1/6
1 Do Spaniel & Pointer 1/6

9 July 1785 Mr Thos Dickins (p182)
16 Tortoises & pairs 2.8

28 Sept 1785 to Mr Saml Ward (p199)
1 Toby Enamiled Jug 4.-

26 Oct 1785 to Mr Charles Hayward (p203)
2 Toby jugs coloured 5/-   1 Do Enamiled 5/-

9 Nov 1785 to Mr James Atkinson (p207)
2 Toby Jugs coloured 5/-   2 Do plain 4/-   9. -.
1 Do Enamiled —

9 Dec 1785 to Mr John Edwards (p221)
4 Toby Jugs coloured 10/-   2 China Glaze 4/-   14. -.
Image Toys
3 sets faith hope & charity 1/6   4. 6
2 Van Tromps   1/3   2. 6
2 pair Spaniel & Pointer   1/6   3. -
4 Game keepers   1/3   5. -
3 pair Sportsman & Lady 1/4   4. -
6 pair Boy & Girl with Baskets 10d   5. -
2 pair Neptune & Venus 2/6   5. -
5 pair Mower & Haymakers with rakes for the women   8. 4
5 pair Gardener & Mate   1/-   5. -
3 Dianas & 1 Apollo   1/3   5. -
3 pair Stag & Hind   1/6   4. 6
2 Sets faith hope & charity China Glaze & Gilt 2/6   5. -
1 pair Sportsman & Ladie Do   2. 4
1 pair Mower & Haymaker Do   2. 6
1 pair Diana & Appollo Do   3. 6
1 pair Gardener & Mate Do   2. -
1 pair Lyon & Panther with cupids coloured & Gilt   4. 6

Dec 1785 to Mr George Phillips No. 135 Oxford Street (p230)
13 Toby jugs Color'd   1. 9. 3

10 Jan 1786 to Mr John Davis (p231)
4 Toby jugs colour'd   10. -

20 Jan 1786 to Mr George Phillips (p231)
36 colour'd Toby Jugs   2/3   4 --. -.

11 Feb 1786 to Mr Saml Ward (p237)
Figures & Toys &c Viz
1 pair Stag & Hind coloured   1. 6
4 Do Mower & Haymaker 1/8   6. 8
4 Do Sportsman & Lady 1/2   4. 8
4 Do Boy & Girl with Basket & Fruit 10d   3. 4
4 Gamekeepers with Hare & Dog 1/3   5. -
1 Houdibras on Horse   2. -
1 Set Faith Hope & Charity   1. 6
6 Dianas & Appolo's 1/3   7. 6
6 Bagpipers 6d   3. -
3 Pair Gardeners & Mates 1/-   3. -
1 Pair Neptune & Venus   2. 6

1 Pair Fox & Greyhound		1. 6
1 Pair Mower & Haymaker Enamd.		4. -
1 Pair Sportsman & Lady Do		4. -
1 Pair Diana & Appolo —		5. -

One set White & Gold

1 Appollo	1/9)	
1 Pair Sportsman & Lady	2/4)	5. 9
1 Pair Boy & Girl	1/8)	

One Set Do.

1 Minerva	3/6)	
1 Pair Bacchus & Venus	4/-)	10. -
1 Pair Mower & Haymaker	2/6)	

8 Mar 1786 to Mr John Edwards (p243)

10 Toby Jugs colour'd	1. 2. 6
2 Do Enamiled	8. -
1 Pair Lyon & Panther with Cupids & Gilt	4. 6
1 Pair large Lyons Gilt	7. -
2 Bacchus Jugs	7. -
1 King David with Harp coloured	1. 9
2 Colourd Bulls with dogs	1. 8

18 Mar 1786 to Mr James Ewer (p246)
Image Toys

1 Minerva white & gold with spear	3. 6
1 Pair Bacchus & Venus Do	3. 6
1 Pair Mower & Haymaker Do	2. 6
1 Pair Boy & Girl with fruit Do	1. 8
1 Set Faith Hope & Charity Do	2. 6
1 Pair small Boy & Girl Do	9
1 Appollo colour'd 1/3	
1 Pair Mower & Haymaker 1/8	3. 9
1 Pair Boy & Girl with Basket 10d	
1 Game Keeper 1/3	
1 Pair Stag & Hind 1/6	2. 9
1 Pair Neptune & Venus White & Gold	4. -
1 Pair Dianna & Appollo Do	3. 6
	1. 8. 5

8/10 Apr 1786 to Mr George Philips or Philips & Martin (p252)

21 Colour'd Toby Jugs	2. 5. 3
3 Enamiled Do 3/3	9. 9

16 Apr 1786 Mr John Letts (p253)
2 colourd Tobys   4. -

2 May 1786 to Mr Wm Mortlock (p257)
6 Toby Jugs   13. 6

11 May 1786 to Mr James Ewer (p259)
1 Minerva White & Gold   3. -
1 Pair Bacchus & Venus Do   3. 6
1 Pair Mower & Haymaker Do   2. 6
2 Pair Dutch Boy & Girl Do   3. 4
2 pair least Boy & Girl Do   1. 6
1 Venus to Neptune   2. -
1 Pair Diana & Appollo   3. 6
1 Pair Stag & Hind colourd   1. 6
1 Game Keeper —   1. 3
1 Pair Derby? Boy & Girl   1. -
1 Pair Lyon & Panther with Cupids
   when perfect & Gilt   4/6 a pair

1 June 1786 to Mr Thos Uphill (p271)
1 Appollo white & Gold   1/9)
1 Pair Mower & Haymr   2/6)   5.11
1 Pair dutch Boy & Girl   1/8)

1 Diana color'd   1/3)
1 Pair Mower & Haymaker   1/6)   3. 7
1 pair dutch Boy & Girl   10d)

1 Appollo coloured   1/3)
1 Pair Sportsman & Lady   1/4)   3. 5
1 pair dutch Boy & Girl   10d)

16 June 1786 Mr Stephen Mundy (p277)
1 Pair Appolo & Venus painted   2. 6
3 Pair Mower & Haymaker   3. -
1 Pair Man with lost sheep   1. 6
2 Pair dutch Boy & Girl   1. 8
1 Pair Sportsman & Lady   1. 4
2 Bagpipers   1. -
1 Gamekeeper   1. 4
1 Pair Stag & Hind   1. 6
1 Pair Do Gilt   2. 6
2 Sets faith hope & Charity 1/6   3. -

1 Pair Neptune & Venus white & gold		4. -
1 Diana Do	1/9)	
1 Pair Mower & Haymaker	2/6)	5.11
1 Pair dutch Boy & Girl	1/8)	
1 Vicar & Moses		2. 6
1 Pair Derby? Boy & Girl colour'd		10
2 Sets faith hope & charity white & gold		5. -
		4.16. 9

23 June 1786 Mr Saml Dunbibbin (p.280)

3 Toby's 6/9 3 Do sitting on a barrel 6/9	13. 6

14 Septr 1786 Mr Wm Mortlock

1 pair Diana & Appollo colourd	2. 6
1 Pair Bacchus & Venus wth Grapes & dove	2. 6
1 Do Shepherd & shepherdess 2/ 1pair Gardener & wife 10d	2.10
2 Do Dutch boy & Girl with fruit Baskets	1. 8
1 Do Man with lost sheep and Woman with lost piece	1. 6
1 Do Mower & Haymaker with Scythe & Rake	1. 6
2 Clowns	6
2 Pair Stag & Hind	3. 0
2 Spanish figures carrying jugs	2. 0
2 Shepherd with sheep 2/ 1 Do carrying music 1/3	3. 3
2 Shepherd & Shepherdess on Rock Candlestick	8. -
2 Vicar & Moses	5. -
1 Jolly Sailor & jug	2. 6
Set white & gold	
1 Diana 1/9 1pr mower & haymaker 2/6)	5. 9
1 Dutch boy & girl 1/6)	

26 Sepr Mr Saml Ward (p.311)

4 Toby jugs coloured	9. -
1 Vicar & Moses 2/6 1 Do gilt 3/-	5. 6

16 Decr 1786 Mr Charles Hayward (p.339)

6 Tobys 15/- 2 Vicar & Moses 5/6	1. 0. 6

18 Jany 1787 Mr Ebenezer Nevil (p.349)

Image Toys Viz

1 Set faith hope & charity white & gold	3. -
1 Shepherd & shepherdess on a rock colour'd	4. -
1 Pair Spanish dancers	2. -
1 Pair Do Do gilt	3. -

1 Pair Shepherd & Shepherdess not gilt		2. -
1 Pair Gasconian & Galigo wt & gold		3. 6
1 Diana wt & gold)		
1 Pr Sportsman & Lady) a Set		5.10
1 Pr small figures with music)		

Enoch and Ralph Wood

All known documentary sources relating to Ralph Wood's figure production date from 1783 to 1787 and relate to the period when he was in partnership with his cousin Enoch. The orders are addressed to Ralph in his capacity as 'sales manager' in the partnership.

16 Nov. 1783 Wedgwood Archive 11496-1. (By kind permission of the Trustees of the Wedgwood Museum.)
Messrs. Josiah & Thos Wedgwood

Bought of Ralph Wood

No 358	12 George & Dragons	2/-	a pair	£1. 4. -.
356	6 Venuses purple lining	15d	"	7. 6.
357	6 Neptunes Do	15d	"	7. 6.
355	6 Do blue lining	18d	"	9. 0.
360	24 Dolphin Flowerpots	1/-		1. 4. -.
341	12 Shepherds	6d	"	6. -.
352	12 Apollos	10d	"	10. -.
351	12 Men with lost Sheeps	9d	"	9. -.
350	12 Charities	8d	"	8. -.
339	12 Gardeners	5d	"	5. -.
371	12 Apollos Gilt	15d	"	15. -.
344	12 Sailors Lasses	5d	"	5. -.
367	12 Stags white spotted	9d	"	9. -.
368	12 Hinds Do Do	9d	"	9. -.
366	12 Hinds spotted Black	9d	"	9. -.
365	12 Stags Do Do	9d	"	9. -.
369	12 Goats	10d	"	10. -.
370	12 Sheep & Rams	10d	"	10. -.
372	1 Pair Neptune & Venus Gilt			3. 6.
373	1 Elephant			1. 3.
374	Man with a boy sitting on a rock			1. -.
375	Do with a Boy in his hand standing			1. -.
	6 Doz. small coulord figures 18 pr Doz			9. -.
	2 Saters Head Drinkg cups flatt Bottom			1. -.
	2 Do Do Do with a Round Foot			1. -.
	Do Do Cream Ewers			1. -.
				£10. 4. 9.

Cask 2/-

Discount 1. 0. 5.

9. 4. .

Cask 2.0

£9. 6. 4.

Received 26th Jany 1784 the Contents inful

Ralph Wood

Several orders are appended to lists in John Wood's sales ledger in the collection of the City Museum & Art Gallery, Stoke-on-Trent.

20 Oct. 1784 John Wood's sales ledger to Mr. John Shaw (p.128)
      'Toys from Bro.Ralph   £1.17.1d'   [not detailed]

25 Jan 1787 John Wood's sales ledger to Mr. Andrew Barr
Bought of Ralph Wood for Andrew Barr

1pr	Neptune & Venus	wt & Gold	4. -.
1pr	Shepd. Shepdess	Do	3. -.
1pr	Spanish figures suppose dancing	Do	3. -.
1pr	Do small Do with Music	Do	1. 9.
1pr	Mower & Haymaker	Do	2. 6.
1	Spanish Woman with Water Pitchers	Do	1. 9.
1pr	Man with lost Sheep & Woman with lost piece	col'd	2. -.
2	Spanish Peasants Worshipping		1. 8.
1	Do Woman Spinning		1. 3.
1pr	Old age with crutches		2. -.
1	Spanish Shepherd with Sheep under his arm		10.
1pr	Do Figures Suppose Dancing		2. 6.
1pr	Stag & hind		1. 6.
			1. 7. 3.

1 Feb. 1787 John Wood's sales ledger Mr. Isaac Swan
Images as per Bror Ralphs Bill 2.11.9 [not detailed]

Sent to Mr Swann Burslem 8th Feby 1787
John Wood
    Bought of Ralph Wood

1	King David	white & Gold	3. -.
1	Minerva	Do	3. -.
1pr	Spanish Gasconian with music)		3. 6.
	& Galego Woman with Water Jars)		
1pr	Spanish Dancers with Music		3. 0.
1pr	Diana & Apollo		3. 6.
1pr	Baccus & Venus		3. 6.

1pr	Sportsman & Lady	2. 4.
2pr	Boy & Girl play with Cat & Blowing Charcoal	3. 4.
1pr	Small Spanish Figures with Music	1. 9.
1pr	Dutch Boy & Girl with Basket of Fruit	1. 8.
1pr	Derby Boy & Girl	1. 2.
1pr	Shepd & Shepdess on a rock could.	8. -.
1pr	Large Obelisks Pebble Gilt	10. -.
1pr	Old Ages wt. & Gold	3. -.
		2. 10. 9.

1 Pebble Gilt Teapot 24 @ 1/-

26 Feb. 1787 John Wood's sales ledger
     to Mrs Sarah Barlow
'Figures which she bought from Brother Ralph. . . .' [not detailed]

Enoch WOOD and James CALDWELL

The ledger of a London retailer named Wyllie includes lists of items supplied by Wood and Caldwell, including a number of figures; they are all listed below. (Information courtesy Ann Eatwell, Victoria and Albert Museum.)

January 6th 1810		£. s. d.
12 pair Justice & Peace	2/-	1. 4.
24 pair Sportsman & Archer	1/4	1.12.
3 pair Village Songsters	3/-	9.
2 pair Horn & Tambourine	3/-	6.
20 pair Stag & Hind	1/3	1. 5.
12 pair Cupid & Dove	1/4	16.
15 doz Flower baskets	2/6	16.
15 doz Pheasants	2/6	1.17. 6.
6 doz Lying figures	2/6	1.17. 6.
3 sets Elements		8.
1 pair Pointer & Spaniel		2.

May 26th 1810		
4 doz Swans	2/6	10.
3 pair Cooks	2/6	7. 6.
6 pair Spaniel & Pointer	2/-	12.
6 setts Seasons	2/6	16.
12 pair Neptune & Venus	2/-	1. 4.
24 pair Andromache & Hygia	2/-	2. 5.
12 setts Faith Hope & Charity	2/6	1.10.
12 dz Flower Baskets	2/6	2. 5.
12 dz Lying Figures	2/6	1.10.

2 Dianas	1/6	3.
2 Floras	2/6	5.
3 pr Cow & calf	3/-	9.
3 pr Foxes	1/-	3.
3 pr Large Leopards	1/6	4. 6.
6 pr small Leopards	5d	2. 6.

August 14th 1810

36 Pr Stag & Hind	1/3	2. 5.
24 Pr Andromache & Hygia	2/-	2. 8.
12 Pr Neptune & Venus	2/-	1. 4.
12 Pr Justice & Peace	2/-	1. 4.
12 Setts Elements	2/8	1.12.
12 Faith Hope & Charity	2/6	1.10.
6 Pr Village Songster	3/-	18.
6 Pr Large Leopards	1/6	9.
4 Pr Cow & Calf	3/-	12.
2 Pr Lions	2/6	5.
3 Pr Cooks	2/6	7. 6.
2 [St. Johns?]	5/-	5.
3 Small Stags 2@2/3, 1@1/-		4. 3.
1 doz Foxes		6.
3 doz Swans	2/6	7. 6.
6 Foxes		3.

October 22nd 1810

20 Pr Stag & Hind	1/3	1. 5.	
24 Pr Sportsman & Archer	1/4	1. 12.	
16 doz Pheasants	2/6	2.	
4 doz Summer & Spring	4/-	16.	
4 doz Flower baskets	2/6	10.	
7 doz Lying Figures	2/6	17.	6

April 3rd 1813

2 doz Pomona & Flora	4d	8.	
8 doz Lying figures	2/6	1.	
8 doz [squatt?] baskets	2/6	1.	
8 doz Large pheasants	2/6	1.	
20pr Stags	1/3	1. 5.	
12 odd Stags		7.	6
4 doz large Pheasants	2/6	10.	

February 12th 1814

16 doz Large Pheasants	2/6	2.	
6 doz Small flower Baskets	2/6	15.	
6 doz Lying figures	2/6	15.	

September 30th 1814

12 Setts Faith Hope & Charity	2/6	1.10.	
12 Pair cupid with Dove	1/4	16.	
12 Stag Hind standing	2/-	1. 4.	
6 Village Songsters	3/-	18.	
3 Cow & calf	1/6	4.	6
12 Sportsman & Archer	1/4	16.	
12 Neptune & Venus	2/-	1. 4.	
2 Tailor & Mate	4/-	8.	
6 doz Large Pheasants	2/6	15.	
12 doz Lying Figures	2/6	1.10.	
3 Setts Elements	2/8	8.	

April 29th 1815

5 Pair Cow & calf	1/6	7.	6
8 doz small Flower Baskets	2/6	1.	
8 doz Large Flower Baskets	4/-	1.12.	
6 Pair Sportsman & Archer	1/4	8.	
12 Pair Andromache & Hygia	2/-	1. 4.	
8 Setts Faith Hope & Charity	2/6	1.	
4 Seasons (new)	1/6	6.	
4 Pair Venus & Cupid	3/-	3.	[sic]
4 Large Cow with Brass nozzle		9	[candlestick?]
4 Hunting horses		9.	
4 Pair Churches		5.	

August 5th 1815

30 pr Stags standing	2/-	3.	
12 pr Justice & Peace	2/-	1. 4.	
17 doz Flower Baskets			
12 size 4, 5 size 6		2. 3	9

November 25th 1815

40 pair standing Stag & Hind	2/-	4.	
20 pair med. Stag & Hind	1/3	1. 5.	
12 large flower baskets	8d	8.	
12 doz small flower baskets	2/6	1.10.	
6 Pair Cow & Calf	1/6	9.	

3 Pair small Jobson	3/-	9.
5 Pair sheep & goat	10d	4. 2
12 Pair small sheep & ram	8d	8.
6 Shepherd & Shepherdess	1/-	6.
1 Hercules & Bull	2/6	2. 6

For other figures detailed in this ledger see p.??

Appendix 2

Impressed numerals on the base or the reverse of figures have been the subject of great speculation: they are usually considered to be mould numbers and as such each subject should have its own unique number. It has been suggested that the numbers indicate the work of Ralph Wood and a list was prepared by Frank Falkener in his *Wood Family of Burslem,* but I think it highly unlikely that the numbers are the product of one factory. In collecting mould numbers I have found several subjects with more than one number, and several numbers with more than one subject, which indicates that there is more than one sequence of numbers involved. It has not been possible to assemble large quantities of impressed numeral figures to examine differences of type face, etc., nor has it been possible to come to any conclusions about the number of factories involved; during the 1780-1800 period John Wood, Ralph and Enoch Wood, Ralph Wood II and III, Enoch Wood and James Caldwell, were just four of the individual companies producing figures.

Two lists of numbers follow: the first is a compilation from various sources and where examples have a maker's name this has been noted, future research may enable further classification within the list, but at the moment no classification is possible; the second, shorter list, includes impressed numerals known to have been in use at Enoch Wood's factories in the 1820s.

Impressed Numerals

Abbreviations used in descriptions

c/c	cream coloured
c/g	coloured glaze
ch/g	china glaze
/g	and gilt
e/p	enamel painted

Abbreviations used in sources, books and catalogues are followed by reference
numbers, if known; auction houses are followed by date of sale, if known;
museum collections are followed by accession number, if known. Private
collections which have been used are not named.

AS	Alistair Sampson
BM	British Museum
Bur	Burnap Collection, Kansas City
Bur2	Burnap Collection, 2nd ed. catalogue
Ch	Christie's
CMAG	City Museum & Art Gallery, Stoke-on-Trent
CP	Creamware & Pearlware CMAG/NCS exhibition catalogue 1986
CW	Colonial Williamsburg
Dor	International Antiques Fair, Dorchester Hotel
Dub	Catalogue of figures in the National Museum, Dublin
Ea	Earle Collection catalogue
FF	Frank Falkener list in *The Wood Family of Burslem*
Gl	Glaisher Collection, Fitzwilliam Museum, Cambridge
Ho	Hoare Collection, Art Gallery & Museum, Brighton
JH	Jonathan Horne
LG	*The Weldon Collection* by Leslie B. Grigsby
LR	Leonard Russell
Mack	Mackintosh Collection catalogue
Mint	Mint Museum, Charlotte, USA, Delhom Collection
Part	Partridge Collection catalogue
PC	Private collection
Price	Price Collection catalogue
S	Sotheby's
SP/B	Sotheby Parke Bernet, New York
S/pt	Southport Museum
TJ	Tristram Jellinek, Lindsay Antiques
V&A	Victoria and Albert Museum
W&F	Wisbech & Fenland Museum
Wil	Willett Collection, Art Gallery & Museum, Brighton

Mould no	Description	Dec	Mark	Source
1	Gardener, sq.base	c/g		FF,CMAG 272.P.49
2	Lady Gardener, sq. base	c/g		FF
2	Hope, mound on sq. base	ch/g	Ra.Wood Burslem	S 7.7.69

Mould no	Description	Dec	Mark	Source
3	Charlotte weeping	c/g e/p		FF
4	St. John	e/p		G1 946
5	Winter/clown/sweep	e/p		PC
6	Winter/clown/sweep	c/g e/p		PC
8	Gardener	e/p		FF S.14.1.69
9	'& Mate' [Gardener's?]	e/p		CMAG 273.P.49
9	Lost sheep	c/g e/p c/c	Ra.Wood Burslem	FF
10	Lost Piece	c/g e/p c/c	Ra.Wood Burslem	FF
11	Neptune			PC
11	Venus	e/p		G1 890
12	Nun	e/p		Dando Dor 1988
13	Woman, mandolin	e/p	27	PC
13	Man hurdy gurdy player	e/p	13	PC
16	Baby elephant drinking at stream, tree stump			S 29.7.71
16	Fair Hebe jug			S 17.1.70
18	Old man			Wil 7
18	Old woman, dog			Wil 7
19	Reclining hind	e/p		FF
20	Oliver Cromwell	e/p		JH 1984 cat.
21	Bagpiper	e/p		CMAG 329.P.49
21	Venus & Cupid, pedestal	c/g e/p		FF
22	Neptune, pedestal	c/g e/p		FF
23	St George & Dragon	c/g e/p	Ra.Wood Burslem	FF, S 27.4.76 Mack 36
25	King David & harp	c/g		FF
27	Nell (pair to Jobson)	e/p		CMAG 3173
27	Sportsman with gun & dog	e/p		FF
28	King David & harp	c/g		FF, V&A 109.1874
29	King David & harp, sq. pedestal	e/p/g		CMAG 623
29	Jupiter & eagle	c/g	Ra.Wood Burslem	FF, Price 62 Bur 1/401 2/501
30	Man Haymaker	c/g	Ra.Wood	Price 74
31	Woman Haymaker	c/g		CMAG 48.P.70
31	Youth leaning on stick	c/g		
32	Lion, paw on ball	c/g e/p		FF, S.17.4.74 Bur 2/522
33	Lion, paw on ball	c/g		Ch 13.2.78 Mack 78,81

Three figures, pearl glazed earthenware with overglaze enamel painted decoration, made in Staffordshire, 1780-1800; left, titled 'Van Tromp' impressed '38' on reverse, ht.275mm; centre, titled 'St Andrew' impressed '122' on reverse, ht.375mm; right, titled 'King David' impressed '29' on reverse, ht. 305mm. *City Museum & Art Gallery, Stoke-on-Trent 328.P.1949, 614, 623.*

Reverse of Van Tromp and King David with impressed numerals '38' and '29'.

Mould no	Description	Dec	Mark	Source
33	Bull attacked by dog	c/g e/p		FF
36	'Roman Charity'	c/g		S 25.3.74
36	Game keeper with gun sq. pedestal	c/g c/c	Ra.Wood	FF,BM,H71 Mack 84 Bur 2/517
37	Van Tromp, sq.pedestal	c/g e/p		FF
38	Van Tromp, sq.pedestal	e/p		CMAG 328.P.49
41	Houdibras rope bead base	e/p		CMAG 317.P.49 V&A C6.1930
42	Houdibras	c/g c/c e/p		FF W&F 1900-22
43	Dr. Franklin	c/g e/p		FF
44	Houdibras	e/p		CMAG 317.P.49
44	Diana, drawing arrow from quiver, dog at feet mound on sq. base			Ch 7.7.75
44	Apollo & lyre	c/g		FF
45	Cupid on lion	c/g		FF, Price 70
46	Cupid on panther	c/g	Ra.Wood Burslem	FF, LG
49	Boy, bird's nest, basket fruit	c/g		Price 68
49	Boy, fruit	c/g e/p		FF
49	Boy, basket veg. (as last?)	e/p		Wil14 Hoare 320005
49	Pr. Boy & girl, mounds on sq. bases	c/g	Ra.Wood Burslem	S P/B 3.12.75 L.134
50	Girl basket	c/g e/p	R.WOOD	FF, LG
51	Toby jug & cup to lip	c/g	Ra.Wood Burslem	FF, Price 88 & 92
53	Satyr head jug, figure handle	c/g e/p	Ra.Wood Burslem	FF, Part 154
53	Minerva	e/p		CMAG 336.P.49
54	Man Old Age crutch & stick	c/g ch/g		Part 92, S 9.1.73 S 8.2.72
55	Woman Old Age basket & stick	c/g		FF, Part 71, LG
56	Juno with bird	c/g		FF
56	Bacchus	ch/g		PC
57	Bacchus	c/g		FF
58	Minerva	c/g		PC

Mould no	Description	Dec	Mark	Source
59	Minerva	e/p		PC
59	Boy, basket flowers	c/g		FF, Part 189
62	Vicar & Moses	c/g e/p	Ra.Wood Burslem	FF, S 23.10.79 S 5.6.68
63	Satyr head jug (see 53)	c/g		Price 78
63	Toby on barrel	c/g		Price 96
65	Toby on chest	c/g e/p		FF, Price 96
66	Girl, basket flowers	c/g		FF, Part 189
66	Man, hurdy gurdy	ch/g c/g	Ra.Wood Burslem	Burnap 408 Wil 11
66	Spanish dancer			Bur 2/515
66	'Gasconian'	e/p		B.Hoare 320008
67	'Gasconian'	e/p		AS, Dor 87
67	Woman, Jar on head	ch/g	Ra.Wood Burslem	CMAG 202.P.49 Bur 2/516 Price 56
68	Gasconian			CMAG 326.P.49
68	Peasant worshipping	c/g e/p		CMAG 321.P.49
69	Worshipper (as 68)	e/p		CMAG 605
70	Old woman feeding birds	c/g	Ra.Wood Burslem	Price 56,TJ, DOR
71	Spanish Musician		Ra.Wood Burslem	Gl 861
71	Troubador	c/g		FF
72	Winter			Mint cat.121
73	Spanish Dancer	c/g e/p		CMAG 262P49
73	Man, hurdy gurdy	c/g		W&F 1900-55
74	Woman with castanets	c/g		W&F 1900-54
74	Sweep boy	c/g e/p		FF
78	Boy with pipe (musical)	ch/g	Ra.Wood Burslem	S/pt 109
79	Jupiter (not as 29)	e/p		Price 62, Gl 914
80	Bust of Handel	c/c e/p ch/g	Ra.Wood Burslem	BM, CMAG 3011 Bur 2/548 S 7.10.68
81	Bust of Milton (see 82 & 90)	c/c e/p	Ra.Wood Burslem	BM H74, CMAG Mack 149, Wil 877
82	Bust of Milton (see 81 & 90		Ra.Wood Burslem	Dub 50
82	Bust of a divine	e/p		FF

Mould no	Description	Dec	Mark	Source
83	Obelisk	e/p		FF
84	Obelisk	e/p	Ra.Wood Burslem	FF
86	Boy feeding chickens		Ra.Wood Burslem	SD
87	Girl with bird in hand	ch/g		CW
88	Rural group, flute	ch/g c/g e/p	Ra.Wood Burslem	FF, S. 30.1.79
89	Rural group, birdcage	ch/g	Ra.Wood	FF, Bur 1/406 2/512
		c/g e/p	Burslem	CP.166
90	Candlestick group Matrimony [as 89?]			Ea.169
90	Bust of Pope	ch/g	Ra.Wood Burslem	FF, CMAG 3012
90	Bust of Milton (see 81 & 82)	e/p		V&A C571-1921
91	Bust of Matthew Prior	ch/g		FF
92	Roman Charity, rocky base	c/g		Bur. 1/399 2/514
92	Zingaria	e/p	Ra.Wood Burslem	JH, Dor 1988 V&A 70.1874
92	Roman Charity	ch/g		LG
93	Roman Charity	c/g		FF
94	Stag, standing	c/g		FF
95	Hind (with strange bocage)	c/g		FF V&A
95	Boy (Simon)	ch/g		V&A C23.1930
96	Boy (Simon)	c/g e/p		Part 95, FF
96	Girl (Iphigenia)	c/g e/p ch/g		Part 95 V&A C25.1930
97	Archeress, bow, quiver & target [Pair to mould 27]	e/p		FF
98	Girl (Iphigenia?)			FF
99	Gasconian	c/g e/p		FF, S. 24.7.56
103	Hercules	e/p	Ra.Wood Burslem	FF
112	Bust Shakespeare	e/p		FF, Mack 148 V&A 2476. 1901 W&F 1900-15
118	St Peter, sq.pedestal	e/p		FF
119	St Philip, sq.plinth	e/p		Wil 791

Two figures, pearl glazed earthenware with overglaze enamel painted decoration, made in Staffordshire, early 19th century; left, girl with a goose titled '& Partner' impressed '136' on reverse, ht. 235mm; right, group titled 'Friendship' impressed '154' on reverse, ht. 180mm. *City Museum & Art Gallery, Stoke-on-Trent 276.P.1949, 1636.*
Friendship with triple leaf spray bocage and triple florets.

Reverse of goose girl and Friendship with impressed numerals '136' and '154'.

Mould no	Description	Dec	Mark	Source
119	St John, sq.pedestal	e/p		FF
120	St Paul, sq.pedestal	e/p		FF
121	St Philip, sq.pedestal	e/p		FF
122	St Andrew, sq.pedestal	e/p		CMAG 614
123	Bust of Voltaire	e/p		FF
127	Bust of Milton (not as 81)	e/p		FF
131	Boys scuffling (not as 133)	e/p		FF, CMAG 390.P.49
132	Girl, musical instrument	c/c e/p		FF
133	Three children scuffling	c/c e/p		FF
134	Companion to 133	c/c e/p		FF
135	Falconer, mound sq. base	e/p		AS, Dor 87
135	Cymon (see 96 & 98)	e/p		FF
136	Iphigenia (see 96)	e/p		FF
136	'& Mate' goose girl			CMAG 276.P.49
137	Sir Isaac Newton	e/p	Ra.Wood Burslem	FF, Wil 970 S 32.2.87
140	Mother & Child sq.base	c/c		FF, Mack 143
153	Group 'Tenderness'	e/p		FF, S 2.6.67
154	Group 'Friendship' with bocage	e/p		FF, S 2.6.67 CMAG 1636
155	Chaucer	e/p	Ra.Wood Burslem	FF
164	Spill vase, Tree, boy, dog bird's nest	e/p		FF
165	Spill vase, Tree, boy, squirrel	e/p		FF
169	'Fortune' Woman, cornucopia	e/p		FF

Impressed numerals from figures and fragments found on sites in Burslem and attributed to Enoch Wood.

No.3 on reverse of St. Barabara
No.6 on reverse of Pieta
No.11 on reverse of St. Sebastian
No.20 on reverse of Biblical subject
No.24 on reverse of clerical figure (two sizes)

2   Small figure of a man seated on box
2   Andromache (on complete figure with bocage matching excavated fragments)

Excavated figures from the Burslem Town Hall site, deposited by Enoch Wood about 1828, boy with basket impressed '12', girl with lamb impressed '15', ht. 150mm. *City Museum & Art Gallery, Stoke-on-Trent.*

Mould Description
no

10   Hygeia (on complete figure with bocage matching excavated fragments)
12   recumbent deer
12   Man with large basket
13   Figure of a man in Turkish dress
14   Figure of a woman in Turkish dress
15   Figure of Shepherd
15   Figure of shepherdess
15   Circular base titled 'DUSTY BOB'
15   rectangular base of Billy Waters figure
18   Man representing Old Age
18   Woman representing Old Age
19   Faith, Hope & Charity
28   Virgin & child

Bibliography

MSS Sources
Collections of documents relating to the pottery industry can be found at the following institutions:

City Museum & Art Gallery, Stoke-on-Trent.
County Record Office, Eastgate Street, Stafford.
Horace Barks Reference Library, Hanley, Stoke-on-Trent.
University of Keele, North Staffordshire.
William Salt Library, Eastgate Street, Stafford.

Trade directories with contemporary information about the pottery industry to 1840 include the following:

1781 Bailey's *Northern Directory*
1784 Bailey's *British Directory*
1787 William Tunnicliffe's *Survey of the County of Stafford*
1796 *The Staffordshire Pottery Directory*, Chester & Mort
1800 *A View of the Staffordshire Potteries*, T. Allbut
1802 *The Staffordshire Pottery Directory*, T. Allbut
1805 Holden's *Triennial 1805-1807*
1809 Holden's *Triennial 1809-1811*
1818 *Commercial Directory 1818-20*, J. Pigot & R.W. Dean
1818 *Staffordshire General & Commercial Directory*, W. Parson & T. Bradshaw
1822 *London & Provincial New Commercial Directory 1822-23*, Pigot & Co.
1822 *Newcastle and Pottery General and Commercial Directory 1822-23*, T. Allbut
1828 *National Commercial Directory 1828-29*, Pigot & Co.
1829 *New Commercial Directory of Staffordshire...*, Pigot & Co.
1830 *National Commercial Directory*, Pigot & Co.
1834 *History, Gazetteer and Directory of Staffordshire*, W. White
1835 *National Commercial Directory*, J. Pigot
1841 *Royal National and Commercial Directory and Topography of the Counties of...
    Staffordshire*, Pigot & Co.

Books
Bradshaw, P., *18th Century English Porcelain Figures 1745-1795*, Antique Collectors Club, 1981.
Dudson, A.E., *Dudson: A Family of Potters since 1800*, Dudson Publications, 1985.
Edwards, D., *Neale Pottery & Porcelain*, Barrie & Jenkins, 1987.
Falkner, F., *The Wood Family of Burslem*, Chapman & Hall 1912, reprinted EP Publishing, 1972.
Freeth, F., *Old English Pottery*, Morgan Thompson & Jamieson, 1896.
Godden, G.A., *The Illustrated Encyclopedia of British Pottery & Porcelain*, Herbert Jenkins, 1966.

Grigsby, L.B., *The Henry Weldon Collection of English Stoneware and Earthenware (1650-1800)*, Philip Wilson, 1990.

Haggar, R.G., *English Country Pottery*, Phoenix, 1950.

Haggar, R.G., *Staffordshire Chimney Ornaments*, Phoenix, 1955.

Haskell, F., and Penny, N., *Taste & the Antique*, 1981 (revised 1982).

Lewis, G., *A Collector's History of English Pottery*, Antique Collectors' Club, 4th revised edn., 1987.

Lewis, J. & G., *Pratt Ware: English and Scottish relief decorated and underglaze coloured earthenware 1780-1840*, Antique Collectors' Club, 1984.

Mankowitz, W., and Haggar, R.G., *The Concise Encyclopedia of English Pottery & Porcelain*, Andre Deutsch, 1957.

Oliver, A., *The Victorian Staffordshire Figure*, Heinemann, 1971.

Oliver, A., *Staffordshire Pottery: The Tribal Art of England*, Heinemann, 1981.

Pitt, W., *A Topographical History of Staffordshire*, 1817.

Pugh, P.D. Gordon, *Staffordshire Portrait Figures and Allied Subjects of the Victorian Era*, Antique Collectors' Club, 1981.

Read, H., *Staffordshire Pottery Figures*, Duckworth, 1929.

Reilly, R., and Savage, G., *The Dictionary of Wedgwood*, Antique Collectors' Club, 1980.

Rhead, G.W., *The Earthenware Collector*, Herbert Jenkins, 1920.

Shaw, C., *When I Was A Child*, Methuen 1903, reprinted Caliban, 1977.

Shaw, S., *History of the Staffordshire Potteries*, author 1829, reprinted David & Charles/SR Publishers, 1970.

Turner, H.A.B., *A Collector's Guide to Staffordshire Pottery Figures*, MacGibbon & Kee, 1971.

Ward, J., *History of the Borough of Stoke-upon-Trent*, Lewis, 1843, reprinted Webberley, 1984.

Catalogues

Clifford, T. and Friedman, T., *The Man at Hyde Park Corner, Sculpture by John Cheere 1709-1787*, Temple Newsam House, Leeds, 1974.

Earle, C., *The Earle Collection of Early Staffordshire Pottery*, Brown & Sons, 1915.

Hobson, R.L., *Catalogue of the Collection of Pottery in the Dept. of British & Medieval Antiquities of the British Museum*, British Museum, 1903.

Horne, J., *A Collection of Early English Pottery*, Annual volumes.

Lockett, T.A. and Halfpenny, P.A., *Creamware & Pearlware*, Stoke-on-Trent City Museum/NCS 1986, reprinted, 1989.

Mackintosh, H., *Early English Figure Pottery: A Collection of Ralph Wood & Contemporary Pottery*, Chapman & Hall, 1938.

Soden Smith, R.H., *Catalogue of the Collection of English Pottery and Porcelain exhibited on loan at the Alexandra Palace*, R.K. Burt, 1873.

Partridge, *Ralph Wood Pottery: Mr Frank Partridge's Collection*, (no publisher or date).

Poole, J., *Plagiarism Personified,* Fitzwilliam Museum, Cambridge, 1986.

Price, R.K., *Astbury Whieldon and Ralph Wood Figure and Toby Jugs,* John Lane, 1922.

Rackham, B., *Catalogue of the Glaisher Collection of Pottery & Porcelain in the Fitzwilliam Museum Cambridge,* 1935 reprinted Antique Collectors' Club, 1987.

Taggart, R.E., *The Frank P. and Harriet C. Burnap Collection of English Pottery,* Nelson-Atkins Gallery of Art Kansas City 1953, revised 1967.

Walton, P., *Creamware and other English Pottery at Temple Newsam House,* Leeds, Manningham Press, 1976.

Willett, H., *Catalogue of Pottery & Porcelain Illustrating Popular British History,* HMSO, 1899.

    Catalogue of a Collection of English Pottery Figures deposited on loan by Frank Falkner, National Museum Dublin, 1911.

    Henry Boswell Lancaster Bequest of English Porcelain and Pottery Figures, Bootle Museum, 1949.

Museums and Galleries with figure collections

Many museums have examples of pottery figures in their collections, often these are kept in store but are available by appointment. Do not make a special journey to any museum to see specific objects without first telephoning to check whether they will be available on the day you intend to visit. Even if something has been on show for years there is no guarantee it will be there for your next visit, nor can you be sure that the gallery you need will be open, therefore always make enquiries before travelling.

Museums and Galleries with figure collections in England include:

Brighton Art Gallery & Museum
Cambridge, Fitzwilliam Museum
Leeds, Temple Newsam House
London, The British Museum
          Victoria and Albert Museum
Northampton Museum
Saffron Walden Museum
Stoke-on-Trent, City Museum & Art Gallery
Southport Museum
Wisbech & Fenland Museum

Museums and Galleries with figure collections in USA include:
Atlanta, Historical Society
          High Museum
Chicago, Art Institute
Colonial Williamsburgh, Virginia
Detroit, Art Institute

Index

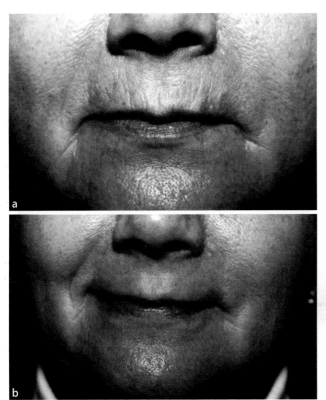

Fig. 82.8a,b Pre- and 6-month postoperative views of perioral carbon dioxide laser resurfacing

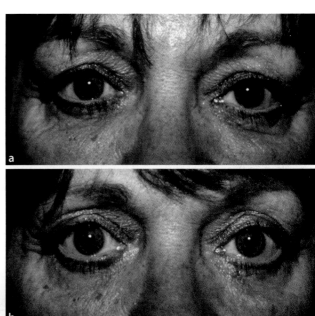

Fig. 82.9a,b Preoperative (**a**) and 6-month postoperative (**b**) views of periorbital carbon dioxide laser resurfacing

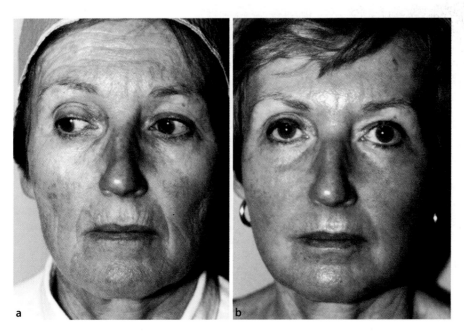

Fig. 82.10a,b Preoperative (**a**) and 3-month postoperative (**b**) views of full face carbon dioxide laser resurfacing

82